Who Owns What Is in Your Head?

Who Owns What Is in Your Head?

How to Protect Your Ideas

Stanley H. Lieberstein

Foreword by D. Bruce Merrifield

HAWTHORN/DUTTON
New York

For information contact: Elsevier-Dutton Publishing Co., Inc., 2 Park Avenue, New York, N.Y. 10016

Library of Congress Catalog Card Number: 76–56527

ISBN: 0–8015–8577–5 (cl.)
     0–8015–8576–7 (pa.)

Published simultaneously in Canada by Clarke, Irwin & Company Limited Toronto and Vancouver

10 9 8 7 6 5 4 3 2 1

For Judy,
with love

Contents

Foreword

Arnold Toynbee has pointed out that the West is dominated by two institutions, industry and democracy. And it is a remarkable fact that the industrial democracies, which represent less than 10 percent of the world population, have gained a degree of ascendancy and a quality of life out of all proportion either to their numbers or to the antiquity of their cultures. In fact, why is it that the great Eastern cultures, which predate those of the West by thousands of years, do not today dominate the civilized world?

I believe that the form of human organization that Toynbee calls the industrial democracy is unique in its ability to harness an enormous array of diverse skills, interests, and individual motivations into a form of concerted action more productive than any authoritarian socialistic form of government can ever be. Basically the industrial democracy—imperfect as we all know it to be—tends to provide both better materialistic and psychological rewards to the individual than any other system. It is based on a concept of participative goal setting and goal implementation, which respects and protects the uniqueness of each individual and his physical and intellectual integrity. Of no small significance in this scheme of things is the concept of "intellectual property," recognized even in the Constitution of the United States in the form of provision for patent rights. Moreover, the concept is in a continual state of evolutionary development, designed to protect on the one hand a corporation or sponsoring institution that may spend considerable amounts of money and time to develop a competitive technological edge, and on the other hand the rights of an individual to earn a living, and therefore to use information to which he has been exposed as an employee of that corporation or institution, even though he leaves to go into the same business for himself or joins a competitor.

Complicated as the judgments can often be in cases in this area, the basic principle of equal justice under the law applied in them has been a powerful stimulant to the entrepreneurial spirit and seems to have contributed in no small measure to the successful emergence of the industrial democracy. To the extent that we are concerned for its future, it would seem important that all of us who are involved in the industrial-democratic process should have a clear understanding not only of the past contributions, but also of the continuing significance of the concept of intellectual property. And implicit therein is that each of us has a reasonably detailed understanding of the operating principles under which the concept currently operates.

This book, *Who Owns What Is in Your Head,* provides a thorough and pragmatic analysis of the critical features of intellectual property rights. It contains surprising, if sometimes disconcerting, case histories to illustrate court interpretations of the law. It fills a void that exists in understanding and resolving the sometimes conflicting rights of the individual and the organization in an industrial democracy. It is a valuable contribution to business administration and to business law. As a reference text it should be on the shelf of every technical and business manager and should be a part of every MBA curriculum.

D. BRUCE MERRIFIELD, Ph.D.
Vice-President, Technology
Continental Group, Inc.
New York, New York

Chairman, Research and
Development Council
American Management Associations

Acknowledgments

Through the years, many people have provided me with valuable information and advice and I would like to think that some of that has found its way into this book. I would like to extend my warmest thanks to each of them. In particular, I would like to thank Professor John Stedman of the University of Wisconsin School of Law and Herbert Burstein of the New York Bar for generously agreeing to review this text to help ensure its technical accuracy; Maxwell Breslau of Gillette Corporation for his assistance with the section on unsolicited ideas; Evelyn Sommer of Champion International Corporation for her assistance with the forms in the appendixes; Armand Gazes of the Rockefeller Foundation and Norma Levy of Interactive Systems for their suggestions on computer security, as well as many others, some of whom are mentioned in the text. I would also like to express my gratitude to Irene Killoran, my secretary, and to the many typists who helped type the original manuscript.

And finally a special note of thanks to my editor, Robert Oskam, for his patience, helpful suggestions, and continual encouragement.

Who Owns What Is in Your Head?

Introduction

Executive turnover is a frequent source of business for lawyers and the courts, primarily because executives who switch jobs tend to stay in their industry and their field of expertise. They tend either to join a competitor or to establish a competitive enterprise. Take, for example, the case of C. Lester Hogan, who resigned as executive vice president of Motorola to become president and chief executive of Fairchild Camera and Instrument Company, and brought along with him a team of seven top men from Motorola. The impact of this personnel shift was such that within a week Motorola stock dropped in value by 10 percent. Motorola's response was to sue the Fairchild Company, Hogan, and its former executive employees who joined Hogan. The company sought an injunction prohibiting Hogan and the others from working for Fairchild and prohibiting disclosure to Fairchild of any Motorola trade secrets. (Curiously, at about the same time Motorola hired John Welty from the Philco-Ford Corporation, apparently to buttress managerial strength in the semiconductor industry.) Motorola eventually lost to Fairchild. Largely because of the way information was handled internally, Motorola was unable to prove that the information its former employees could pass on was a "trade secret."

Modern corporations are extremely sensitive to the potential impact of the loss of key employees to competing companies, and the dollar figures in suits stemming from a shift in allegiances on

1

the part of such employees can be astronomical. In the case of several executives who left IBM to join the Telex Corporation, a court award of $21,900,000 was granted IBM in compensation of alleged damages suffered through misappropriation of IBM trade secrets by Telex. Telex had hired several former IBM employees to help it design and develop peripheral equipment compatible with the central processing units of IBM's computers. On appeal the award was reduced to $18,500,000, and ultimately the dispute was resolved by private settlement between the two companies. But this case remains an example of the sensitivity that business and industry demonstrate on the question of who owns what is in a key employee's head. And while the amount of financial damages, alleged and assessed, may have been exceptional in this dispute, the dispute itself is but one example out of a myriad that have arisen in the past and of the many such that crop up in increasing numbers in the present.

The problem that exists with reference to executives and employees who have access to trade secrets and other confidential information is not one defined only in terms of the rights of employing companies. Assuming that it is inherent in a free society that men and women shall, for whatever reason, have liberty to take employment where they may, it is important to understand what rights an individual has as well. Of course, these rights must not encroach on the rights of others affected by the individual's actions. Thus in examining the rights of the employee one must look as well to the rights of the original employer and those of a third-party employer, i.e., a company that hires an employee away from a competitor, as Fairchild did when it hired Hogan from Motorola.

Basics of the Employer-Employee Relationship

Over a century ago, in 1868, a Massachusetts manufacturer, Joseph Peabody, sued a former employee of his, John R. Norfolk. Peabody had developed a process to manufacture gunny cloth from jute butts, and he claimed to have perfected his process at great expense after many years of secret inventing and then had built a factory in which to practice his process. When Norfolk was hired, the latter agreed in writing to "consider all of said machinery as secret to be used only for the benefit of said Peabody or his assigns, and that by all means in his power he will prevent all persons from obtaining any information in regard to it such as would enable them to use it."

Norfolk subsequently left Peabody and made arrangements with a third party to build a factory for manufacturing gunny cloth—with machines similar to Peabody's and utilizing Peabody's process. Peabody sued, and the suit was reviewed by the Supreme Judicial Court of Massachusetts. After review of the facts, the ruling that emerged was that one who develops "a process of manufacture, whether a proper subject for a patent or not . . . has a property in it, which a court . . . will protect against one who in violation of contract and breach of confidence undertakes to apply it to his own use, or to disclose it to third persons." Thus the court sided with Peabody, finding that Peabody's process of manufacture was secret and, as such, constituted a valuable property right. Norfolk did not have the right to take such property from Peabody and convert it for his own use.

Courts ever since have cited *Peabody* v. *Norfolk* in employer-employee trade secret cases, and the very definition of a trade secret which is most often used in the courtroom is one that essentially evolved from that case. For one thing, Peabody was the inventor of the process, not Norfolk. Peabody had invested substantial sums of money in the process and in the factory where manufacturing took place. Peabody had hired Norfolk and advised him of the confidentiality of the information, which Norfolk acknowledged in a written agreement. Furthermore, Norfolk was more than just another employee of Peabody—he was not the chimneysweep but rather a high-level employee who was effectually made a confidant to Peabody. As such, his relationship to Peabody could be seen as that of a fiduciary, one who owes a special duty of trust stemming from the confidential nature of the relationship. The fact of these or similar circumstances and limitations has since played an important role in the matter of resolving trade-secret disputes.

It may be worthwhile at this juncture first to review basic terms that will be used throughout the discussions that follow. These designate either a particular legal tradition or define a principle of relationship between employer and employee.

In law, the distinctions made are primarily between *common law* and *statute law*. The "common law" is that body of case law based on custom and precedent, which the English followed and applied at the time of the *Mayflower,* as modified by judicial opinion in this country. It is the basic foundation of the British legal system and that of countries sharing the heritage of that system, including the United States. Statute law is law specifically enacted through legislation (federal or state) designed to apply in certain defined situations and to serve as the governing rule for the particular circumstances covered. Most situations involving the employer-employee relationship, however, are governed by the common law rather than by statute. In the course of time, the common law has been amended through the courts on a slow case-by-case, precedent-setting basis to fit the needs of our changing times. (It is a mistake to regard the common law as inflexible or fixed for all time.)

Common law recognizes a special relationship, often described as a fiduciary relationship, between master and servant or between a principal and his agent. Thus, under the common law a master is entitled to entrust his servant with confidences with the expectation that those confidences will not be revealed. The same is true of a principal and his agent. And in many of the contemporary cases involving the employer-employee relationship, the relationship is referred to as one of master-servant or principal-agent.

The definition of "trade secrets" is not universally agreed upon. It is not statutory, although some states have enacted criminal laws relating to the theft of trade secrets wherein the term is defined in a limited manner for criminal purposes, to include principally the theft of that which is *tangible,* e.g., drawings, plans, written formulations, etc. Civil litigation often involves confidential relationships and information that does not necessarily take some tangible form.* The definition to which most judges look for guidance in resolving a trade-secret dispute is contained in the standard legal reference known as The Restatement of Torts. The Restatement

---

*Although recent criminal laws of some states (e.g., New York) may be interpreted so as not to require the taking of a *tangible* object, the author has been unable to find a single reported conviction *not* involving the taking of tangible property. Furthermore, informal discussion with the District Attorney's office indicates a strong skepticism that such a conviction can be obtained.

is an attempt by legal scholars to distill the case law, as developed from the common law, into basic principles. The following excerpts are the closest we come to agreeing on the meaning of the term "trade secret."

> A trade secret may consist of any formula, pattern, device or compilation of information which is used in one's business, and which gives him an opportunity to obtain an advantage over competitors who do not know or use it. It may be a formula for a chemical compound, a process of manufacturing, treating or preserving materials, a pattern for a machine or other device, or a list of customers . . .

> . . . An exact definition of a trade secret is not possible. Some factors to be considered in determining whether given information is one's trade secret are: (1) the extent to which the information is known outside of his business; (2) the extent to which it is known by employees and others involved in his business; (3) the extent of measures taken by him to guard the secrecy of the information; (4) the value of the information to him and his competitors; (5) the amount of effort or money expended by him in developing the information; (6) the ease or difficulty with which the information could be properly acquired or duplicated by others.

If you think the above definition is a bit cumbersome, you are probably right. As a sort of shorthand most lawyers who practice in this field will speak of a trade secret as something that is *not generally known* in the trade or industry to which it applies, *and which provides its owner with a competitive advantage.* Those two elements, not being generally known and affording a competitive edge, are the most vital elements of a trade secret. Note that the word "known" is used here in the broader sense that the secret is not readily observable or easily deciphered. The Restatement itself says "a substantial element of secrecy must exist, so that, except by the use of improper means, there would be difficulty in acquiring the information."

In the *Peabody* v. *Norfolk* case, noted above, the secrets were a result of Peabody's work, and application of the common law principle noted above is clear. But what if Norfolk had gone to work for Peabody and in the course of his employment had developed the secret technology himself? Assume for the moment that Norfolk did not enter into any written agreement with Peabody—what effect would that have had? Suppose further that Norfolk could not gain useful employment elsewhere because his only skill resided in the same type of work that he had been doing for Peabody. What effect would that have had on Norfolk's right to work for a competitor or to set up a competitive business?

These questions become increasingly important in today's mobile society where the increasing sophistication of technology and business practices has resulted in a massive proliferation of confidential processes and information in virtually every industry. In a recent front-page article entitled "Moving Days—Again," *The Wall Street Journal* quoted a number of management recruiters to the effect that there is an increasing number of people changing jobs, whether for larger salaries, increased responsibility, or simply a desire for change. Whatever the reason, it is a fact that in America an employee or manager can seek his fortune with a company of his own choosing and can change jobs or set up his own business subject only to certain limits. It is those limits that constitute the boundary line between the rights of an employee and the rights of an employer.

This book is written with an eye to presenting employers and employees with a clearer sense of where the boundary line lies, and to do so in light of a wide range of circumstances that may comprise or affect a particular employer-employee relationship. We will specifically deal with those aspects of the employer-employee relationship that involve:

1. trade secrets, be they of a business nature—personal business relationships, including valuable customer lists and client contacts developed through the auspices of an employer—or of a technical nature, i.e., relating to manufacturing processes;

2. ideas, patentable or not, created in whole or in part by the employee.

This book will review and analyze many actual cases that were vigorously fought because of the substantial business interests involved. In the process we shall attempt to answer such questions as:

What are the rights of an employee to compete with his former employer or to join a competitor of his former employer?

What are the rights of the former employer?

What are the rights of the new employer?

How may an employer protect himself against the possible loss of trade secrets or proprietary data or customers when an employee leaves the firm?

What are the benefits and risks of an employment contract and when and how is it best used?

What goes into an employment contract and what should you look out for?

What are the rights of the executive manager or employee to knowledge he acquired during the course of his employment or to ideas or inventions of his creation during the course of his employment?

In short, whether you are an employer or employee, who owns what is in your head and what is created by it, and how may those rights and creations be best protected?

1 □ Who Owns Rights to What?

If you have ever awakened in the morning with a hangover and if you have read about what causes a hangover, then you are probably aware that it is partially due to a loss of water from the body. Many of the popular hangover remedies that we hear about aim essentially at restoring the balance of fluids in the body.

In the mid-1960s Dr. J. Robert Cade, associate professor of medicine at the University of Florida, discovered a liquid having most unusual properties. It entered the bloodstream about twelve times faster than water. That liquid is now sold under the name "Gatorade." Today Gatorade is not only popular as a thirst quencher among athletes, but is often prescribed by physicians to prevent dehydration, particularly among infants. It is also a somewhat useful remedy for hangovers. The rights to Gatorade are now owned by the Stokley-Van Camp Company, which pays royalties to a special trust.

It wasn't long after Dr. Cade made his discovery and its commercial potential was realized, that both the U. S. government and the University of Florida got into the act. The government, through the Department of Health, Education, and Welfare, laid claim to Gatorade on the ground that it had provided Dr. Cade with two government grants and therefore, it argued, had funded the research by Dr. Cade that resulted in Gatorade's discovery. The University of Florida maintained that it owned the rights because at the time of Dr. Cade's discovery he was an employee of the university. Dr. Cade, on the other hand, contended that he alone owned the rights to Gatorade because he said he developed Gatorade on his own with his own funds.

A vigorous three-party lawsuit soon followed. Ultimately the dispute was resolved by private settlement between the three parties. But the case presents some interesting basic questions concerning the rights of an employee to his discoveries as opposed to the rights of the employer, here the University of Florida. And what are the rights of an employee operating under a government grant vis-à-vis the rights of the government agency? Of what significance is it if the discovery is outside the field of the grant or outside the field of the employer's scope of business but depends for its existence, at least in part, on the utilization of materials or the knowledge acquired while working within the scope of the government grant or within the scope of the employer's business? In short, who has rights to what?

To Ideas and/or Inventions Made During the Course of Employment

The "hired to invent" test

Briefly stated, when an employee is specifically engaged to do something, whether it is to help solve a problem or develop something new, e.g., a product, process or machine, and he is provided with the means and opportunity to resolve that problem or to achieve the desired objective and is paid for that work, then that employee is said to have been "hired to invent." The employee is hired and paid to accomplish a defined task—and it is no different if the task is to build a new house or a new machine, design a bridge or a package, create a toy or a composition of matter. Assuming in each instance the employee is specifically assigned to accomplish a defined task and is furnished the means (tools or equipment, laboratory or other facilities, assistants, and so forth) and is paid for the efforts involved, then the employer is entitled to own outright the fruit of the creative tree he planted and paid for.

The employee receives his financial reward in the form of pay for the work done. All financial risks are borne by the employer. Thus, in a sense, the employee, like TV's Paladin, is a "hired gun." The results of his efforts belong to the employer.

This principle is well accepted not only in the United States and the United Kingdom but in most countries of the world, even those having legal systems that otherwise depart radically from ours. What then is all the fuss about? Well, let's go back to the Gatorade case for a moment.

The effect of government contracts and grants

The University of Florida said that research was one of the things for which it hired and paid Dr. Cade. No, said Dr. Cade, he was hired as a professor of renal physiology. As he saw it, he was never assigned or expected to engage in work leading to Gatorade.

The government agency involved, the National Institutes of Health (NIH), also sought title. Its claim was not that of an employer, but based on the terms of the grants under which Dr. Cade was performing research. Those grants provided for certain rights to NIH to inventions that resulted from the research being funded. But, Dr. Cade argued, those funds were for research on "aldosterone," an electrolyte-controlling hormone. The discovery of Gatorade, according to Dr. Cade, was made independently of those grants and did not use government funds. In other words, contended Dr. Cade, he was not "hired to invent" Gatorade; that is, it was not part of what he was being paid to do by either the University of Florida or NIH.

It's worth noting here that the government is no different from any other employer when it comes to deciding who owns employee inventions. But when the government funds a private research project, it does so according to a written agreement. In theory the terms of the agreement govern who owns what. All government agencies operate under essentially two sets of rules: they either take title outright or they let the contractor-grantee take title subject to a government right to take over if the invention is not being used in a fair manner for the overall benefit of the public. The Department of Energy, for example, usually seeks outright title, whereas the Department of Defense will allow the contractor to keep title, particularly where he contributes funds out of his own pocket, so long as any development or invention is commercialized within a reasonable time frame. And, if new products are developed and sold, the price structure must also be reasonable. The prime objective of the Department of Energy is to encourage creativity by its contractors, to the profit of the public. So long as the public ultimately benefits from newly created means of using energy, the department may "waive" its claim of title on request.

NIH generally operates under a contract with a university permitting the university the option to take title. Should the university not elect to take title, then NIH will take title. NIH may obtain patent rights and license them or it may simply dedicate the invention to the public—public dedication can take place merely by publishing the discovery without restriction and not filing an application for patent. NIH employs contract administrators who will review the work of its grantees. Unlike government contracts that define the scope of the work to be performed, NIH grants are relatively wide open as to what research the money is to be used for. The only limitation is the statement of the purpose of the funds in the application for a grant. But that is not necessarily a binding limitation on NIH in the sense that other research is excluded. The purpose of the vagueness as to what the grant covers is to permit the research project to alter course in midstream without the necessity of government approval. This helps cut red tape in the event that a research project unintentionally leads to an important development in another area and the researcher wants to pursue this new development. But it can create confusion in some instances, such as when the researcher simultaneously and independently pursues a private project. Unless the researcher keeps accurate and detailed records of both projects so as to show that government funds are not being diverted to the private project, the researcher may later find the government claiming rights to discoveries from that private project too. Essentially that was the hub of contention in the Gatorade case. Dr. Cade argued that Gatorade resulted from a privately financed, independently conducted research project. The government said his work resulted from the use of the grant funds. But to the University of Florida, Dr. Cade was an employee and in their eyes his discovery of Gatorade was part of his job. This raises an important topic, namely the significance of the scope of an employee's work.

The scope of the employee's responsibility

Although the questions raised by the Gatorade case are interesting, the case was settled privately, and the courts never did sort out who owned what. It appears they each got a share of the pie. But let's look at another case that is often referred to as one of the leading cases on this point of law. Francis W. Dunmore and Percival D. Lowell were government employees, working for the U.S. Bureau of Standards (Department of Commerce) when they discovered how to apply principles of radio communication to the remote control of airplane bombs and submarine torpedoes. They assigned their rights to the Dubilier Condenser Corporation. The Bureau of Standards laid claim to the invention on the ground that it was made by their employees in the course of employment. The dispute went into litigation, finally winding up before the Supreme Court. The Court found that although Dunmore and Lowell were employed in research and testing, and that work on remote control devices was one of several "navy" problems before Dunmore's group, the Bureau of Standards had not specifically engaged Dunmore and Lowell to work on and resolve that particular problem. (Dunmore and Lowell had told officials at the Bureau of Standards of their work.) Looking at past practices at the Bureau, they were justified in believing that they would own the rights to their work in this area. Their work was outside the scope of their employment because it was neither generally nor specifically assigned to them among their tasks. The government was left with a shop right.

Contrast this case, *United States* v. *Dubilier Condenser Corp.*, with *Houghton* v. *United States.* Harry W. Houghton, when employed by the U.S. Public Health Service, was assigned to a research project for the combination and safe control of certain dangerous gases. Houghton succeeded in that project and later argued it was his because it was not part of his duties when hired. He was hired as a chemist, he said, and *not* to invent that combined gas. But the federal Court of Appeals in Baltimore, Maryland, did not agree. It said that the government owned the rights here because Houghton had been specifically assigned this task as part of his job—it was what he was being paid for. Thus "hired to invent" is not limited to the initial reason for being hired—it applies to whatever duties are assigned an employee throughout his or her employment.

In cases of patentability and patent rights

A classic case on the subject of "hired to invent" is *Standard Parts Company* v. *Peck.* William J. Peck sued Standard Parts for infringement of a patent issued to him. True, we are using the patented device, said Standard Parts. But, we are entitled to do so, they said, because the Peck patent should rightfully belong to us. And indeed when the Supreme Court was finished with the case, William Peck was only the nominal owner of the patent. The court imposed a "constructive" trust on Peck—a legal fiction, the effect of which was to make Peck a trustee for Standard Parts and require him to assign his rights to Standard.

The whole mess grew out of an agreement between Peck and the forerunner of Standard Parts, the Hess-Pontiac Spring and Axle Company. The Hess company hired Peck to develop "a process and machinery for the production of the front spring" used by the Ford Motor Company. The agreement didn't say anything about who would get title to any new developments, or to any inventions. Peck assumed that he would get title. Standard Parts, which acquired Hess-Pontiac and thus succeeded to the latter's interests, argued that they owned any ideas Peck came up with while working for Hess-Pontiac. The Supreme Court agreed with Standard, saying that Peck did "nothing more than he was engaged to do and paid for doing."

As we can see, the basic rule is that if you hire or assign someone to do something, work on a project, perform a task, or accomplish a stated objective, and you pay for that work, then you own the result. If you pay for someone to solve a problem, if that is part of his job, then the solution is yours. Peck was assigned to work on and develop certain machines. He was paid for doing that. Title to those machines, therefore, belonged to his employer, Hess-Pontiac (Standard Parts after they acquired Hess). Peck is a classic example of an employee "hired to invent." And ownership is not altered by an issued patent. If the employer owns the invention or discovery, he owns the patent rights too.

There is a lot of litigation in this area and much of it involves the question of just what an employee was hired and paid to do. That is something that must be resolved with attention to the particulars of a case. But if an employee was not hired to invent, does the employer have any rights to his discoveries?

The "shop-right" concept and its limits

Warren H. Lockwood had been employed as a sales manager for the Coleman-Petterson Corporation when he conceived the idea for bakery receptacles that could be stacked one on top of the other when filled and nest into each other when empty. An essential feature of that idea was that the nesting and stacking could be accomplished without turning the receptacle.

At the time he thought of the bakery receptacle idea, Lockwood was in charge of Coleman's Cleveland plant, directing its salesmen selling bakery equipment items including a flat wire-and-metal bakery tray and a delivery cart housing the trays. From the testimony at trial, it appears that Lockwood had been alone in a motel room one weekend when he started drawing sketches "and silhouettes, and, after cutting them out and using pins, worked paper models of receptacles together." A few days later Lockwood went to see a patent lawyer to discuss his idea. He prepared some models and instructed his attorney to conduct a patent search and prepare a patent application, which he paid for out of his own funds.

Coleman-Petterson Corporation had no employment contract with Warren Lockwood, and when it sold its business to Fanner Metal Products Company, Fanner continued to employ Lockwood as its salesman in Cleveland, without a contract.

After his patent application was filed Lockwood disclosed his invention to William Coleman, who was then a vice-president of Fanner. Coleman expressed no interest in the invention and nothing further happened until Lockwood was transferred to Los Angeles and met with Vincent Ryan, the general manager of Fanner's Los Angeles plant. Lockwood told Ryan of his invention and proposed a license. After discussion, Ryan suggested that the matter "slide a little bit longer," primarily because there was no apparent market for the invention.

A few months later, Safeway Stores, Inc. had a problem to which Lockwood's invention seemed applicable. However, another Fanner employee, named Wilson, developed an open rack on wheels into which the trays sold by Fanner could be placed. Lockwood permitted Fanner to make a set of samples of his receptacle to offer Safeway, but they chose the Wilson rack. Ryan then told Lockwood

"I don't see any interest in that invention of yours. I don't know that it has any value."

Eventually Lockwood quit his job at Fanner to exploit his invention. He licensed it to a company called Mid-West, which agreed to help develop it to a commercial stage. Mid-West succeeded in developing Lockwood's receptacle, and started selling it in competition with the Wilson rack sold by Fanner.

Subsequently, Banner Metals, Inc. acquired the Fanner Company. A few months later it started marketing a receptacle, incorporating Lockwood's invention, to Safeway Stores in Los Angeles. When Mid-West accused Banner of infringing the Lockwood patent, Banner said it either owned the Lockwood patent or at least had a "shop right" to use the invention. Banner (having acquired the rights of Fanner which, in turn, had succeeded to the rights of Coleman-Petterson) argued that Lockwood had made his invention while an employee of the company. According to Banner, since Lockwood was an employee, he was familiar with the company's business, its problems, and customer needs. Therefore, Banner reasoned, Lockwood had an obligation to his employer—either to assign full rights to the employer or, at the least, to permit Banner to use the invention royalty-free.

The California District Court of Appeal noted first that Lockwood was hired to sell, not invent, and second, that he was not under any contract to assign his inventions to his employer. Furthermore, the court observed, Lockwood made his discovery on his own time, utilizing his own resources and, with the single exception of permitting Fanner to make some samples to display to Safeway, bearing all costs himself.

The California court also stated that you do not necessarily give up your rights to any ideas or inventions merely because you become an employee. And that holds true even if the employment furnishes the opportunity or occasion for the conception of the idea, or enhances your mechanical skill or scientific knowledge and inventive faculties so as to enable you to develop and perfect the idea. This also holds true for improvements the employee may make to a device or process used by the employer. Merely because an employer furnishes an employee with the opportunity or setting in which to come up with a new idea does not, of itself, mean that the employer owns the idea.

The California court, after denying Banner Metals' claim to ownership of the Lockwood invention, proceeded to discuss Banner's claim to "shop rights." First the court set the background for a shop right, namely the employee who is not hired to invent but invents anyway, using his employer's facilities:

> . . . the discovery of an invention by an employee, whose duties to his employer do not require him to make any inventions, during the course of his employment through the use of the employer's equipment, materials and labors does not deprive the employee of his invention although the employer may have a shop right in the invention which gives him a non-exclusive, irrevocable license to use the invention.

Then the court defined the shop-right concept:

> The limits of the shop right doctrine have been thus defined: Where an employee (1) during his hours of employment, (2) working with his employer's materials and appliances, (3) conceives and (4) perfects an invention for which he obtains a patent, he must accord his employer a non-exclusive right to practice the invention.

A shop right, then, is a royalty-free, nonexclusive and irrevocable license to the employer (and his successors in interest) to use the invention. But since it is based on an equitable principle of fair play it is generally regarded as personal in nature. That is, it goes along with the business of the employer (had there been a shop right it would have gone along with Coleman's business to Fanner and then Banner) but the employer can't sell or license it to third parties—that could destroy a "secret" if secret, and if patented it would destroy the exclusivity (except for the employer's personal use) that a patent would otherwise confer.

Let us return to the Dubilier case for a moment. Remember that the Supreme Court said that even though Dunmore and Lowell were government employees, they and not the government owned the inventions they came up with. But the court went further and also said that since Dunmore and Lowell made their discoveries on the job, using the facilities of the Bureau of Standards, the bureau had a shop right to the use of those discoveries. So while Dunmore and Lowell got title to the patents, the government wound up with a royalty-free, nonexclusive, permanent license.

In contrast, Banner Metals received no rights whatever to Warren Lockwood's idea, even though it was suggested to Lockwood by a problem he saw while working for his employer (Coleman-Petterson, now Banner Metals). The fact that the job suggested the problem and that it was solved by Lockwood while still an employee did not give his employer any rights to the solution. Lockwood was not hired to solve that problem; it was never part of his assigned duties.

And because Lockwood did not make any material or significant use of his employer's facilities, he did not even have to give up a shop right to his employer.

In summary, the basic common-law principles that govern ownership of ideas, inventions, and discoveries of employees are:

1. When an employee makes an invention or discovery within the scope of his employment, and he was hired to invent, i.e., employed to solve the problem or think of the idea underlying that invention or discovery, that invention or discovery belongs to the employer. The theory is that the employee was only doing what he was paid to do. Coming up with that invention or discovery was part of his job.

2. When an employee makes an invention that is outside the scope of his employment, something he was not hired to do, but utilizes his employer's resources, i.e., equipment, labor, materials, and/or facilities in making the invention, that invention is owned by the employee subject to a "shop right" on the part of the employer. That employer has a nonexclusive, irrevocable license to use the invention indefinitely, without having to pay a royalty.

3. When an employee makes an invention working outside the scope of his employment and does not use his employer's resources, then the invention belongs to the employee and there is no shop right reserved to the employer.

To Inventions the Employer Does Not Use

It's interesting that Lockwood offered to make a deal with his employer but was turned down. Initially, the employer saw no commercial potential to the invention. So Lockwood went elsewhere—and finally entered into an agreement with another company. But what if Lockwood had assigned his rights to his employer and the latter did not use it?

Each year thousands of inventions are made by employees and assigned to and patented by their employers. Only a minute fraction (estimates by Department of Commerce officials range from about 1 to 5 percent) are ever commercialized. Almost every patent lawyer has met his share of inventors eager for a patent primarily as a testimonial of brilliance. Once obtained, the inventor may be satisfied to frame the patent and hang it on the wall reserved for trophies. There is no requirement in the law that an inventor commercialize his discovery. He must reduce it to practice, but that can take the form of a crude working model or may be accomplished "constructively."*

Our legal system contains no requirement that a patent owner must commercialize or work his or her patent. And it makes no difference whether the employer patented the employee's discovery or not. If the ownership rights belong to the employer, whether because the employee was "hired to invent" or because of an employment contract requiring employees to assign their inventions to their employer or because of a voluntary transaction— whatever the reason—there is no legal obligation on the part of the employer to do anything with it. The employer may choose not even to apply for a patent, but to prefer a trade secret.

In contrast, legal systems throughout much of the industrialized world, particularly in countries in Western Europe, impose such a requirement. Failure to use or work a patent will result in forfeiture of that patent in virtually every country in Western Europe. In West Germany, for example, if an employer fails to make use of an employee's discovery within a five-year period, the employee may reclaim the rights to it.

Although not legally required to do so, many companies, Exxon

*A "constructive" reduction to practice is a legal fiction having meaning only within the context of patent law. An invention is said to be constructively reduced to practice, even though the idea never went further than having been put to paper, by the act of filing an application for patent. That patent application constructively reduces the invention to practice for all legal purposes, for example, determination of a dispute between two (or among several) claimants as to who has priority (who thought of the idea and reduced it to practice first).

and Ciba-Geigy among others, have adopted a policy of returning to employees after a period of time (usually several years) the rights to unused inventions made by those employees. General Electric will even help its employees start up new business ventures based on inventions or discoveries that General Electric can't use itself, and will help finance them in return for a share of the equity (usually a minority share).

To General Background Information and Skill Acquired During Employment

Can an employee ever leave his job and use the information he acquired on his former job in competition with his former employer and yet live happily ever after? The law says maybe. Under common-law principles the answer would be yes, assuming there are no elements of unfair competition involved. But even that may be modified by an employment contract. Let's look at how it works under the common law so that we can appreciate the impact of an employment contract.

A good illustration of the point involved may be taken from the case of *Wexler* v. *Greenberg.* Alvin Greenberg had been hired as chief chemist by the Buckingham Wax Company, owned by Irving and Mildred Wexler. Greenberg spent about half of his time working in Buckingham's laboratory, where he analyzed and duplicated competitors' products and then used the resulting information to develop various new formulas. The remainder of his time was spent ordering necessary materials, talking with chemical salesmen concerning better or cheaper ingredients for Buckingham's products so as to lower costs and improve quality. The products Greenberg was improving were those sold by Buckingham, namely chemicals for sanitation and maintenance purposes, such as floor waxes and cleaners.

Among Buckingham's customers was Brite Products Company, Inc. Brite purchased exclusively from Buckingham.

The fireworks started when Brite hired Greenberg to work for them. After Greenberg joined Brite, the latter no longer limited its business to selling a complete line of maintenance and sanitation chemicals but now started manufacturing them. Greenberg was, of course, instrumental in getting Brite into the manufacture of cleaners and floor waxes, using some of the formulas he had worked with during his employment by Buckingham.

At the trial level the lower court found that Greenberg had appropriated formulas acquired during his employment with Buckingham and went on to enjoin him and Brite from using those formulas. But the case was appealed to the Supreme Court of Pennsylvania and that court reversed. The court made particular note of the fact that the formulations involved were not *disclosed* to Greenberg by Buckingham. The court went on to say: "the fact is that these formulas had been developed by Greenberg himself . . ." That court also commented:

> This problem becomes particularly significant when one recognizes that Greenberg's situation is not uncommon. In this era of electronic, chemical, missile and atomic development, many skilled technicians and expert employees are currently in the process of developing potential trade secrets. Competition for personnel of this caliber is exceptionally keen, and the interchange of employment is commonplace. One has but to reach for his daily newspaper to appreciate the current market for such skilled employees. We must therefore be particularly mindful of any effect our decision in this case might have in disrupting this pattern of employee mobility, both in view of possible restraints upon an individual in the pursuit of his livelihood and the harm to the public in general in forestalling, to any extent widespread technological advances.

The Supreme Court of Pennsylvania said that in order for Buckingham to prevail it had to show two things: (1) a legally protectible secret; and (2) a legal basis, either a covenant or a confidential relationship, upon which to predicate relief. The court said that Buckingham could not stop Greenberg from simply using his aptitude, his skill, or the general knowledge he acquired during the course of his employment.

The Pennsylvania court went on to recognize that in the usual situation "an employer *discloses to his employee* a pre-existing trade secret." (Emphasis placed by the court in its opinion.) In that case the employee is said to be bound by a fiduciary duty to keep the information confidential. In the court's words, a pledge of secrecy is applied. But the formulas in issue were merely the result of Greenberg's routine work of changing and modifying formulas.

The modifications involved were the fruits of Greenberg's own skill as a chemist. There was no indication that Buckingham had specifically hired Greenberg to make the formulations he had made while at Buckingham and was now using on behalf of Brite. Therefore the Pennsylvania court concluded that Greenberg violated no trust or confidential relationship in continuing to use those formulas. That court said that the information involved was merely a part of Greenberg's technical knowledge and skill, which he acquired by virtue of his employment with Buckingham, and which "he has an unqualified privilege to use."

The court also went on to exonerate Brite, saying that former customers are legally entitled to compete with their suppliers "as long as they do so properly." Since there was no evidence that Brite had actually enticed Greenberg away from Buckingham or that Brite was specifically out to get Buckingham's trade secrets, there was no evidence of unfair competition on the part of Brite. The significant aspect of the case is the court's recognition of an employee right to use his general knowledge, experience, and skill when he leaves an employer.

The *Wexler* v. *Greenberg* case stands out a bit because most courts would find that developments including new formulations by an employee, in the course of his employment, so long as that was expected of him, belong to the employer. Since it appears that it was part of Greenberg's job to develop new formulations, most courts would find that those formulations belong to the employer. But the Supreme Court of Pennsylvania brushed that aside, saying it saw no evidence that the particular formulations involved were "the goal which Buckingham expected" Greenberg to find. The upshot of the case left Buckingham with the continued right to use those formulas—essentially a shop right—but it left Greenberg with possession of those formulas since they were a product of Greenberg's mind. Since Greenberg discovered those formulas, he alone, for example, had the right to file a patent application. The case stands strongly in favor of the right of an employee, when leaving one job, to continue to use his general knowledge, experience, and skill.

Other courts have recognized that right too. But there is a controversy in the law, a relatively unsettled point, with respect to the right to rely on "memory." There are a good number of court decisions saying that it makes no difference whether the employee takes his employer's trade secrets in a written form or memorizes them. The rules applicable to the right of the employee to use the information involved remain the same. That is, if the information is truly a trade secret then the employee can expect to be enjoined from using the information and it is no answer that he memorized the information. That reasoning was noted by a California appellate court in the case of *Alex Foods, Inc.* v. *Metcalfe and Torgerson,* described more fully in the next section on customer lists. But it may be worthwhile noting here that an appellate court in New York has held just the opposite.

In the case of *Anchor Alloys, Inc.* v. *Non-Ferrous Processing Corp.,* the Appellate Division, Second Department, of the New York State Supreme Court said: "a former employee, without the use of a list belonging to his former employer, may solicit the latter's customers and that remembered information as to specific needs and business habits of particular customers is not confidential." The New York court cited a number of cases in support of its position. The point is simply that when reviewing the right of an employee to quit a job and go someplace else and continue to use his general knowledge, experience, and skill it is important to keep in mind that what he takes with him as part of his memory may or may not be considered part of that background knowledge. Roger Milgrim in his treatise *Trade Secrets,* and David Bender in a comprehensive law review article on the subject, are of the opinion that it makes no difference whether the information is taken by tangible means or memorized. In other words, courts are likely to apply the same rules to memorized information as to information gathered on paper. David Bender notes that customer lists provide the most troublesome aspect in this area and with that let us now turn to that subject.

To Customer Lists and Client Contacts

The difference between stealing an employer's trade secrets and taking his customers, it is said, is like the difference between stealing an employer's car and taking his wife, too. One reason for the acute sensitivity of top management to the threat of losing its customers is that more often than not top management cultivated those customers. A look at the chief executives of *Fortune*'s list of the top five hundred industrial companies reveals that marketing and finance are the principal routes to the top. And usually both backgrounds share a strong affinity for the firm's customers. The loss of customer relationships to a firm may have more of an immediate impact than the loss of manufacturing secrets—however prized those secrets may be.

An employee who leaves with his former employer's valued manufacturing know-how may indeed do considerable damage. But that damage will frequently take the form of a long-range threat. That is, the "lost" secrets may enable a competitor to enter a field and threaten the former employer's market share or price structure. Certainly that is important—important enough to give rise to prompt and substantial litigation to enjoin disclosure and prevent the use of that information against the best interests of the former employer. But no matter how threatening that situation may seem, no matter how vigorously it may be pursued in and out of the courts, it still rarely provokes the peak of intense fury that seems to be reserved for a direct threat to take away a firm's customers. An attack on a customer list can bring out the summit of emotion from management. It can trigger strategy sessions worthy of a third world war or at least of a campaign for mayor of New York. The sheer outrage involved has sometimes contributed new words to our vocabulary. And that is understandable, since the loss of a significant number of customers is not something that shows up the balance sheet a couple of years later; its impact can be immediate and may even be felt in the next quarterly report.

According to William B. Barton, author of "A Study in the Law of Trade Secrets," an in-depth article for the *University of Cincinnati Law Review* tracing the historical development of trade-secret law, "Cases involving customers' lists have been productive of more litigation than any other type of case in the trade secret category."

The basic rule (assuming, for the moment, there is no employment contract in force) is that to protect a customer list an employer must establish that there is something special about the list, that it is not merely a compilation of names and addresses that almost anyone can obtain from a trade directory. For example, in a case decided in Texas in 1970, an employee, A. C. Crouch, had left his employer, taking both customer and supplier lists. When the employer asked for an injunction, the Texas court distinguished between the two and refused an injunction as to the list of suppliers. The identity of the suppliers, it turned out, was readily available to anyone who cared to consult the appropriate trade directory. Virtually everyone in that business knew how to compile that list of suppliers. There was nothing unique or confidential about the supplier list. Sometimes the customer list can also be compiled easily from trade directories. But in this case the list of customers contained private information about each customer— the names of key men in the company who had authority to issue purchase orders or to instruct their purchasing departments to issue purchasing orders. The customer list also contained some personal information about those key executives, background information of the sort that sometimes proves helpful in a sales call. The latter information is not found in published directories and would not normally be available to a competitor. Thus permitting Crouch, the ex-employee, to take advantage of it would be indulging a form of unfair competition.

In another case, in New Jersey, a manufacturer of rectifiers lost two employees of long standing. One had been with the firm for about nineteen years and the other for over twenty years. Both left the company to start their own rectifier business. What angered the former employer even more than the new competition was that his customer book was missing. The employer was sure his former employees had taken it. Indeed, some witnesses indicated they had seen the former employees remove cartons of book from their offices when they left the company and that they believed the customer book was among them. The significance of the customer book was that aside from identifying the customers for rectifiers, it indicated such business information as the volume of purchases and the dates when purchases were made and by whom, and also provided a basis for determining when replacement parts would be needed.

Because of the unique characteristics of the customer book, that employer succeeded in obtaining a temporary injunction against his former employees. In granting the injunction the New Jersey court verbally indicated to counsel that it saw nothing wrong with the former employees going off on their own and starting a new business in competition with their former employer. But the nature of the information contained in the customer list it regarded as particularly sensitive and confidential. The case ended in a settlement soon after the injunction issued. Trial was avoided when the former employees agreed not to call on certain customers—the one hundred best customers on that list—for a period of one year. That settlement permitted the former employees to try to get started in business calling on smaller customers but safeguarded the better customers for the former employer—at least for a year. That one-year lead time proved to be enough for the former employer to solidify relationships with its better customers and later made it difficult for the fledgling company to penetrate the cream of the customer marketplace.

It is not always necessary that the customer list contain unique information about the customer. In fact, it is sufficient if the customer list is simply not readily obtainable or discoverable without considerable effort by those who work in a trade or field. Take, for example, the case of *Hecht Foods, Inc.,* v. *Sherman.* Hecht Foods paid about $38,000 for a coffee servicing business operated by Dellwood Dairy Company, Inc. in the metropolitan New York City area. Dellwood had approximately 250 accounts. Murray Sherman was Dellwood's sales manager and he was responsible for soliciting new accounts and servicing customers. After Hecht bought the business, Sherman stayed on for about three weeks and then quit. It wasn't long before Sherman was out soliciting the same customers for his own account and Hecht brought suit.

At first the lower court decided against Hecht. It ruled that there was nothing confidential about the customer list. The Appellate Division in New York disagreed. It said that "a coffee servicing business . . . is not focused toward one particular segment of industry; rather, its potential customers are those employing a number of persons for whom coffee machines are made available during business hours at coffee breaks." In that circumstance, said the court, telephone or other directories are simply of no help in isolating and identifying those customers who have or want coffee machines. Therefore, the New York appellate court ruled that the list of customers involved was "a valuable asset of the business." The court went on to say that it made no difference that Murray Sherman neither had a written agreement nor might simply have memorized the customer list. Since Sherman had built up many of the customers while employed by Dellwood and had been paid for that work and, in the process, while being paid by Dellwood, had built up a close personal relationship with those customers, it would have been inequitable for Sherman now to call on those customers. In doing so, Sherman would have deprived Hecht Foods of a major asset that it had bought from Dellwood and paid for.

One member of the New York appellate court dissented, saying that the coffee service business involved virtually every business concern, that all such business concerns were listed in the telephone directory and that therefore there was nothing special about the customer list involved. Thus the dissenting judge would have permitted Sherman to have solicited those customers unless Sherman had signed an employment agreement containing a restriction on his doing so subsequently. (An employment contract may be used for any number of reasons, one of which is to impose a restraint on an employee—prohibiting that employee from calling on customers after he leaves the company. There are certain limits as to the scope of that restriction; that is, in terms of the time it will be enforced after the employee leaves and the geographical area in which it will be enforced, and there are other limitations relating to individual laws in the various states. A more extensive treatment of the application of restrictive covenants and employment contracts as well may be found in chapters 5 and 6.)

The Appellate Division of New York had decided another case involving customer lists a few years before the *Hecht* case. In the case of *Public Relations Aids, Inc.* v. *Wagner,* the defendant, Hyman V. Wagner, had been employed by Public Relations Aids (PRA) as its sales manager and later as its vice-president in charge of client relations. He left PRA after several years and started his own firm in the public relations field in competition with PRA. PRA sued and obtained an injunction against Wagner. Wagner appealed and the New York Appellate Court said that the injunction should not have been granted. In its opinion, said the court, "PRA's mailing lists and lists of its customers were not secrets." In fact, the court noted, PRA had often boasted of some of its well-known customers. "The names of such customers would be well-known to anyone in the business of public relations and any list of prospects could be easily and readily compiled from various available sources." Once more we see that customer lists which can be readily compiled and which contain no special or unique information about the customers cannot be protected—at least, not in the absence of an employment contract.

Sometimes a court will order an injunction to prevent a former employee from approaching customers, not so much because the customer list is itself confidential but because in order for the employee to approach those customers he must make use of information that he learned in confidence. For example, in the 1973 case of *Schwayder Chemical Metallurgy Corporation* v. *Baum*, the Michigan Court of Appeals ruled that Charles S. Baum and the company he had set up should be enjoined from competing with Schwayder, his former employer, with respect to customers located through Schwayder's customer lists. The key to this case is not that the customer list was itself confidential but that Baum could not make use of that customer list and call on those customers without, in the process, necessarily using information with respect to Schwayder's manufacturing process that had been given to him in confidence. For Baum to use that information would require a breach of a confidential relationship with respect to Schwayder.

Among other considerations that a court will look to when deciding whether to enjoin an employee from soliciting customers of his former employer is the nature of that customer relationship and whether the employee is interfering with a relationship that otherwise would have continued normally. In other words, is the customer someone who normally buys only from the former employer and would ordinarily be expected to continue in that relationship? To illustrate, take the case of *Alex Foods, Inc.* v. *Bill Woodson Metcalfe and Lloyd Torgerson,* decided in Los Angeles, California. Alex Foods, Inc. manufactured perishable Spanish food products, salads, etc., and sold them throughout southern California. Torgerson sold a competing product line. Metcalfe was a salesman who had worked as a delicatessen manager prior to becoming a route salesman for a distributor of Alex Foods.

After joining that distributor, Metcalfe was issued a small list of markets and cafés within a given route and told to build up the route by calling on all the additional markets and cafés within that geographical area. Soon thereafter the distributor for whom Met-

calfe worked was "merged" into Alex Foods, Inc. Metcalfe continued as a salesman for Alex. He was eventually promoted to
supervisor and his duties included developing routes in new areas
as well as serving as a relief route driver when necessary. Metcalfe
would also train new drivers. Thus Metcalfe had access to all route
lists. Those lists contained the names and addresses of the customers, what they normally bought, and the dates they were called
upon. As a result of his experience with Alex, Metcalfe became
acquainted with the price of products, discount policy for quantity
purchases, the types of products, and difficulties encountered with
respect to their perishability.

Several years later, because of a dispute with Alex's sales manager, Metcalfe was fired by his supervisor. Metcalfe then tele-
phoned Torgerson and told him he was no longer working for
Alex and was looking for a job. He and Torgerson had a meeting
on the afternoon of the day that Metcalfe called, and Torgerson
told Metcalfe of a reorganization of routes in Orange County to
permit more intensive coverage of that area. A few days later, after
continued discussions, Torgerson and Metcalfe met again and
Metcalfe was offered a job as a route salesman to help reorganize
the Orange County routes. Metcalfe was assigned several routes
within Orange County, routes which had formerly been serviced
by a different salesman for Torgerson. Torgerson also gave Metcalfe a route list and a price list but essentially left Metcalfe largely
to his own discretion in developing the routes to their maximum
capacity.

Within a period of four days Metcalfe obtained thirty-five new
customers for Torgerson, all of them customers who had been
handling Alex products. Metcalfe had had business dealings with
thirty-three of these thirty-five customers when he worked for
Alex. The evidence showed, however, that the great majority of
those customers continued to sell the Alex line of products alongside the new Torgerson line. On that fourth day, Alex filed a
lawsuit against both Metcalfe and Torgerson. Torgerson immediately fired Metcalfe in the hope of avoiding "trouble."

In court, Torgerson argued that the list of customers was general knowledge and pointed to a route list of retail grocery stores
in Orange County put out by the local newspaper. That newspaper
list showed the name of the store, address, name of manager or

owner, rating, and buying connection. Similar route lists for neighboring counties were also put into evidence. The names of most of the customers that Alex complained of were contained on that list except for a restaurant or two and a few delicatessen stores. After a hearing the trial court issued an injunction preventing Torgerson and Metcalfe from soliciting any more of Alex's customers and from selling or delivering any food products competing with those that Metcalfe had sold on behalf of Alex to the very same customers. Thus Torgerson not only could not seek out new customers on his own in competition with Alex but he was enjoined from dealing with or selling to those customers that Metcalfe had just begun to develop. Metcalfe and Torgerson appealed, arguing that the customer lists were simply not confidential—they were available from newspapers, all of the customers were generally known to the trade, and furthermore the nature of the business was such that a customer would not ordinarily patronize only one supplier.

The California court referred to a section of its labor code, Section 2860, which provides that everything that an employee acquires by virtue of his employment, except the compensation due him, belongs to the employer. And that holds true whether acquisition was made during or after the expiration of the term of employment, so long as it arose from that employment. The court then went on to say that a customer list built up by the employer over a period of years is his property, and its use by a former employee for his own advantage will be enjoined.

"On the other hand," continued the California District Court of Appeal, "every individual possesses a form of property, the right to pursue any calling, business or profession he may choose. A former employee has the right to engage in a competitive business for himself and to enter into competition with his former employer, even for the business of those who had formerly been the customers of his former employer, provided such competition is fairly and legally conducted." Thus the California court recognized the apparent conflict between the rights of the employer to protect property acquired over a period of years at considerable expense and the right of an employee to enter into a competitive business with his former employer. The resolution of that conflict, said the court, depended on whether Metcalfe was guilty of unfair competition in soliciting the customers of Alex. Metcalfe had a right to go out into a business competitive with Alex's, but he could not engage in unfair competition in order to do so.

If we stop for a moment and refer back to the case in New Jersey involving the two employees who had decided to set up a competing rectifier business, the unfair competition element involved there was their knowledge of just whom to call upon, specific information about customers and their past purchasing habits, and specific information as to when replacement parts would be needed. That kind of information courts will recognize as not being part of what competitors normally have. Thus it was not fair to say that those employees were just like anyone else deciding to go into the rectifier business. They carried with them more than the ordinary skill and years of experience they had acquired while working for their former employer. They carried with them specific details that a new competitor in the field would not ordinarily have. That constituted unfair competition. By analogy, did Metcalfe have anything that was beyond the ordinary knowledge acquired through experience? Was Metcalfe in a position to utilize information that came to him in confidence and that he would not otherwise have been aware of and that competitors would not normally have been aware of?

In deciding the case the court drew a distinction—between a handful of customers of Alex Foods that had switched to the products sold by Torgerson as a result of Metcalfe's sales efforts and the large group of wholesale buyers who normally dealt in competitive lines and who continued to remain customers of Alex Foods even though a portion of their business was given to Torgerson. As to the wholesale buyers, it was clear that they normally carried more than one brand of Spanish food products so that they could furnish their customers a choice or selection.

Although the California District Court of Appeal that decided this case referred to several criteria for determining whether to protect a customer list, it particularly focused on one, namely the question of whether the business involved was such that a customer would ordinarily patronize one concern so that the business involved would have continued but for the interference. In other words, was it likely that Torgerson might have obtained the customer's business anyway without Metcalfe because the customer tended to patronize more than one concern. It appears that a few of the retail customers actually fell into that category—they normally patronized only one concern, and if they had not been solicited by Metcalfe they would have continued to be customers of Alex. But the vast majority of the customers that Metcalfe called on were wholesalers. Since those wholesalers normally carried competing brands, and since they continued to carry the product line of Alex even after Metcalfe called on them, it was not fair to say that they would not have carried Torgerson's product line but for Metcalfe's intervention and use of his special knowledge acquired while employed by Alex. Therefore, the court modified the injunction, saying that it should be limited to the category of customer of Alex Foods that did not carry competing lines and whose business with Alex would normally be expected to continue unless interfered with. Thus, Metcalfe and Torgerson were now free to call on wholesalers who carried competing lines, and on retailers with whom Metcalfe had not directly conducted business for Alex.

Another twist to the customer relationship problem comes where the former employee simply sends out a notice to the customers with whom he has been dealing on behalf of his former employer and merely says that he is going into business for himself. So long as the employee goes no further, does not make any effort to solicit the business from those customers, there is very little likelihood of getting an injunction. There have been several cases along this line that have indicated that a former employee may *receive* business from customers of his former employer even though he is prohibited from soliciting that business. James A. West, for example, had been employed as a salesman by Aetna Building Maintenance Company, Inc. West had signed an employment contract with Aetna agreeing not to "solicit, serve and/or cater to any of the customers of the Company [Aetna] served by him" as an employee for a period of two years after termination of his employment.

The evidence showed that when West decided to leave Aetna, he let a few of the customers he had been calling on know that he was going into business for himself. There was specific evidence of at least one instance where he had advised a customer of Aetna of his plans before he left the company. In other instances he advised the customers after leaving Aetna. But the evidence failed to show that there was any active solicitation of business.

Samuel Zaegel, president of Aetna, testified that Aetna had taught West how to estimate and sell a job and trained him in the techniques involved. That kind of practical information was vital to the successful estimation of a contract in order to avoid financial loss.

A trial court found for Aetna. It enjoined West from diverting any more of Aetna's customers (he apparently had already taken three), and he was also enjoined from "soliciting, diverting, or taking away, directly or indirectly, any customers of" Aetna.

On appeal, however, the Supreme Court of California reversed. The latter court said that West had a right to notify customers of the fact that he was going into business for himself, and that "West was entitled to accept business from Aetna's former customers and such acceptance, by itself, did not constitute solicitation." Although the California Supreme Court recognized that Aetna was entitled to protection against West's use or disclosure of trade secrets given to him, the court could find no evidence that the information involving building maintenance and janitorial-type services actually constituted a trade secret. Although Aetna's methods of estimating a contract may have been well refined by then, there was no evidence that they were secret or that competitors in the business did not use essentially the same methods of computing costs. It appears that the court was convinced that anyone who went into the business would sooner or later develop the same costing method for determining the price of a contract and that there was nothing unusual about the way Aetna did business. There was no evidence that others in the trade did not do business in the same way.

One interesting aside here is that the employment contract appears to have been worded broadly with the intent to prevent West not only from soliciting but actually from serving any of Aetna's customers for a two-year period after he left the company. But the Supreme Court of California chose to construe the contractual language in it narrowly, so that it applied only to instances where West would actually seek the business of those former customers of Aetna. The court's reading did not preclude West from servicing those customers when they came to him. One interesting and unanswered question is whether West would have been prevented from *receiving* business from customers he had serviced while working for Aetna if the employment contract he signed actually and *specifically* said that he would not solicit or accept such business. The chances are that in some states such a contract would be enforced literally and in others it would not.

In general, courts take a stricter and more protective attitude toward enforcing restrictive covenants in employment contracts, including restrictions against an employee either soliciting or accepting business with customers of his former company, where that employee is a principal of a company and where he participates in the sale of that company. For example, the *New York Law Journal* reported a case decided by the Supreme Court of New York where an individual, Edward Casey, had sold his business and along with it its goodwill. As part of the sale he agreed that he would not solicit business with or accept employment from customers. (Actually the covenant not to compete was even broader than that.) After the sale of the business Casey found himself out of work and when he couldn't get another job in his field, he asked the Supreme Court of New York to declare his covenant not to compete void. But the New York court said absolutely not. Here the restrictive covenant wasn't just a part of an employment agreement, but part and parcel of the sale of the business and part of the goodwill of the business. Casey had been specifically paid for that restrictive covenant—he had sold for a fee his right to compete in this area for a certain period of time; this right was specifically bargained for. In other words, when you buy a company and its goodwill and the principals who sell the company to you agree not to call on that business' customers for a reasonable period of time—which is set out in the agreement—then you will find that in virtually every jurisdiction you will be able to enforce that restriction, at least with respect to those principals.

Be careful here, because as to the employees of those principals, the general rules apply. After all, they did not participate in the sale of the business and they did not give up any specific rights as part of the sale of the business or its goodwill. Keep in mind that the term "principal" refers to those who have significant financial interest in the business sold, and not merely to any minority shareholder, such as an employee with a very small interest but no real authority to influence the transaction one way or the other.

In summary, it may be helpful to quote from Rudolf Callman's well-known treatise *The Law of Unfair Competition, Trademarks and Monopolies:* "The obvious cannot be secret. Thus, every man, woman and child knows that barbers, butchers, bakers and grocers use white coats, aprons and towels." Although one may quarrel as to what barbers and grocers are wearing these days, the point is clear. Where a customer list is nothing more than a compilation of names and addresses that can be obtained readily from published sources such as a trade directory or the yellow pages of a telephone book, then the law will not recognize that list as a trade secret and will not enforce it as such.

Where a customer list—such as the names of individuals along a milk route, or a list of homeowners who regularly have their rugs shampooed—is carefully culled out with considerable effort, then the law will step in and protect that list. There simply are no trade directories or other sources from which one can simply look up those who regularly have their milk delivered or their rugs shampooed.

Where the customer list incorporates specific information on the customers—such as personal information about key executives and details about the type of purchases they make—then that too can constitute a trade secret and be protected because, once more, it is not the kind of information that is generally available.

A customer list may be protected under circumstances where the former employee cannot possibly call on any of the former customers that he once called on without violating another obligation, such as a requirement that he not use or disclose other information, e.g., manufacturing process information. In the latter case it's not really the customer list that the court is protecting but the customer list is nonetheless the beneficiary of a primary objective: to protect other trade secrets.

Remember, too, that in deciding whether to protect a customer list a court will not only look to whether the customers are known or whether the list is generally available to the trade, or can easily be ascertained, but will also look at the nature of the customers. Where the customers tend to buy only from one source and the element of loyalty is significant, there is more of a tendency to protect that relationship. But where the customers are accustomed to dealing in competitive lines, such as the wholesale buyers in *Alex*

Foods v. *Metcalfe,* then the likelihood is that the courts will not protect that type of customer relationship. Furthermore, even when all the other elements are satisfied, the law recognizes a difference between a former employee who actively solicits customers of his former employer and one who merely notifies those customers of the fact of his availability as a competitior but goes no further. The courts are not likely to enjoin an employee from receiving business from customers of his former employer even though the circumstances are such ʰat they will prohibit that same employee from soliciting such business.

Most courts are far more protective of customer relationships with respect to the principals of a company who sell the company and its goodwill and who agree contractually that they will not compete with or call on the customers of that business for a specified period of time.

The above principles are common-law principles, but they may be modified by contract. Most of the states will enforce such a contract, subject to certain qualifications. Those qualifications are significant—many devolve from basic common-law considerations —and the further chapters of this book will help throw them into focus.

2 □ The Right to Compete and Take Competitive Employment

In looking at the subject area of trade secrets and their protection, there is a diversity of factors to be considered. But common to every one of these is the central fact that it is always through the actions of people that confidential information is threatened or lost. Those actions may be accidental or deliberate; they may grow out of ignorance or result from planned behavior. Whatever they are, it is clear that without the agency of a person with knowledge of and/or access to a trade secret, there would be no threat of divulgence. So the most obvious route towards controlling the flow of secret information is to control those people who have knowledge of it and/or access to it.

Employers have long realized that the protection of their interest does require the exercise of control over those in their employ. The difficulty that arises for them in this context, however, is that in a free society individuals are acknowledged the right to take employment where they can and will. That includes the recognition of a common liberty to resign from one's position of employment in order to assume a more attractive position elsewhere, even if that is with a previous competitor firm. And there is perhaps no area of the law of trade secrets that has given rise to a greater number of lawsuits than that associated with competitive activities by former employees. But as ours is a mobile society in which economic mobility and personal freedom are highly valued, before one can realistically discuss the controls today's employers can consider or rely on in an effort to protect vital trade secrets, it is important first to understand what limits are imposed by the employee's rights.

In a survey of about five thousand MBAs, graduates of twelve of the nation's leading business schools, published by the *Harvard Business Review,* November–December 1971, under the title "Job-Hopping and the MBA" some interesting statistics were uncovered. The survey involved four consecutive graduating classes from such leading business schools as Harvard, Wharton, Columbia, Indiana, Carnegie-Mellon, Virginia, UCLA, Michigan, Northwestern, Tulane, and Amos Tuck. Of some thirteen thousand questionnaires, 5,022 MBAs responded—a response rate of 40 percent, which also reflected nearly 10 percent of the total number of those who received MBA degrees in the United States during the four graduating years 1965–68. By 1970, more than half the graduating class of 1965 had left their first employer. The survey indicated that about 10 to 13 percent of each graduating class left their first employers within the first year after graduation. Within the first two years of graduation, approximately 23–26 percent of each of the four graduating classes had left their first job, and by the end of the third year, 34–37 percent had taken new employment. Among the reasons given for leaving were limited opportunity for promotion, limited job responsibility, underutilization of their MBA training, and inadequate salary. Although still other reasons were given, those four were the reasons most frequently mentioned.

A quick look at those four reasons most frequently cited by the so-called job-hoppers reveals a common thread. Three of the four reasons most frequently cited reflect an apparent desire for greater use of one's talents, that is, a desire to maximize opportunity and responsibility. Salary ranked next to opportunity and responsibility in terms of its importance to those who sought new jobs.

The survey indicated a tendency of many MBAs to move into smaller companies on their second and third jobs. Reflecting on that tendency to move into smaller companies, the *Harvard Business Review* comments: "Although some of this movement can be explained by the MBA's desire to form his own company or to gain a greater equity share in the company for which he works, many MBAs believe the opportunities for rapid advancement, for more substantial job responsibility, and for more freedom of action are greater in the smaller company." (One interesting observation that is worth noting is that the survey indicated "that turnover is *not* related to age, marital status, and several other variables with which it has often been linked.")

Not only do employees seek greater opportunity elsewhere, but often employers seek greater talent elsewhere. And quite often that talent is sought from among the employees of one's competitors. For example, *The New York Times,* on Sunday, May 14, 1978, reported on the first page of its Business and Finance section that "the nation's most prestigious brokerage firms are wooing their competitors' star brokers with huge bonuses, inflated commissions, and paid-up insurance policies. Some are pirating entire brokerage offices, paying a bounty to office managers for each employee brought along in the switch. Hired headhunters are conducting massive telephone recruiting campaigns."

That article, entitled "Body Snatching on Wall Street," reported that body-snatching was hardly new to Wall Street, and it described specific instances of employee "piracy." Indeed it quoted Richard McFarland, President of Bain, Kalman and Quail, a Minnesota-based regional brokerage firm that is taking legal action against raiders, as saying that big brokerage houses proselytize "like a bunch of piranha."

In an October 9, 1978, article entitled "The Head Hunters Are After *You,*" *Fortune* magazine reported that "the closely guarded data banks at Boyden and at Heidrick & Struggles [both executive-search firms] each contain more than 100,000 names; data banks at the other big firms hold between 50,000 and 100,000 names apiece." That article described the increasing success in the executive-search field and attributed it, in part, to "the rising demand for talent [that] has coincided with a falling supply of talent. . . ."

Among the leading executive-search firms mentioned in the *Fortune* article is Spencer Stuart & Associates. Roger M. Kenny, a vice-president of Spencer Stuart, is quoted in an article in the Business and Finance section of *The New York Times* for Friday, September 9, 1977, as saying, "when I started in this business ten years ago, the books on Management I read advised that I could become Chairman of a company if I stuck to it. This is false. It's a timeworn adage." Kenny then proceeded to explain the double standard of loyalty that often prevails in a company. That double standard involves the expectation by the company of an executive's loyalty that is greater than the company's loyalty to the executive. To illustrate his point, Mr. Kenny cites the example of a company seeking to replace an executive. It will often initiate a search to find a replacement without notifying that executive, and the unwitting executive is usually shocked to learn that his job is gone. That very same company, on the other hand, cannot tolerate the unhappy executive who is seeking employment elsewhere. That employee must go about his business of finding other employment discreetly for fear of being dismissed summarily.

And yet it is clear that for a company to invest capital in the development of a business, for a company to be able to afford substantial investments to stimulate research and to improve business methods, it is necessary to have some degree of protection against the unscrupulous misuse and abuse of information—some means of protecting data that has been acquired at a high price. Without that protection, much of the motivation behind many substantial investments in research and new technology would be lost. Much of the impetus behind capital investment in newly developing areas of endeavor would be lost if that business, once developed, could be taken away at the blink of an eye by unscrupulous competitors or once-trusted former employees. True, some protection exists in the patent laws, but not everything can be patented. Indeed, the subject matter of patents is quite limited by statute. Most of the know-how developed by industry is not patentable. Customer relationships and the goodwill of a business cannot be patented. Business methods cannot be patented. Indeed, the wheels of business for the most part turn on information and data that are not patentable. And even that subject matter that is patentable provides protection of a limited nature, limited in scope and duration. Thus, to stimulate capital investment it is essential that some means of protection be afforded investors so that they may realize the kind of return on their investment at least adequate to encourage continued and repeated investment, so that commerce and industry may continue to grow.

The conflict between the need for mobility on the part of employees and the need for protection on the part of industry ade-

quate to justify continued capital investment requires a balancing
act on the part of the law. The law's approach must be realistic and
pragmatic. Most judges recognize the sensitivities involved and
their decisions reflect a social awareness as well as a knowledge of
specific law and the facts and arguments presented in the particular cases before them. This area of the law and cases in this area
seem to give rise to lengthier opinions by judges; many of those
opinions could qualify as social commentary as well as legal analysis. For example, Judge Frank B. Ellis of the Federal District Court
for the Eastern District of Louisiana sitting in New Orleans said in
Standard Brands, Inc. v. *Zumpe:*

> An employer who discloses valuable information to his employee in
> confidence is entitled to protection against the use of these secrets
> in competition with him. But the employee who possesses the em-
> ployer's most valuable confidences is apt to be highly skilled. The
> public is interested in the reasonable mobility of such skilled persons
> from job to job in our fluid society, which is characterized by and
> requires the mobility of technically expert persons from place to
> place, from job to job, and upward within the industrial structure.
> And the employee himself must be afforded a reasonable opportu-
> nity to change jobs without abandoning the ability to practice his
> skills.

Because times have changed and because judges sitting on the
bench today recognize that change, a new and more pragmatic
attitude toward the employment relationship has been adopted by
the courts. As a result courts have refused to enforce restraints that
are too broad, and lawyers have become increasingly sensitive to
contracts that appear to provide greater restraints on competitive
activities by the employee than are reasonably necessary for protection of the employer. For example, in *Solari Industries, Inc.* v.
Joseph Malady, decided by the Supreme Court of New Jersey in
1970, the court decided to revise an employment agreement so as
to provide a limited form of protection, limited to the extent that
appeared to the court to be reasonable or reasonably necessary for
the protection of the employer under the circumstances.

Joseph Malady had signed an agreement with his employer,
Solari, to the effect that for one year after termination of his employment he would not, without Solari's written consent, engage

in promoting or selling equipment or products similar to or competitive with those of Solari Industries, nor engage in business with customers of Solari with whom he might have had dealings in connection with the sale of Solari products.

After some difficulties with his employer, involving questions of his authority in view of a corporate reorganization, Malady left the company and went to Italy, where he obtained a franchise from a competitor of Solari Industries. That franchise was for the distribution of products competitive with Solari's products in the United States and Canada. Malady proceeded to visit customers and prospective customers of Solari, after first obtaining a legal opinion from his attorney to the effect that the noncompetitive provision in his agreement was unreasonable and void because it was too broad—it "failed to define an area." Solari brought an action to obtain an injunction but this was denied on the basis that the provision in the agreement contained "no express geographical limitation." The court said the restriction involved was "unreasonable and void per se and is not in any part enforceable in our courts." In reviewing the lower court's opinion, the Supreme Court of New Jersey stated that "while a covenant by an employee not to compete after the termination of his employment is not ... as freely enforceable [as a covenant not to compete that accompanies the sale of a business], it will nonetheless be given effect if it is reasonable in view of all the circumstances of the particular case. ... When an employer, through superior bargaining power, extracts a deliberately unreasonable and oppressive noncompetitive covenant he is in no just position to seek, and should not receive, equitable relief from the courts."

The Supreme Court of New Jersey then proceeded to review the prior law and the circumstances and decided that equity justified "blue-penciling" the agreement—a term of art used when a court arbitrarily revises the terms of an agreement so as to make them fit the circumstances. In the case of Joseph Malady, the New Jersey Supreme Court found that his activities had centered in New York and concluded that there was ample justification for blue-pencilling the employment agreement so as to limit the restraint against Malady's activities to those of Solari's actual customers or prospective customers in the United States with whom he had substantial dealings on Solari's behalf while under Solari's employ. The court proceeded to send the case back to the lower court with instructions to provide a limited injunction based on the actual circumstances and needs of the parties involved.

The Solari case represents a case of first instance for the state of New Jersey and is important because it is representative of the current tendency on the part of the courts to take a pragmatic view of employment cases and to try to resolve them by balancing the equities involved. It is particularly illustrative of the application of a rule of reason to a situation where an employer attempts to control the competitive actions of a former employee.

Early Background

Cases like *Solari Industries* v. *Joseph Malady* can be traced back over five hundred years. In 1414 a case was decided in England that became well known in this area of the law. It is called the Dyer's Case. The Dyer's Case is the first known case dealing with restrictions on the practice of a trade or craft. To understand it, it is necessary to recall the system of apprenticeship that prevailed in medieval times. In the late fourteenth and fifteenth centuries, a system of craft guilds developed, wherein those guilds became the dominant forces of economic growth. A craft guild was composed of three classes of members: masters, journeymen, and apprentices. The master was able to obtain most of his labor through a system that involved the indenture of an apprentice. During the period of indenture, the apprentice would work primarily for the skill he acquired, his training being his essential or primary form of payment. Any other payment would, at best, be nominal. By tradition he was essentially a servant of the master for a limited period of time. Although precise terms of indenture varied from guild to guild, a custom of a seven-year period of indenture developed. At the end of the apprentice period the apprentice was free to practice his trade as a journeyman. Although he was free to provide his services for hire to whoever would pay for them, most often the apprentice would eventually become a master craftsman in the same town in which he had served his apprenticeship. One reason was simply that in time the guild developed a clublike atmosphere and membership—hence also competition—would be restricted. It took many years for one to become known and re-spected by other craftsmen and, therefore, it was not a simple matter for a journeyman to travel to a town where he was not known and join a guild.

Though it worked well throughout its first century of develop-ment, some time during the sixteenth century the guild system began to show signs of strain. A rapid increase in the number of journeymen who sought to become craftsmen made it all too sim-ple for masters who sought relatively cheap labor to take advan-tage of the system. Some guilds, using various subterfuges, would extend the period of apprenticeship beyond the seven-year term called for by the Statute of Apprentices. One means would be to bind the apprentice for a year or more after the term of apprentice-ship as consideration for the training provided during apprentice-ship. Many guilds would refuse admission to journeymen who received their training outside of the particular town or village involved. Furthermore, guilds began to require examinations of increasing stringency, and to impose fees for admission into the guild. Those fees served to increase the difficulty of admission and made it all the easier for masters to extract additional obligations from both apprentices and journeymen.

The Dyer's Case is actually the first reported case dealing with restrictions relating to the right of an employee to practice his craft. It appears that the employee, a dyer, had agreed as part of his "indenture" that he would not practice his craft for a period of six months in the same town as his master. The dyer said that he had satisfied that requirement, but the judge said that it didn't matter whether the employee had satisfied it or not, because the condition involved was illegal. The judge made a statement which, translated into today's language, reads "By God, if the plaintiff [i.e., the master] were here he would go to prison until he paid a fine to the king." The court expressed vigorous indignation at what it considered an oppressive master. By today's standards, however, a restraint of six months for a well-defined and limited geographical area, would probably be upheld in most states.

In 1536 an Act for Avoiding of Exactions Taken Upon Appren-tices was adopted. That act acknowledged that masters had "by cautil and subtil means compassed and practiced to defraud and delude" apprentices so as to make it difficult for them to work as

journeymen without the consent of the master. The law made it
illegal to compel or cause an apprentice or journeyman to agree
that when his apprenticeship term expired he would not set up or
keep shop in his craft. In 1563 the Statute of Apprentices set a
formal period of seven years for apprenticeship, after which the
apprentice would by law be free to practice his trade as journeyman. Thus England in the mid-sixteenth century recognized the
need to protect employees against restrictive covenants that would
prevent them from practicing their occupations or professions in
competition with their employers after their employment term
expired.

The attitude of the courts against restraints on an apprentice
from practicing his craft after the apprenticeship expired continued for a long time in England. In case after case involving
apprentices, even in cases where courts would specifically note that
the restraint was not a broad one, the ruling would be that it was
unlawful to restrain the practice of a trade. To illustrate how
strongly the courts felt about this issue, the case of the blacksmiths
of South-Mims is worth noting. That case was decided in 1587.
The employee, who was identified only as "another black-smith"
had agreed not to compete with his employer; that is, not to practice his craft in South-Mims after his apprenticeship. There was no
time limit; he was simply not to practice his craft in South-Mims.
The employee apparently violated that covenant and when a suit
was brought to collect on a bond that the employee had apparently
given, the local justice of the peace threw the employer in jail. It
appears that the employer was eventually freed on a writ of habeas
corpus, but the court held that the bond given by the employee was
"void, because it was against the law."

The Transition Phase: Part I
The Agreement Not to Compete as an Incident to the
Sale of a Business

One of the most celebrated cases in this area of the law, *Mitchel*
v. *Reynolds,* was decided in England in 1711 by the Earl of Macclesfield. In that case Reynolds, a journeyman baker, had agreed not
to practice his baker's art in the parish for the full term of the lease

of a bake shop that he gave to Mitchel. When he violated his word, Mitchel sued and Reynolds claimed that the restraint was illegal because it interfered with the practice of his craft. But in that case, Lord Macclesfield said that notwithstanding the ordinary presumption that restraints of trade are invalid, a special situation existed. In the case at hand, Reynolds had received valuable consideration and "by his own consent, and for his own profit, give [sic] over his trade and part with it to another. . . ."

Mitchel v. *Reynolds* has been cited for almost three centuries as the classic case involving a restraint imposed in conjunction with the sale of a business, and which is voluntarily accepted in consideration for a profit. The opinion by Lord Macclesfield specifically noted that the effects could be different in a case of restrictive covenants in employment agreements. But the latter, said Lord Macclesfield, are subject to "great abuses . . . from masters, who are apt to give their apprentices much vexation on this account, and to use many indirect practices to procure such bonds [restrictive covenants] from them, lest they should prejudice them in their custom, when they come to set up for themselves." Thus the stage was set for distinguishing between a restriction on one's right to practice his field, craft, or profession as part of an ordinary employment relationship, and a restriction voluntarily accepted for profit as part of, or in conjunction with, the sale or lease of a business where goodwill was involved.

The law has continued to recognize the practical effect of a restrictive covenant that is an incident to the sale of a business as opposed to such a covenant when it is incorporated in an employment agreement. When you buy a business and that business involves a certain amount of goodwill or reputation of a personal nature, then it is clear that the success of the business depends, in part, on the goodwill established by the seller. It follows that if the seller turns around, just after having sold his business to you along with its goodwill, and starts to compete with you—utilizing the reputation that he established in the business that he sold—the seller is actually taking back part of what he sold to you. Assume, for example, that John Smith sells his retail men's clothing store along with its goodwill. Now, if John Smith is well known in the town or locality in which his business was situated, it is apparent that if he moves across the street and sets up a competing retail business, he is continuing to trade on the goodwill that he previously established and presumably sold. Of course, if the transaction did not involve goodwill, if all that he sold was the inventory of the clothing store and the location of the store, and the buyer intended to establish his own reputation independently of John Smith, or intended to trade on a different name—perhaps a franchise name obtained by license from some large franchise operation—then it would not matter that John Smith opened up a competing operation nearby. In the latter instance, goodwill was simply not part of the transaction.

The more classic example that occurs frequently involves the so-called route cases. That is, the owner of a milk delivery route, or a delivery route involving the cleaning of laundry or the shampooing of rugs, decides to sell his business. His business has been built up by word of mouth and is based almost entirely on his personal knowledge of the particular customers involved and the personal relationship that he has with those customers. In this instance the element of goodwill stands out as the dominant feature underlying the entire operation of the business. If that owner sells the business, including the goodwill associated with it, then it is clear that if he were to solicit those customers again, he would be taking back what he sold. In route cases it is obvious that goodwill is the key to the sale of the business, and since the owner who sold the business was paid for its goodwill, then it is only reasonable that he be expected not to trade on that which he sold. Therefore, a court will enforce a restriction in the agreement of sale which says that once the owner parts company with the goodwill associated with a business, he will not thereafter trade on that goodwill, although he may engage in the same business in areas where he is not known.

The courts will almost always enforce a restriction on competition that is an incident to another transaction such as the sale of the business, assuming it appears to be a reasonable restriction, The word "reasonable" is an important one. Reasonableness is central to the whole system of Anglo-Saxon law. Recall the importance of it in *Solari* v. *Malady,* cited above. And note that the antitrust laws in the United States prevent unreasonable restraints on trade or commerce, and that unreasonable restrictions on competition among businessmen—those which are actually part of a scheme to divide markets or fix prices—are likely to run afoul of the antitrust laws. But that is another subject.

The Transition Phase: Part II
Freedom of Contract and the Industrial Revolution

As noted, the covenant not to compete that is often found in employment agreements and in employment relationships today was generally considered a restraint on trade and unenforceable in England during the medieval era. But a change slowly evolved in the late eighteenth and nineteenth centuries. Whereas the guild craftsman was at the mercy of his trade and the restriction on his ability to practice his craft could literally deprive him of basic sustenance, the workers coming out of the Industrial Revolution could often obtain other gainful employment. The economic doctrine of laissez-faire began to take hold in an environment that prized liberal economic concepts. The nineteenth century philosophers particularly placed value on the principle of freedom of contract. Although Lord Macclesfield was concerned with the basic inequality of bargaining power between the apprentice and the master, judges in the nineteenth century were primarily concerned with balancing the freedom of the market against freedom of contract. As the apprentice system disappeared in favor of factory labor, the long training periods associated with the skilled craftsman disappeared in favor of jobs that often involved little skill and perhaps no special training. Unlike the apprentice, who was virtually pinned down to his town by economic considerations, laborers could leave one economic region in favor of another and find labor in a local factory wherever industry was growing. Economic mobility developed.

A new conflict arose. Employees desired the freedom to travel about at will and take employment wherever it suited them. The employers, on the other hand, became concerned with the possibility of future competition from their own employees and with the possible loss of customers or trade secrets to their past employees.

In 1853 the Court of Queen's Bench decided that thereafter a covenant not to compete would not be considered invalid on its face but rather that anyone challenging such a covenant would have the burden of showing that the covenant involved was unreasonable. The key element here was the strong freedom-of-contract views then prevailing in England. That view prevailed in England until 1913, when it was finally discarded and the old rule holding that all restraints of trade are prima facie invalid was reinstated. But in the meantime virtually all contracts involving a restrictive covenant were upheld and enforced. To illustrate the feelings prevalent at the time it is interesting to read the comments of one judge writing in 1875 in a case that was important then, *Printing & Numerical Registering Co.* v. *Sampson:*

> ... if there is one thing which more than another policy requires it is that men of full age and competent understanding shall have the utmost liberty of contracting, and that their contracts when entered into freely and voluntarily shall be held sacred and shall be enforced by courts of justice. Therefore, you have this paramount public policy to consider—that you are not lightly to interfere with the freedom of contract.

In 1880 an important decision was arrived at in England. It set the stage for a period of about thirty years thereafter, during which time virtually all restraints of trade, including post-employment restrictions, were assumed to be valid and enforceable until proven otherwise. That case, *Rousillon* v. *Rousillon,* involved the nephew of two men who owned a champagne distribution firm. The nephew had worked for the owners as a clerk and had represented them in England as well as in other countries. He had agreed that if he left their employment he would not represent another champagne house for two years. But when the owners gave up their retail business, he decided to set himself up as a retail wine merchant. It appears that the problem arose when the nephew represented that he was from a city in Champagne although he actually had no business there. His former employers sued and the court enforced the covenant not to compete even though there was no limit of a geographical nature. In other words, the restraint was against competition for a two-year period and applied throughout the world.

The Transition Phase: Part III
The Rule of Reason

According to the Columbia Law School's Professor Harlan Blake, a prominent legal historian who has written extensively on this subject, the pendulum began to swing back again to a more moderate viewpoint in the early twentieth century, particularly with certain decisions that were arrived at around 1913–20. Keep in mind that up to this point the pendulum had swung from one end, which held all covenants not to compete in employment agreements to be unenforceable and void, to the other extreme where virtually all post-employment restrictions were assumed to be valid until proven otherwise. In the early twentieth century certain rules, which moderated the extreme viewpoints began to be formulated. Professor Blake describes those rules as follows:

> First, that the rule of reason required different measures to be applied in employee-restraint cases; second, that the employer must affirmatively show that the restraint sought to be enforced is no broader than needed for his reasonable protection; third, that the restraint must be reasonable, taking into account the interests of the employee as well as the employer; and finally, that a restraint could not be justified if its only purpose is to protect the employer from future competition.*

The law in the United States seemed to develop along lines parallel to English law, but in America greater emphasis was placed on protecting the employee from overly heavy burdens imposed by contract. U.S. courts did not hesitate to enforce covenants not to compete and restrictions against employees, but seemed to adopt the test of reasonableness more readily.

The test of reasonableness is a judge-made test and not a law enacted by any legislature. After being defined and refined over many, many years of court decisions, it was incorporated in a summary of the law known as the Restatement of Contracts. That Restatement was first formulated in 1932 and has been generally

*Harlan Blake, "Employee Agreements Not to Compete," 73 *Harvard Law Review* (February 1960): 643.

followed by most U.S. courts since. The Restatement itself is quite complex but Professor Blake condenses the essential elements applicable here in the following statement: "A restraint is reasonable only if it (1) is no greater than is required for the protection of the employer, (2) does not impose undue hardship on the employee, and (3) is not injurious to the public."

That very condensation is reproduced in the opinion by the Supreme Court of New Jersey in the Solari Industries case against Joseph Malady described earlier. The Supreme Court of New Jersey there analyzed the facts in the light of that test and concluded that there was no reason why an injunction could not be fashioned that would be operative only as to reasonable space and time, that is, reasonable in terms of the limitation imposed from a geographical standpoint and from the standpoint of duration. There was no reason to preclude Malady from competing with his former employer, Solari, throughout the United States, when, in fact, Malady's activities as an employee had been confined to the New York area. The test of reasonableness required modifying the covenant not to compete so as to impose a geographical limitation on the restrictive covenant. Once so revised by the court, an injunction could be issued based on a now "reasonable" restriction.

The Current Attitude of the Courts Toward the Right of Employees to Compete

As noted earlier, most courts today strive for a pragmatic analysis of the facts before them. Most judges seek to balance the interests of the employer, the employee, and society. In the absence of an overriding statute (some states have passed laws that specifically govern the employment relationship and determine whether an employer can prevent an employee from competing with him) a court will generally apply the test of reasonableness found in the Restatement of Contracts and paraphrased by Professor Blake. Let's look at a few recent decisions that illustrate the point.

In 1976, the Supreme Court of Georgia decided a case involving Frank Miller Associates, Inc. trading as Snelling & Snelling, an employment agency, and Mary C. Dunn, a former employee. It appears that Dunn had worked for Frank Miller Associates and had signed a contract at the time she was employed to the effect that within one year of the date of termination she would not compete with her former employer. The Supreme Court of Georgia in a *per curiam* opinion (the opinion of the court and not any one judge) said that covenants against competition in employment contracts are "considered in partial restraint of trade and are to be tolerated only if reasonably limited as to time and territory, and otherwise reasonable." The Georgia court said that the restriction in the contract that applied for a time period of one year in an area of a twenty-five mile radius was reasonable. But the phrase "in any capacity" was unreasonable. In the eyes of the court that phrase "would prohibit [Mary Dunn] from being employed as a book-keeper, secretary, or filing clerk by a competitor." That contract, said the Supreme Court of Georgia, was unreasonable because it imposed greater limitations on Mary Dunn than were necessary for the protection of the employer.

In 1976, the United States Court of Appeals for the Fifth Circuit (encompassing Georgia) reviewed a case brought by the well-known tax preparation firm of H & R Block, Inc. H & R Block had sued to enforce a restrictive covenant prohibiting a former employee, George R. McCaslin, from soliciting customers or preparing tax returns or in any way engaging in a competitive business with them for a five-year period in an area twenty-five miles from their office. Once more, the decision was *per curiam.* Five years was an unreasonably long period of time under the circumstances and furthermore, the covenant was unnecessarily broad in that it prohibited McCaslin from working in any capacity for a tax preparation business, however minor.

It is interesting to observe that unlike *Solari* v. *Malady,* neither the Georgia court nor the Federal Court of Appeals for the Fifth Circuit would modify the contract and impose an injunction to the extent that it considered reasonable. The Florida District Court of Appeals in July 1973 faced a somewhat similar problem in that a former employee, G. Brett Railey, Jr., had signed an agreement with his employer, containing a covenant not to compete or divulge trade secrets for a period of five years. There was no limitation geographically. Therefore, Railey argued, the clause was too broad and too indefinite, and should be held void and unenforceable. The court reduced the time period from five to three years, and limited the geographical area to the state of Florida, and to within one hundred miles of those areas in the state of Georgia where the employer, Kenco, was engaged in business. It may be of interest to observe that Florida is one of the states that has a statute specifically prohibiting contracts restraining anyone from exercising a lawful profession, trade, or business, but that this statute contains an exception. The exception is for a restraint in conjunction with the sale of a business or the sale of shares of a company. It seems that in this case, Brett Railey had been an employee and had signed an agreement with the unlawful restrictive covenant in 1968. But in 1970, he signed a new agreement which called for the sale of his stock to his employer. That agreement also contained the restrictive covenant that he complained of. The Florida court, in an opinion by Associate Judge Carroll, recognized that the original covenant not to compete was invalid but the covenant not to compete in conjunction with the second agreement, i.e., the one involving the sale of stock, was enforceable. On that basis the Florida court decided to do some blue-penciling.

What happens when an employer decides to hire someone *primarily* to prevent that person from competing? Would a covenant not to compete be enforced in that situation? It appears not—at least not according to the case known as *Lektro-Vend Corp.* v. *Vendo Co.* Judge Richard W. McLaren, sitting on the federal district court bench in Chicago, noted in his opinion: "Vendo's President admitted the major purpose and intent of the employment contract was to obtain the anti-competitive benefits accruing from the covenants." Judge McLaren concluded: "it appears to the court that this course of conduct was adopted by Vendo in an attempt to limit Mr. Stoner's activities for the full planned term of the post-employment agreement, showing that protection of goodwill was not a significant goal in obtaining the covenant." The sale of a business was involved, but the facts showed that the sale of the business was actually a facade to cover up the "primary" consideration, which was to be able to assert a restrictive covenant against Harry B. Stoner. Under the circumstances, the restrictive covenant was held to be an unreasonable restraint of trade and in violation of the antitrust laws. Once more, we have evidence of a pragmatic approach by a contemporary judge prepared to look through the apparent structure of the transaction and get at the true facts.

Special Provisions to Extend the Life of a Covenant Not to Compete

Some companies have experimented with ways in which to hold the loyalty of an employee beyond the term of employment. In the course of doing so some have successfully restrained the employee from joining a competitor. One clause that is quite popular is a consultant's clause, sometimes made optional on the part of the employer. That is, the agreement recites that the employee will continue as a consultant in the event that the employment terminates. As a consultant, the employee will be paid a certain fee and in return for that fee, agree to render certain expressly defined services, or provide his or her talent for a certain minimum number of hours per month, and will, of course, agree not to work for or join a competitor during the period of consultancy. The difficulty with such a clause is simply that it is a one-way street. It attempts to impose a mandatory consultancy on an employee even when that employee does not wish to shoulder it. But even though its enforceability is questionable as a mandatory condition for employment, if the former employee accepts the fee associated with the consultant clause, he does bind himself not to compete. The assumption here is that the agreement provides for a reasonable period of time, perhaps a year or so, after a normal period of employment terminates, during which the former employer may continue to call on the ex-employee to obtain the benefit of know-how acquired by the employee and to gain the employee's cooperation with respect to certain post-employment activity, the signature of various documents, including patent documents, and in general to have the ex-employee available for discussion so as to be able, symbolically, to "pick his brain" for a limited period of time after the employment ended. Now, if there is a fee associated with that clause and the fee is commensurate with the amount of effort or time involved, and assuming further that the clause does not work the kind of hardship that would preclude the employee from obtaining gainful employment, then there would seem to be no reason why the consultancy provision would not be enforceable. If the employee accepts the benefits involved, that is, by accepting the fees involved, then the employee in effect accepts the obligations involved.

Another means of inducing an employee to remain loyal after employment is by contingent benefit plans. Many companies have adopted savings plans whereby they will match contributions by the employee or even more than match the contributions. But there is no payout for a period of at least five years after the initial deposit. The employee's right to the employer's share is said to vest in the employee after a period of five years, but then only to the portion that has been in the savings plan for that five-year period. The point here is simply that such a plan can be so structured as to provide for a continued payout even after the employee leaves but be contingent on the employee's not joining a competitor. Similarly, deferred compensation plans can be arranged or deferred bonus schemes can be structured whereby the payouts are forfeited if the employee joins a competitor within a certain number of years after termination of employment.

Another side of essentially the same coin is an option reserved by the employer in the contract to continue the employee's salary for a limited period of time while that employee is unemployed and presumably prevented from obtaining gainful employment because of the restrictive covenant. This option simply enables the employer to offset or preclude the arguments sometimes raised by the employee and sometimes asserted by courts in their opinions that the restrictive covenant is unreasonable because it prevents the former employee from earning a livelihood. Some of the most clear-cut agreements that attorneys would regard as being eminently reasonable have been held unreasonable under "hardship" circumstances. For example, in one case described by a well-known practicing lawyer, a court was faced with a somewhat unusual set of circumstances. The lawyer was representing a company and asserting a covenant not to compete in what seemed to be a very reasonable employment contract. The covenant not to compete was limited in time to one year and geographically to the state involved. The case law by the highest courts in that state seemed ample to justify the validity of that contract. But the circumstances showed that the former employee had an extremely ill daughter, that the child was being treated by specially equipped medical facilities in a certain locality, that it was hard to reproduce the facilities involved, and that the former employee had made considerable effort to obtain employment in his particular field outside of that area but had been unable to do so—at least unable to do so in those few select areas where adequate treatment could be had for his daughter. Under the circumstances of that case, as reported by the lawyer, the judge said the restrictive covenant was simply unreasonable. Thus it appears once more that a judge was applying a pragmatic approach—and with heart.

The case of *Post* v. *Merrill Lynch, Pierce, Fenner & Smith, Inc.*, is a classic example of a common-sense approach by a judge to a situation without precedent. Jack Post worked for Merrill Lynch from 1959 to 1974, when he joined Bache & Company, a competitor. Subsequently Merrill Lynch advised Post that his rights in the company-funded pension plan had been forfeited under a provision in the plan that permitted forfeiture in the event an employee joined a competitor. But, said Post, this was not fair in his case because he didn't leave voluntarily—he was discharged without cause. Merrill Lynch said that was irrelevant. Post sued.

In the Court of Appeals of New York, Judge Sol Wachtler, after noting that there was no precedent for distinguishing between an employee who leaves voluntarily and one who is terminated by an employer without cause, went on to draw such a distinction. The restrictive covenant preventing an employee from joining a competitor is based upon a "mutuality of obligation," he said. "Where the employer terminates . . . without cause, however, his action necessarily destroys the mutuality of obligation on which the covenant rests as well as the employer's ability to impose a forfeiture. An employer should not be permitted to use offensively an anti-competition clause coupled with a forfeiture provision to economically cripple a former employee and simultaneously deny other potential employers his services. . . . it would be unconscionable to tolerate a forfeiture. . . ."

This case will almost surely serve as precedent for future cases whenever an employee is involuntarily dismissed and the employer seeks to prevent him from working for a competitor.

In summary, courts will generally apply a test of *reasonableness* to determine whether to enforce a provision in an agreement that would preclude an employee from competing with his former employer.

3 □ How Are Trade Secrets Lost?

Trade secrets are lost through the actions of individuals who have access or gain access to the confidential information that makes up the secrets. That is, of course, the obvious answer to the question above. And the nature of some or even many of those actions will be evident to employers. But often employers who indicate a concern for protection of confidential information fail to take cognizance of one or several ways in which secrets get out. And equally frequently, many employers with some awareness of how secrets can be lost fail to appreciate the total potential for damage in a situation in which they think themselves relatively invulnerable.

If a company is truly concerned to prevent the loss of valuable confidential information, then it behooves that company to be on guard on all fronts. Any security program that fails realistically to take into account the whole range of circumstances in which secrets may be compromised runs the risk of failure. What follows here is a broad overview of many of those circumstances, some of which may seem obvious—which does not mitigate the potential for eventual problems—and several of which are probably routinely overlooked in many a company's security program.

Loss Through Espionage and Corporate "Intelligence Data Gathering"

Is industrial espionage any kind of problem other than one used to provide a plot element in pulp thrillers? Just who cares anyway?

Well, E. I. duPont de Nemours & Co. showed how much they care when a small plane was spotted circling low over a plant site under construction. DuPont was building a multi-million dollar plant in Beaumont, Texas to make methanol, a basic ingredient of antifreeze and a fundamental starting chemical for many processes in the chemical industry. DuPont elected to keep the method secret instead of applying for a patent.

The plane was actually spotted by construction workers. When duPont succeeded in tracking down the plane, it found Rolfe and Gary Christopher, aerial photographers, who freely admitted they had been hired by a third party they refused to name to take aerial photographs of the plant as it was being built. The type of construction and layout apparently would have permitted that third party to calculate backwards and determine the particular secret process that duPont planned to use.

The Christophers argued that the air space in which they were flying was "public airspace." Therefore, they reasoned, anyone was at liberty to fly around and, naturally, to look around; and, of course, since you can look, you can also photograph.

Both the trial court and the U.S. Court of Appeals for the Fifth Circuit at New Orleans refused to buy that argument. Judge Irving Goldberg of the court of appeals ruled that while anyone is free to try to "reverse engineer" a product if he lawfully obtains it, by breaking it into its components mechanically or by chemical analysis and thereby discovering secrets, "our devotion to free wheeling industrial competition must not force us into accepting the law of the jungle as the standard of morality expected in our commercial relations."

In ruling for duPont in the civil suit against the Christophers, Judge Goldberg stated: "This is a case of industrial espionage in which an airplane is the cloak and a camera the dagger. . . . In taking this position we realize that industrial espionage of the sort here perpetrated has become a popular sport in some segments of our industrial community." But the judge refused to condone it.

That "popular sport" can prove and has proven fatal. In August 1968, a pretty twenty-two-year-old secretary for Hoffmann-La Roche, an international pharmaceutical firm—best known to many executives as the home of Librium and Valium—was murdered. She had been working on a Saturday in the company's medical library in Nutley, New Jersey. Although the case was not solved, police could find no plausible motive behind the murder other than the possibility that she surprised someone in the act of stealing trade secrets. Hoffmann-La Roche has since tightened its security, but if the police theory on the motive was true, the lesson was expensive.

Jacques Bergier, in his book *Secret Armies: The Growth of Corporate and Industrial Espionage* (Bobbs-Merrill, 1975) points out that the U.S. research budget in the early 1970s had climbed to over $25 billion per year (now about $40 billion), much of it spent by large corporations. That alone can serve as an inducement for corporate spying. Rather than spend hundreds of thousands of dollars to duplicate the work being conducted in the research labs of, say, a major pharmaceutical firm, a few thousand dollars placed in the hands of a corrupt employee or a "hired investigator" may do the trick, or so some firms conclude.

The front page of the *Los Angeles Times* for August 19, 1974, loudly proclaimed: "Industrial Spying: $6 Billion Drain on U.S. Business." Now, it is not unusual for a news story to appear in a major newspaper or news magazine, as it does from time to time, about an individual case of industrial espionage, or about a lawsuit brought by a company to halt a raid on its employees by another, but it is unusual for the subject itself to serve as front-page, first-column news in a paper of general circulation.

The story was not about any individual case but about the impact of industrial espionage on our economy. It pointed out that perhaps "the biggest stimulus to espionage has been the tremendous growth in research and development and the progress in technology." The story revealed such spying techniques as "laser beams fired from an unmarked van" through the closed window of an office building to pick up conversations at a meeting; a "beauty operator" who asked "seemingly casual questions about the work her customer's husband [a chemist] does;" an answering service operator who tapped into a private line. The story described the use of code names, secret drops, infiltration, mini-cameras, spies, blackmail, and other instruments straight out of "Mission Impossible." As a TV program, it would be acceptable fare. But when we recognize that it is all actually taking place, we are suddenly faced with a situation so mind-boggling as to be almost incomprehensible. How does one grasp the meaning of a six-billion-dollar loss?

Dun's Review, in October 1970, interviewed one hired investigator, whom it called "America's Number One industrial spy," Umont O. Cumming. He was described as a "dead-ringer for the late Guy Kibbee," who "with his ruddy complexion, twinkling eyes, and guileless countenance, looks like anybody's favorite uncle." Cummings, describing himself as a professional investigator, said that he logged more than one hundred thousand air miles a year carrying out assignments for major U.S. corporations and for patent-law firms. His specialty: checking to see if patents were being infringed.

How can an investigator like Cummings legitimately be hired? And why will a company—for example, duPont in the case of its plant in Beaumont—choose not to seek patent protection in the first place? Both questions relate to the difficulty of policing "process" patents.

A patent on a product, for example, a pen, can be copied and infringed but at the risk that the patent owner will find the copy on the market and use it to support a lawsuit for patent infringement. Some companies that have had experience with patent litigation might well argue that the cost of defending such a lawsuit is alone a penalty. When subsequent damages are awarded, losing that patent-infringement suit compounds the penalty. But how does a patent owner go about proving that his patent for a method or process has been infringed? A side-by-side comparison to the finished product is rarely adequate. Too often a finished product, particularly a chemical or pharmaceutical substance, cannot serve to prove the method by which it was made. Take Coca-Cola, for instance. Chemical analysis is insufficient to determine the secret process by which it is made.

The difficulty in determining whether a competitor is copying and infringing a given patented process is one reason why some companies shy away from disclosing the process in a patent. Another reason is the relatively short life of a patent compared to a trade secret. Technically, a patent lasts seventeen years in the United States (and about fourteen to twenty years in most industrialized countries in the world) but the startup time, particularly with some complex processes requiring heavy capital investment, time for pilot-plant studies, and the design and construction of a new plant, as was true in the case of duPont's methanol process, may well cut into that patent life. A trade secret, on the other hand, lasts indefinitely: witness Coca-Cola. Of course, there is the risk that someone will try to learn the secret or that it will be disclosed by a disgruntled employee who learned it during his employment, but that risk must be weighed against outright disclosure in a publication such as a patent application, particularly if the patent may be difficult to enforce.

There is still another reason why a firm, such as duPont with its methanol process, may prefer not to seek patent protection. The basic elements of the process may already be known and, hence, the overall process not patentable. Or, the overall process may even have been the subject of a patent application. But the way in which the component steps are carried out may constitute additional valuable know-how. Certain details of manufacture may add up to a major economic difference in the form of a savings in production cost, for example. And that savings in cost will permit a price differential that could spell commercial success in the form of market share and profitability. Thus know-how, in the form of collected, specific details of manufacture, may be valuable and yet fail to meet the standards required for a patent. Those details, if disclosed in an application for patent, may simply look obvious to an examiner in the U.S. Patent Office. And, indeed, often details of a process, apart from the basic steps or sequence of that process, may make all the difference in the world in a commercial sense, but little difference when viewed academically. Although the patent laws are not academic, the standards applied by those who measure the difference between what is new and described in the patent and what is old, are sometimes of an academic nature. The United States Supreme Court, for example, in a landmark decision known as *Graham* v. *Deere*, frequently cited by judges and lawyers alike, has ruled that commercial success is, at best, only a secondary consideration in determining patentability. The issue of commercial success may not even be reached or considered if the invention does not satisfy the primary conditions of novelty and unobviousness. Consequently, commercial success is not generally taken into account in establishing whether a new process or product is "obvious." But that same commercial success may be the direct result of specialized "know-how" and, therefore, valuable as a trade secret. Unlike a patent, that trade secret cannot be invalidated, but it can be lost through disclosure.

In the course of his interview with *Dun's Review,* Cummings, the professional investigator alleged to be America's number one industrial spy, admitted that he gained entrance into plants and factories through several ruses. He became "a kindly old stockholder curious to know more about a process his company is using;" an "overindulgent father" out to help his hobbyist son whose hobby happens to fit the needs of his client; a fire or building inspector making his rounds, or a workman. He apparently succeeded in getting into at least one plant by punching someone else's time clock. After a quick inspection, he punched out. On another occasion he succeeded in getting the police to help him get inside a plant—ostensibly to investigate something of a suspicious nature. Once in, he also managed to inspect a certain machine on behalf of a client. He also used his wife to help him on occasion. In one instance his wife, representing herself as a magazine reporter, succeeded in interviewing executives of a mining company and learned what the company was using to dispel poisonous fumes from diesel engines in the area. Those are but a few methods used by "professional investigators." The use of electronic "bugging" devices is frequent enough, and other methods used by industrial spies might even impress the CIA.

Some industries, ever fearful of the espionage game, hire counterespionage agents. That is suspected to be particularly true in the toy industry, where secrecy concerning next year's Christmas models is the byword. The auto industry is also quite sensitive about revealing next year's models. Counterespionage agents may serve the dual role of providing information to the client so that he can at least keep abreast of his competitor, and maybe gain a competitive edge, and learn of any espionage activities that the competitior may be engaged in against the client.

Stephen Barlay, in his book *The Secrets Business: The Lucrative Racket of Espionage in Big Business and How It Operates* describes several interesting "cloak-and-dagger" corporate espionage cases including one involving conventions and "hostesses." Apparently, in at least one case, seemingly innocent hostesses hired by a company for an annual sales convention were actually on the payroll of a professional investigator. The hostesses had been primed to elicit certain information.

Barlay also describes the use of female "escorts" who have been planted to provide company and "sympathy" to business executives while acquiring some valuable information. Such women are sometimes described as female "operatives." He tells the story of one such female operative who posed as a lesbian as part of a plan to trap a certain research scientist. That scientist's private life had been investigated and he had been found to have problems concerning his sexual adequacy. The female operative got a job where he worked, got to know him and at the first pretense revealed her "secret" to him. She apparently challenged his ability to turn her into a heterosexual. The scientist, it seems, welcomed the challenge (in what Barlay describes as fulfilling the old Walter Mitty fantasy) and in the process became "hooked" on the girl. She needed money to buy freedom from her "past." He had no money but he had access to information that was worth a lot of money. He managed to provide the needed funds via the arranged sale of that information. Things seemed to go along smoothly until a hitch developed—the girl fell in love with the scientist. According to Barlay, she was "dealt with."

The tale of Dr. Robert S. Aries is the one most people associate with industrial espionage. It is described in many texts on the subject, including Jacques Bergier's *Secret Armies,* and in studies published by the National Industrial Conference Board in New York (see Study No. 199). Its plot has all the trappings of a made-for-TV movie.

Dr. Aries had been a faculty member at Brooklyn Polytechnic Institute, teaching on the graduate level. Many of his students worked in the laboratories of large companies, including Merck & Co, Inc., a major pharmaceuticals company. Dr. Aries' approach to teaching was to encourage students' use of their everyday work experience, as opposed to library research, in the classroom and in writing term papers.

Merck had spent about one-and-a-half-million dollars developing Amprolium, a coccidiostat for killing parasites in poultry. Just about the time Merck decided to put the drug on the market, it learned that Dr. Aries was scheduled to give a lecture in Canada announcing his discovery of a new coccidiostat called Mepyrium. From the published abstracts of the talk, Merck suspected that Mepyrium was similar to or the same as Amprolium.

At about that time, Merck was negotiating the acquisition of a French chemical company. That company told representatives of Merck that Dr. Aries had licensed them to manufacture Mepyrium, for a fee, of course. He had also given the company scientific and production data. When Merck compared this material with their data for Amprolium, they realized that Mepyrium was a direct copy.

Merck immediately went to the federal courts to obtain an injunction barring further disclosure. They got their court order but, in the meantime, Dr. Aries, who had been born in France, suddenly found it convenient to return there. France refused to extradite him on the ground that, as a French national, he should be tried in France.

When Merck investigated the source of the leak, they discovered that one of their employees had been a student of Dr. Aries at Brooklyn Poly Tech. A comparison of his handwriting with the handwriting on the flow sheets that Aries had given to the French company revealed that the sheets were written by the same person. The employee had a peculiar way of writing the ampersand (&), which showed up repeatedly on both his employment records at Merck and on the flow sheets given to the French company. Dr. Aries, evidently, hadn't. even bothered to rewrite the material given him.

Other students, it developed, had also cooperated with Dr. Aries to pirate research secrets from their companies. Dr. Aries succeeded in learning the formula for new oil additives from Rohm & Haas Company, and the components of an electrical device used in computers and developed by the Sprague Electric Co. Some students disclosed trade secrets as the result of Dr. Aries' encouragement to make full use of their work-day experience. Others were bribed. Curiously enough, while under criminal indictment in the United States and Switzerland, Dr. Aries brought suit in France, charging Merck with stealing his trade secrets. He was last seen living in luxury on the French Riviera.

The theft of trade secrets does not relate only to formulas and processes. Trade secrets can encompass business information, customer lists, and marketing plans, as well. The case of *U.S.* v. *Mayfield* illustrates what can happen when a marketing plan is stolen.

One day Colgate-Palmolive received a call from a Eugene Mayfield. Mayfield reported that he had been an executive with Procter & Gamble (which later proved to be true) and that he had access to P & G's marketing plan for Crest toothpaste. He offered to sell that marketing plan to Colgate for twenty thousand dollars. Colgate promptly notified the FBI, then, under direction from the FBI, negotiated a "deal." An arrangement was made to meet in a men's room at Kennedy Airport in New York City. When the meeting occurred, Mayfield was in one partitioned compartment of the men's room and he instructed the Colgate representative to enter an adjacent compartment. The Colgate man then had to pass not only the money under the partition but also his trousers. Unfortunately for Mayfield FBI agents were all over the place outside the men's room.

Mayfield was arrested and charged with carrying stolen goods across state lines. (The marketing plan was in written form and according to P & G was worth over a million dollars.) He was tried in the criminal division of the U.S. District Court for the Eastern District of New York (in Brooklyn, N.Y.) and sentenced to two years' imprisonment. Because of ameliorating circumstances, his sentence was suspended and he was put on probation, but he could have been sentenced to up to ten years imprisonment and fined up to ten thousand dollars.

The Mayfield case is interesting not only because it involves general business information as opposed to technical or scientific data, but also because it illustrates one unique, limiting aspect of how the criminal laws apply to trade secrets. P & G's marketing plan was in written form—it was in a "tangible" form. There is some doubt as to whether the same federal law (the National Stolen Property Act [18 USC 2314]) under which Mayfield was indicted, relating to the transportation of stolen goods across state lines, would have applied to "intangible" goods. For example, in the case of *United States* v. *Bottone,* involving the theft of trade secrets from Lederle, a pharmaceutical company owned by American Cyanamid, the federal district court acknowledged that there was a legitimate issue as to whether any goods had been stolen. Said the judge:

> To be sure, where no tangible objects were even taken or transported, a court would be hard pressed to conclude that "goods" had been stolen and transported within the meaning of Sec. 2314; the statute would presumably not extend to the case where a carefully guarded secret formula was memorized, carried away in the recesses of a thievish mind and placed in writing only after a boundary had been crossed.

Judge Henry T. Friendly went on to examine the facts of that particular case, where employees, Sidney Fox and John Cancelarich, removed documents from Lederle's files at Pearl River, New York, took them to the Fox home within New York State, made photocopies, microfilms, and notes, and then restored the original papers to their file at Lederle. The defense argued that no papers belonging to Lederle had been stolen and no Lederle documents had crossed state lines. But Judge Friendly didn't see things that way. He ruled that the photocopies, and so on embodying the trade secrets represented stolen goods and that "it would offend common sense" to rule otherwise.

Although the law is not crystal clear on this point and much depends on the facts of each case, secrets that are not taken in some tangible, physical form but are stolen by straightforward "memorization" are not likely to constitute stolen "goods" and therefore, the theft is not likely to be subject to criminal punishment. That is true under federal law as well as the law in most state jurisdictions. The underlying philosophy relates to civil liberties and individual freedoms, but even so, it is not of an absolute nature. That is, just as one's freedom of speech does not permit shouting "fire" in a crowded theater, individual liberties can, at best, serve as a narrow shelter for the would-be thief of trade secrets. In the first place, few secrets lend themselves to pure "memorization" and once notes are taken, a tangible embodiment of someone else's property is made. And even when the secret can be fully committed to memory without any tangible aids, that secret must somehow be transmitted and then used. Although it may be possible to avert the *criminal* laws by memorization, the owner of the trade secret may still exercise his *civil* law rights to obtain an injunction and damages, and to prevent the disclosure and the commercial use of his trade secrets by either the "wrongful" taker or a third party.

There is another limitation to the criminal laws, not usually mentioned in books or articles, but one that is, nonetheless, important from a pragmatic business point of view. While a large company, such as Merck or Colgate, may command considerable attention from the FBI and the local district attorney's office, particularly if the trade-secret information appears to be of major significance, the average businessman may not have the same experience. The problem, quite often, is not that the FBI or the district attorney's office does not want to be helpful, but that their offices may be overburdened with work. The district attorney's office in most large cities is faced with a heavy docket of cases, many of which deal with serious personal crimes such as homicide, rape, assault and battery, etc. There is an understandable tendency to give low priority to trade-secret business crimes that may be of less than major importance. Some trade-secret thefts amount to no more than a misdemeanor (punishable by a year or less imprisonment). Some district attorneys report that occasionally employers try to make a criminal case out of an ordinary squabble with a former employee or business partner. Although a particular trade-secret loss may spell commercial disaster for a small businessman, he may find sympathy but little else to comfort him from an overburdened assistant district attorney. Of course, much depends on just how overburdened the district attorney's office is at any given time but, in the normal course of events, in most major cities, it is the exception and not the rule to find an underworked district attorney's office. The point to be made is that, pragmatically speaking, if the trade secret involved is not a major one affecting a primary or substantial interest of a major company, it may be wise to report the crime but to move ahead rapidly on the civil side at the same time to get the necessary injunctions to prevent disclosure and third-party use, even while the criminal case is pending on the district attorney's docket.

Somewhat on the borderline of industrial espionage is the practice of companies that have intelligence-gathering offices or departments operating comparatively openly within the corporate organization. While practices coming to light from within these offices may result in an actual charge or suit being brought against the company, the feeling is evident that monitoring and inquiring into a competitor's operations are licit concerns for a business. But the evidence also indicates that an element of industrial espionage is frequently present.

Business Week, on August 4, 1975, presented a report on corporate intelligence entitled "Business Sharpens Its Spying Techniques." Among other topics, *Business Week* explored the gathering of competitive intelligence data in highly competitive industries, such as computers and semiconductors. "Increasingly," said the article, "the emphasis is not just on the competitor's price cut this week or his product next year, but on his potential far in the future." That report quotes Vincent B. Harris, vice-president of Standard Pressed Steel Co., a maker of specialty nuts, bolts, and screws, as saying: "The most important information to us is 'What is his strategy?' That includes market, construction, financing. We want to find out what the competition's labor relations are, what his credit at the bank is like, what kind of market he has, because they all affect competition. It's a total business battle."

To illustrate its point about data gathering, *Business Week* referred to IBM's Commercial Analysis Department as a "model" of corporate intelligence operations. According to that story, IBM's Chairman Frank T. Cary, in a deposition made public as part of the Justice Department's antitrust suit against IBM, acknowledged that thousands of branch-office representatives were responsible for reporting information about competitors' installations to the unit.

It appears that many others, for example, Texas Instruments, Beckman Instruments, Citicorp, and particularly those in the electronics industry, keep fairly extensive files on the operations of their competitors. Citicorp, parent of First National City Bank, acknowledged it had an executive whose functional title was "manager of competitive intelligence."

Some companies train their salesmen of new equipment to service it as well. That way they get to meet the "back office" people. Not only does that help customer relations, but it also may expose the salesmen to competitive quotes lying around on a backroom desk or posted on a backroom bulletin board.

By finding out what competitors are planning, it may be possible to beat them to the marketplace. For example, Clorox was market-testing a mild, sweet steak sauce, Prime Choice, when Heublein suddenly appeared with Steak Supreme, a similar sauce packaged in a similar bottle. Clorox sued, accusing Hueblein of taking unfair advantage of Clorox's marketing program. That suit was settled but the point it illustrates lingers on. Knowing what a competitor is up to, what his marketing plans are, what new products he is planning to introduce, if any, what products may be downstream based on current research, what pricing policies, promotional activities, advertising strategy, and budget are, all add up to an ability to take the edge away from that competitor in the marketplace. And that is the essence of a trade secret—something not generally known among your competitors that gives you a competitive advantage.

Corporate intelligence gathering is an attempt to collect as much data as possible about one's competitors, data that are not necessarily stolen but may be simply picked up casually by sales and customer representatives, technical people, and scientists, and from publications including issued patents. That data may then be organized and analyzed, possibly with the aid of a computer, to arrive at what the competition is up to. And perhaps to get a jump on them in the marketplace.

Through Mishandling of Unsolicited Ideas—Or How to End Up Paying Someone Else for Your Own Ideas

If corporate espionage, that six-billion-dollar drain, is not enough to make even the most blasé businessman security-conscious, there is more. There is one area sometimes slighted even by those who are normally alert. It is an area that ordinarily does not have a criminal element. And that, perhaps, may account for why it does not receive more attention. But it has given birth to some of the most fascinating cases in the history of litigation over ideas. And it has caused some major corporate headaches. The subject: how to treat unsolicited ideas submitted by a third party.

The Wall Street Journal once ran a feature article on this subject (November 28, 1966) entitled: "Got Idea? Forget It," describing lawsuit after lawsuit stemming from the improper care and treatment of unsolicited ideas. For example, the article noted the settlement of a lawsuit against National Biscuit Co. (Nabisco) for $26,250. That suit was brought by a professor of marketing who claimed to have first suggested to National Biscuit the idea of making crackers with fresh fruits and vegetable bits in them.

In another case, involving a book publisher, Little, Brown & Co., writer Carol Crosswell Smith had submitted a manuscript entitled *Pirate Queen of Connaught,* based on an obscure historical figure. It seems that Little, Brown rejected her manuscript but, sometime later, commissioned another writer to write a book on the same subject and eventually published it as *Pirate Queen.* Smith was successful in her suit against Little, Brown, as was another writer who sued Billy Wilder and Paramount Pictures Corporation on a similar basis. The script writer had tried to reach Wilder by telephone to sell him a movie script based on the story of Floyd Collins, who died after being trapped in a cave for ten days in the 1920s. Although he could not reach Wilder, the writer did talk with Wilder's secretary and related the plot to her. About a year later Paramount made *Ace in the Hole,* a movie about a man who dies after being trapped in a cave for ten days. Paramount wound up paying the script writer ten thousand dollars for his idea.

In the case of *Sloan* v. *Mud Products, Inc.,* the District Court for the Southern District of New York found that John I. Sloan had submitted a novel idea regarding a butterfly valve to Mud Products. In ruling on the suit, the court found that "it would be unconscionable to permit the defendant company, primarily a sales organization, to breach a fiduciary relationship and capitalize upon a mechanical discovery originating in the mind of Sloan. . . ."

What is particularly interesting about the Sloan case is the court's analysis of the law in this area. It spelled out essentially four conditions to be satisfied, namely: (1) that the unsolicited idea be original or novel; (2) that it be submitted in relatively "concrete" form, i.e., in a form sufficiently clear and specific so that there can be no mistake as to just what is submitted; (3) that the disclosure be made in confidence, i.e., with the reasonable expectation that it will be received in confidence; and (4) that the idea be adopted and subsequently used by the recipient.

A further example of problems in this area is illustrated by an employee suggestion plan Boeing Airplane used. It contained certain "exculpatory" language on the suggestion forms, expressly reserving the right to make any final determination as to whether to grant a cash award and how much. An employee, Orin Osborn, submitted a suggestion that was subsequently adopted by Boeing. When a dispute arose over the cash award, the ninth Circuit Court of Appeals ruled that Osborn had submitted the idea in anticipation of a reward and remanded the case to the trial court for a determination of whether a quasi-contract could be implied from the circumstances. The court said that the language used by Boeing, under the circumstances of its suggestion plan, did not grant Boeing the right to appropriate a valuable idea for its own use without reasonable payment. Boeing could have, the court recognized, reserved such a right "at its absolute discretion" but it would have taken more than some exculpatory language on the suggestion form. Thus, if Boeing had made clear, perhaps by the use of larger print and simpler straightforward language on the face of the forms and on all literature about the suggestion system, that it was reserving such a right—so that whoever submitted a suggestion would be fully aware that he might not be paid, and that he was submitting the idea with that risk—then Boeing might have destroyed any implication of contract. The point is that the form language was not adequate to reserve an absolute discretionary right, and an employee who submitted an idea as part of that suggestion system was indeed doing so with the reasonable expectation of a reward.

Where the idea is not novel or original, then it does not matter whether the idea was submitted in confidence or with the expectation of payment. For example, Helen Davies sued the Carnation Company for misappropriating her ideas regarding the use of powdered milk. She had disclosed them in a letter to which Carnation promptly responded, saying it had no interest in her rights to the ideas she disclosed. During the lawsuit Carnation showed that it was familiar with the uses of powdered milk suggested by Davies and had conducted tests regarding such use prior to receipt of Davies' disclosure. Here Carnation's records proved quite valuable for the company.

Where the circumstances indicate that there was no confidential relationship or any right to expect a confidential relationship, then it does not matter whether the idea is novel or original, or whether it was submitted with the expectation of payment. For example, Robert and Edna Rensselaer sued General Motors for "pirating" their ideas concerning devices such as improved sunvisors and improved seats to provide extra comfort, including room and roominess. The evidence showed that as soon as the first contact was made with General Motors, the company promptly responded with a letter and pamphlet stating in simple, clear, and unequivocal terms that General Motors would not accept any ideas submitted in confidence and would not agree to any "confidential relationship" with the submitter. The U.S. District Court, sitting in the Eastern District of Michigan, found that the most critical issue presented in this case was "whether one person, by his gratuitous and unilateral act, may impose upon another a confidential relationship." The court said that a confidential relationship could not be unilaterally imposed, particularly under the facts of that case where the disclosure was made "in the teeth" of a clear statement from General Motors that it would not accept any information in confidence.

So, we can see that companies are exposed to the loss of trade secrets through industrial espionage and to lawsuits from third parties over unsolicited ideas that may cover or duplicate, at least in part, past or current plans or ideas already developed by the company but not yet published or used.

Through Suppliers and Customers

Another common way through which trade secrets can be lost and companies exposed to liability is through ordinary business relationships with suppliers and customers.

Say a company needs special equipment not available in the trade. So that company designs the special equipment. But it takes certain labor skills, tools, and plant space—none of which the company has—to implement the design. Consequently the company goes to a manufacturer of similar equipment, discloses the design, and asks that the equipment be built for it. The manufacturer builds the equipment for that company—but then also for that company's competitors. There is nothing wrong with that if the company truly does not care. But often it does. Often there was no intention on the part of the company to give a supplier new designs and have that supplier use the company's own designs on behalf of its competitor.

In one case that was settled prior to the institution of a lawsuit, a company engaged in electroplating designed a new "plating barrel." The designs were given to a manufacturer of plating barrels with the express but oral understanding that the designs would be kept confidential and not used to make barrels for competitors.* It was not long thereafter that the plating company got wind of certain advertisements of a new barrel incorporating the confidential designs. Once the secret was out, little could be done. The secret designs could no longer be safeguarded. Because of certain personal relationships involved in that particular case, an amicable settlement was soon agreed on. But more often than not, given similar facts, a lawsuit would result. Indeed, the problem might have been avoided had there not been any close working relationship with that supplier. For one thing, the confidential understanding might have been—as it should have been—spelled out in writing and appropriate safeguards built into the agreement and the procedure for handling the information. Giving full faith and credit to the words of the supplier, the "loose" arrangement with the plating company resulted in an accidental misunderstanding whereby several people working for the supplier did not know of the secrecy element and saw nothing wrong with disclosing it to other potential customers, including competitors of the plating company that did the creative work and bore the expense of designing the new barrel—one that overcame certain problems in the industry. [As an aside, it may be of passing interest to note that the plating company had rejected the idea of filing a patent applica-

*Since the barrel was to be distributed only to those who would keep its design secret, the danger of competitors learning the design through reverse engineering was minimized.

tion, preferring to keep the design plans for the barrel a trade secret—trusting in the word and good intentions of its good friends who manufactured barrels for them.]

Sometimes customers, usually not retailers but customers occupying a manufacturing or finishing stage in the chain by which a product is ultimately brought to the marketplace, are a source of trade-secret leakage. If the customer is a manufacturer and needs to be entrusted with confidential information to make the best use of a product he is buying, suppliers will not often insist that their customer sign secrecy agreements. Since it is the salesman who has contact with customers and that salesman may be earning a commission on his sales, it's all quite understandable that he will not press a customer to sign an agreement to avoid a loss of trade secrets. In fact, in his eagerness to gain favor with a customer, a salesman might sometimes go overboard in his enthusiasm and disclose more than is really necessary.

Through the Pen and the Mouth of Valued Employees

There can be no question, however, that the most prominent, most significant, and most frequent manner through which trade secrets are lost is through employees—not only employees lost to competitors but through present, valued, and trusted employees who have no intention of ever leaving their present company, much less revealing trade secrets to their company's competitors. And yet they do—and often.

Let us first recognize that *companies* do not disclose or reveal trade secrets—or anything else for that matter. Companies, after all, are inanimate. Only people reveal information—people who may believe they are acting in the best interests of their company and their profession. People reveal confidential information at meetings—all kinds of meetings. From the chairman of the board addressing a group of security analysts, eager to stress some new developments to help drive up the market for that company's shares, to the custodian talking to friends about the new boilers in the plant, people who work for the company and are its greatest asset, are often its weakest link in its security chain.

Those who get blamed the most are the research scientists,

followed by production management. The research scientist is often accused of having a passion for publishing his work and gaining recognition in his field through lectures and the presentation of research papers. He attends conventions, forums, and seminars and is prey for industrial spies, scalp hunters and those with open minds and no false sense of pride with regard to copying a good idea casually overheard.

The Gordon Conference, an annual meeting held in the United States that is attended by a great many research scientists from around the country and from overseas, is reputed to be one of the most fertile grounds for finding out what your competition is up to. True, a company can't very well deny its research scientists the right to attend conferences, seminars, etc., or to present papers. But unless properly prepared, and unless the scientist genuinely accepts and believes that others may be purposely out to pry secrets loose from his tongue, the scientific attendee may well fall victim to the trained industrial spy.

The methods used vary greatly. At times a few drinks and some casual but flattering conversation can open up many a "top secret" lid. Classified information sometimes accidentally spills out—perhaps as part of a serious discussion with others in the field. In the process of exchanging ideas—a process most research personnel hold dear to their hearts on the ground that cross-fertilization of ideas is the key stimulus to creativity—disclosure of a few choice bits of information may be all the clues a trained mind needs to piece the puzzle together.

Sex—as Stephen Barlay points out in *The Secrets Business*—as well as blackmail and extortion, are devices that have been and will continue to be used. But as a practical matter, their use is reserved. Someone who has established at least modest credentials in a highly specific subject, someone who is associated with a university here or abroad, or has published one or two papers in a narrow specialty, someone who can readily "talk" the subject, will often be able to engage an industrial researcher, seeking advice, in a most intimate scientific conversation. And since industrial spies recognize this, they may hire someone who has the educational background to at least understand the subject, pay him to read up on a narrow phase of it and become familiar with the work of one or two not-too-prominent researchers who, for one reason or another, will not likely attend a given conference, and plant their trained individual at the conference as that successful but not-too-prominent researcher. Of course, that can only work if the physical appearance of the scientist being replaced is not well known. Sometimes, particularly with foreign scientists, a researcher may be known only through his published work and it may be easy to assume his name. At other times it may not even be necessary to masquerade as a real person. Posing as a fictitious member of the faculty of a major university and having the correct appearance— together with the apparent knowledge of the subject—may be all that is necessary to gain the confidence of a research scientist at a particular corporation. Once his confidence is gained, the research scientist may reveal secrets as part of a general discussion of his field, as part of an inquiry in which he believes he will obtain useful information himself, or in response to an intellectual challenge carefully posed (possibly in a manner previously rehearsed and based on that industrial researcher's personality).

A secret, like a good idea, does not care who owns it. Therefore secrets may be, and often are, revealed without any intention to do so—and sometimes without any prying. The accidental disclosure of trade secrets, not to spies, but through innocent conversation at conventions, seminars, and the dinner and cocktail parties attendant on those meetings, is probably the biggest source of trade-secret leakage. "Cross-fertilization" of ideas implies the exchange of ideas. But how does one limit revelation of technology by a scientist so as to avoid giving the opposition clues to just what the scientist and one's company is on to? How does one get a scientist to check himself in the midst of a heated discussion over a point or a topic that is of vital importance to him, that he may have been working on for months or even years, that he has wrestled with both at the lab and in his bed at night before finally falling asleep? It must be remembered that to a dedicated researcher the subject of his work is as important as Procter & Gamble's marketing plan for Crest is to Procter & Gamble. How much that scientist's work is worth financially, or may be worth financially, to his company is at best secondary. At times it may seem even irrelevant to the scientist. But most researchers do recognize that their company is sponsoring their research, for the most part out of a profit motive. Even pure research, it is hoped, will later give rise to new products on the basis of new understanding of previously unexplored principles. Hoffman-La Roche, for example, sponsors basic research in molecular biology that may, one day, give rise to a better understanding of the physiology of the cancer cell. While that fundamental research may not lead to new products directly, the basic information generated may well lead other researchers, particularly those working for the company, to discover new products.

In addition to meetings and seminars, published papers will sometimes provide valuable clues to trade-secret information. Indeed, they may occasionally even reveal trade secrets, although not intentionally. Ask any corporate patent lawyer and he will probably be able to recite more than one occasion when information was precipitously disclosed in a publication before there was an adequate opportunity to prepare and file a patent application. In fact, if that patent lawyer chooses to be candid, he will reveal that quite often research management in a company will apply friendly but ample pressure on its patent lawyer to "get something on file" with the U.S. Patent Office so that a paper can be presented at an upcoming meeting, or so that a paper can meet a deadline set by a journal for publication purposes. Such pressure may reduce the time spent in preparing the application. The old adage about haste making waste will show itself years later, in a courtroom, when weaknesses in the patent are explored, weaknesses that might have been corrected when the application was first drafted, if time for review had been available then.

Through Former Employees

"The easiest way to find out what a competitor is doing is to hire away an employee," says *Business Week*. *Time* magazine reported (February 20, 1978) a lawsuit initiated by Mobil Oil Co. against Superior Oil Corp. Mobil accused Superior of "raiding" its employees, and hiring some thirty-two exploration and production experts to acquire important technical secrets, offering as much as 100 percent pay increases to the Mobil employees. Mobil sought an injunction to prevent disclosure of any trade-secret information, and damages for any information already disclosed.

Mobil sued in Houston, Texas and in Calgary, Alberta. In its

Houston suit, Mobil identified one employee who left to join Superior, H. R. Hirsch. Hirsch had been Mobil's "exploration manager–technical." Mobil said he left with a "specific and detailed knowledge of oil and gas prospects." Thus Superior would save much time and money knowing what areas to avoid and which locations looked best for drilling. Mobil also said that Hirsch knew its secret-bid calculation process. According to *Time,* that secret process involved a complicated method of outguessing the competition in order to make low bids for oil leases and still win them. The lawsuit filed in Canada named another employee, Arne R. Nielsen, president of Mobil Oil of Canada, who, according to Mobil, was thoroughly familiar with its "airborne radar propane seep detector and computer graphics modeling system."

Mobil disclosed that it spent over $200 million a year for exploration and seismographic surveys of land and offshore sites for oil, the kind of money that Superior would not have to spend if it could obtain the results from several former key Mobil employees. Despite its arguments, however, Mobil was unsuccessful in obtaining a temporary injunction. As of this writing, Mobil is considering an appeal after having lost at trial.

The oil industry is a particularly tempting area for gaining access to competitive information through a competitor's employees. Texaco once accused Occidental Petroleum of hiring away two key geologists to help locate desirable sites in Peru. That suit, brought in federal court in Delaware, was resolved with an agreement that Occidental Petroleum would hold profits from any oil discovered in Peru in a constructive trust for Texaco. With sums like $200 million per year at stake, Mobil and other large oil companies are sitting ducks, particularly for smaller companies that cannot afford such huge investments in exploration.

In a twist on the hiring situation, *Business Week,* in its August 4, 1975, story, reported that one California electronics company freely admitted interviewing applicants from competitors, even though there were no job openings available. The vice-president of that company said that he was out to find out whatever he could about the company's competitors. What's more, he encouraged his senior engineers to take interviews with his competitors and try to get plant tours to find out what they could about the competition. In at least one instance, there was a payoff. Through interviewing an applicant from a competitor, even though no opening existed, the interviewer learned that the competitor had been sitting on an appropriation for a certain new product and that the product might never come into the marketplace. Based on that information the California company, which had apparently intended to cut its price in anticipation of the competitive product, held its price and consequently reaped greater profits.

The trash can is also a gem as a source of competitive information. Merck, the major New Jersey-based pharmaceuticals firm, learned to its dismay that its garbage had been regularly collected and sifted through to keep track of its developments. Others, too, have employed the old "garbage can" trick. Most companies have since learned to use shredders, but not for everything. Shredders may be in use in R&D and perhaps in patent departments, but rarely will they be found in marketing, package design, public relations, or in the general executive suite. And yet copies of classified documents are often circulated to those departments and through those channels. Those copies may wind up in files or, depending on the interest of the recipient, in the wastebasket. Wastebaskets still contain much more than waste.

Through Information Provided to The Government

Federal laws such as the Freedom of Information Act, the Federal Advisory Committee Act, and the Sunshine Law all serve useful purposes. But they also serve as a means through which valuable competitive information can be obtained.

Government agencies, operating under such laws as the Occupational Safety and Health Act and the Environmental Protection Act, may collect data relevant to studies of or investigations into certain industries or industrial plants. They may request information such as the raw materials handled by a plant. The purpose may be worthwhile—for example, to find out what chemicals a worker may be exposed to. The uncontrolled handling of vinyl chloride can apparently cause cancer, other chemical products have been known to cause impotency, and there is a legitimate need to protect the industrial worker. But what happens to those data collected by the government? Is it kept confidential? After all, by disclosing your raw materials you may be disclosing the nature of your process or a key ingredient that would not normally show up in chemical analysis of the final product. Knowing the elements of a finished product does not necessarily mean knowing the particular reactants used in the process of making that product. This is particularly true in the chemical, pharmaceutical, cosmetic, and food and beverage industries, where starting ingredients may break down and the constituents may rearrange into new products or substances. In theory, any number of different starting ingredients could be used. The Coca-Cola example applies here as well. The principal chemical constituents may be found on the label. But knowing the starting ingredients to reproduce the product is another matter.

Most of the time, the government will take the position that the information provided it by private industry is confidential. The particular agency will refuse to disclose information, pointing either to laws or its own regulations requiring secrecy. But those laws and regulations may conflict with other laws, such as the Freedom of Information Act. Federal courts have tended to favor openness in government and to resolve such conflicts in favor of disclosure.

Sometimes the federal court will review the nature of the subject matter and conclude it is not really a trade secret. And the court may be right under a strict interpretation of trade-secret law. For example, if the information is contained in publications it is not a trade secret. But a particular use or application may be different. Take the hypothetical instance of a company using starch as a filler for paste. The use of starch as a filler may have been disclosed in several publications and it may be used as a filler for various food products, but competitors in the manufacture of paste may not yet be aware of the application of starch to their product. That kind of information, information that may form part of valuable know-how, may not legally qualify for trade-secret protection. Thus a claim under the Freedom of Information Act from an alert competitor may well produce useful information about another's products and processes.

Although this area of the law is relatively new and still in development, it is an area of increasing importance and a possible serious source of leakage of competitive information.

Through Computer Crime

The advent of the computer has brought a new frontier to the war against crime. But here the criminal is generally a lot more sophisticated than the average stick-up artist or burglar. And the financial consequences of his crime are often higher—monumentally higher. What is at risk includes not only money but private information, information that may constitute valuable trade secrets. It is apparent that just as a computer may store a firm's financial information, it may also store its technical, marketing, and other business information. To understand the nature of the problem let's look at a couple of ways in which computers have been misused.

In its November 20, 1978 issue, *Newsweek,* described how Stanley Mark Rifkin succeeded by computer in arranging the transfer of $10.2 million of funds from a California bank to Irving Trust Co. in New York with instructions that the money be moved to an account in Zurich, Switzerland. The order was executed the very next morning.

Rifkin then flew to Switzerland and used the money to buy nineteen pounds of diamonds—forty-two thousand carats—from a Russian trading group. But it appears that the order was so huge that the Russians couldn't fill it immediately. As a result Rifkin wound up with only $8.1 million in gems and a little over $2 million in cash. Somehow Rifkin managed to smuggle the diamonds through U.S. Customs and for a while set himself up in a plush Beverly Hills hotel. He might not have been caught but for a tip that the FBI received from someone to whom Rifkin had been talking—someone to whom Rifkin evidently said a bit too much.

Thomas Whiteside, in his book *Computer Capers, Tales of Electronic Thievery, Embezzlement and Fraud,* relates story after story of embezzlement from very large companies. He describes, for example, how a chief teller of the Park Avenue branch of New York's Union Dime Savings Bank managed to manipulate accounts through the use of a computer terminal to support his bookmaking habit. He eventually pleaded guilty to a charge of grand larceny for approximately $1.5 million. The chief teller conducted his computer fraud over a period of almost four years and was never detected by auditors. It was only because of a police raid on the bookmaking operation that the teller's embezzlement came to light. Had the bookie not kept the teller's name on a list of customers, it appears that the teller may well have continued on his merry way for many additional years.

One of Whiteside's more fascinating accounts is of an interview he conducted with a man he refers to as James Harlowe. He describes how Harlowe had been convicted of embezzling more than a million dollars from his employer over a six-year period, how there had been regular audits during the six years, and how no one in the company, including those who worked for Harlowe, observed what he was doing. It seems that the only reason Harlowe was eventually caught was because he got tired of the situation and decided to set up and call attention to a particular embezzlement situation. But for that, detection of his computer crime might have continued unnoticed. Harlowe eventually served five and a half years of a ten-year prison term in San Quentin—a sentence that is unusually harsh for a white collar criminal. As Whiteside points out, and as most criminal lawyers know, white-collar criminals rarely serve that kind of time—though their crimes may have far more serious financial impact than most ordinary robberies or burglaries.

According to Frank Lautenberg, president of Automatic Data Processing, Inc., a New Jersey computer servicing company, "a computer may be likened to a DC8, it can get you there, or it can kill you. A company needs audit routines. People are often inclined to believe too religiously in computers." That statement is borne out by Whiteside's description of how "James Harlowe" would take the manipulated computer printouts into management meetings. Instead of questioning the printouts, management would just assume their accuracy and then question the operations and operating people. In one instance employees were chewed out on the basis of Harlowe's computer reports, the manager saying that he had it all down in black and white. There seems to be some magical respect that management has for the computer's printed word.

It is significant of course that computers can be employed to steal money. It is equally significant that just as a computer can be misused for financial benefit, it can also be misused to obtain trade-secret information. Indeed, the government has conducted experiments to determine the extent to which its computers can be penetrated to obtain classified information. In one fascinating account, Whiteside describes how two programmers succeeded in penetrating an elaborate security system that had been designed to protect information in an advanced computer time-sharing system called MULTICS. That system had been developed jointly by Honeywell, Inc. and the Massachusetts Institute of Technology, supported, in part, by the Defense Department. It took the two programmers just half an hour to determine that the MULTICS security system could be penetrated, and it took them only two hours longer to write a computer program to actually carry out the penetration. Whiteside reports that in a paper written by those two programmers, they made the following statement:

> On numerous occasions, programmers have conducted formal or informal projects aimed at testing the security of operating systems by penetration—by writing programs that obtain access to information without authorization . . . In each case, the result has been total success for the penetrators.

Industry, of course, uses computer time-sharing systems to store much valuable information, both about its books and records as well as information of a technical and business nature. The vulnerability of information stored by computers makes the problem of control and security, already extremely important, even more complex.

In addition to the problem of protecting the information stored by computer, there is also the problem of protecting the software itself. There are many companies in the business of designing software, and their programs constitute a valuable product to them. Thus far, the courts have declined to recognize computer programs as being patentable. The primary reason for denying patents is the contention that a program is nothing more than a series of mental steps and that one cannot patent a mental process. So software companies have been relying on both the copyright law and trade-secret law. Copyrights provide limited protection with respect to the program in much the same way that a copyright would protect the text of any book. A copyright does not protect against the use of the ideas contained in the book but merely the particular expression of those ideas. Similarly a copyright on a computer program does not protect against a variant of that program, which essentially utilizes the same concepts but in an altered form. A copyright doesn't really protect against someone who says essentially the same thing but in a different way, and that is equally applicable to computer programs.

To protect software as a trade secret, it is necessary that all other principles of trade-secret law be adhered to. The ownership of the rights to software follows the same rules that govern the ownership of any other idea or discovery or creation. The same rules between employer and employee apply to software as to the discovery of a new machine, for example. And the owner of that software who wishes to retain it in the form of a trade secret must advise any employees or third parties who have access to it of its confidentiality. He must institute some form of control to limit access or to limit distribution, and preferably should restrict distribution to those who sign an agreement to respect its confidentiality. David Bender, in his book *Computer Law,* describes some of the problems associated with maintaining software as a trade secret, and also describes how patents might be obtained by drafting the patent and patent claims around the apparatus involved.

4 □ How to Safeguard
Confidential Information

How does one protect against leaks of confidential information? Is it necessary to shred excess information frenetically, lock all doors and files, clean all desks, hire armies of security guards, forbid employees to publish, make speeches or attend conventions? Should a company hire undercover agents to spy on the activities of its own employees? Who owns the papers in an employee's desk? Can a company search the drawers of its executives' desks without permission? Can a company administer polygraphs to its own employees as a condition of continued employment? At what point does the right of a company to protect its property cross the individual right of an employee to privacy?

These questions and others are faced all the time by companies, not only in the United States, but throughout the world. In a front page story on July 28, 1972, *The Wall Street Journal* reported that efforts by duPont to protect its secrets included having its guards walk the hallways on Saturdays trying doorknobs, looking into offices, rummaging through wastebaskets, and seizing papers on people's desks. It also told of shredding by ITT, of efforts by Polaroid to prevent its own employees from knowing its formulas by using code numbers instead of chemical names on bottles, and of well-guarded vaults to secure high-priority documents at Eastman Kodak. IBM reportedly fired employees "for not being as conscientious about security rules as they should have been."

To understand what should be done about protecting trade

secrets, it is helpful to look at the subject in its proper perspective. In order to do so, it is worthwhile briefly to review some fundamentals. First, it is necessary to appreciate what we are trying to protect. A trade secret is basically any subject matter not known to your competitors and that provides a competitive edge or advantage. Second, it is useful to keep in mind how those secrets are lost. As noted earlier, companies are inanimate, companies do not reveal anything—the employees, including officers and the chairman of the board reveal information, wittingly or unwittingly. No spy, no espionage agent, can pry loose a trade secret unless he gets it from the mouth or the pen of an employee, whether through blackmail, bribery, an inadvertent slip of the tongue, or through an employee who so fails to secure a confidential document that it may be duplicated or even stolen, or by an employee who misplaces a document or files it in the wastebasket, not recognizing its possible value to competitors. Somehow, somewhere, an employee must be the source of the information lost, whether intentionally, through carelessness, or through outright thievery. Now, of course, it makes no sense to blame an otherwise innocent employee who took all appropriate precautions to protect certain marketing plans, designs, or formulas and filed them in a vault, for the work of an outright thief or burglar who stole those plans, designs, or formulas. But, how did the thief know of the existence of such material in the first place? How did the thief know precisely where it was stored and when it would be kept there—if not through some employee, whether directly or indirectly? It stands to reason that an employee must always be the ultimate source of a loss of confidential information—even if no employee actually participated in the crime or knowingly conspired with or intentionally contributed information to the criminal.

The employee stands at the critical pivotal point between confidentiality and disclosure. Therefore, it is essential to start and build any internal security program around a particular company's employees, based on the nature of that industry and the type of business it conducts. First and foremost, a company must define its own security needs in terms of the kind of people it has and in terms of their needs. For example, a company that depends on research, such as a pharmaceutical company, needs creative and talented scientific personnel. A toy company needs creative de-

signers. A consumer-oriented business may especially need creative marketing talent. Those companies must design security programs that take the needs of those creative individuals into consideration, or run the risk of losing the people who generate the
trade-secret information in the first place.

The "security grid" at the end of this chapter may serve as a
useful guide with which to review a current security program or to
start such a program. The security grid must, however, be applied
by someone with an understanding of the nature of the company's
business, its people and its objectives. It is not intended to serve
as a basis or as justification for creating a corporate police state.
A hypercautious atmosphere may not only restrict or destroy
creativity and injure the company's long-term growth; it may even
present a challenge to the ingenuity of a disenchanted employee's
mind. Most professional security officers will frankly admit that it
is just not possible to devise a perfect, foolproof security system.
The best security system is one that is reasonable and that most
employees are likely to accept. That employee acceptance, as opposed to employee challenge, will encourage compliance as opposed to deviousness. Indeed, the key to an effective security system is winning employee compliance.

The scientist or market researcher who feels impelled to discuss
problems with other professionals in his or her field should understand the need for security and genuinely desire to protect his
company's interests. That kind of understanding and desire simply
cannot be imposed "on orders" from above. It has to be instilled.
And the way to instill it involves essentially the same principles of
motivation used to induce other behavior characteristics. According to Ernest Dichter in his book *Motivating Human Behavior,* it is
essential to focus on the employee's needs and adopt a plan that
accepts those ends, rather than ask the employees to deny them.
Once we recognize that the employee stands at the central point
about which discretion and disclosure pivot, we can adopt an effective security plan, effective in terms of the needs of the company
and the needs of its people.

The first step is to determine what is necessary to keep secret
and from whom. Only then do we concern ourselves with *how.*
What are the sources of confidential information in the company,
what is the natural flow of such information? (For example, are

copies made and circulated, and if so, to whom?) What is the disposition of copies of confidential information: are they filed, and if so, where, or are they thrown away? What records are retained and where? Is any of the confidential information classified into categories? Are agreements employed? What efforts are made to advise employees of the significance of trade secrets and when are those efforts made—at the time of hiring or thereafter? Once the confidential information can be identified, its source or origin ascertained, and its natural disposition (or circulation) traced, a plan can be devised. That plan should *start with the employee prior to the time he or she is hired.*

When a candidate for employment is interviewed and the stage is reached at which it is decided to offer that candidate a position, the subsequent discussion of the terms of employment should include a frank discussion of the company's security needs. The employee who first learns of security restrictions (such as formal clearance to present a talk in his own field) after he has quit his previous job and is already on the payroll (even if it is his first day) is likely to develop a deep and abiding resentment for both his new employer's policy and for corporate security in general. All too often an employee is hired with virtually no discussion of corporate security or confidential disclosure agreements (which may even contain restrictive covenants). Then when he shows up for work— perhaps even having sold his house and having relocated to a new city—that employee is confronted with various papers to sign. "Here, John, this will only take a few minutes of your time. Just sign these forms." That kind of presentation is similar to the way some parents talk to their children on their first visit to the dentist —"It will be painless." The employee confronted with that situation, having to some extent burned his past job bridge behind him (and possibly having refused other job offers) may well grimace and bear with it the way he did when he first visited the dentist. But his attitude toward the company is no more fond.

Contrast that with the company personnel officer who tells a prospective employee being seriously considered for employment, "John, the position we are discussing entails exposure to confidential information. The company has adopted certain policies in an effort to prevent needless disclosure and I think you should know about them." That kind of frank talk prior to making an actual offer is likely to generate support or at least cooperation from the candidate should be accept employment. He knows in advance what will be expected of him, what agreements he will be asked to sign and their substance, what clearance procedures, if any, he will be expected to abide by, and what other security measures he will be expected to live with if he joins the company. He may think the security measures a bit stiff, but knowing about them before any commitments are made, he is more likely to regard the company as "fair" and therefore those security measures as more palatable.

Take, for example, the case of a technical salesman. Assuming he is to be exposed to trade secrets about the product he is selling, he should then be told prior to any offer of employment that he will be expected to keep confidential certain information that he will learn on the job; that he will be expected to sign an agreement to that effect; that the information considered confidential includes a list of customers and customer contacts, together with certain technical data about each customer, all of which is to be kept in certain locked files. That candidate should be advised of those aspects of the company's security policy applicable to him. If he is expected to sign an employment agreement that restricts him from calling on those customers for a period of time in the event he works for and then leaves the company, he should be told about that clause before he is hired. (Indeed, failure to advise him in advance of such a provision may destroy its enforceability. This point will be discussed more fully in the chapter on contracts.)

At this point, let's review the elements of a security program.

Invention Assignment

A corporate security policy should have some flexibility. Not all employees will engage in scientific research, in market research, or product design, or will call on customers. Those employees who may reasonably be expected to invent, to create new product ideas, new designs, new methods, those employees engaged in scientific or technical work, should be asked to sign an agreement to the effect that title to all their inventions, ideas, and discoveries related to the company's business will be assigned to the company. (In the absence of such an agreement, the problem of determining who is hired to invent and the problem of shop right, discussed in chapter 1, may cloud the company's right to those inventions.)

Confidentiality Agreement

This, of course, is at the center of any security policy. It need not be a separate agreement. Customarily, a confidentiality agreement is nothing more than a provision in an employment agreement. It may take the form of one or two paragraphs in which the employee acknowledges that he or she is taking a sensitive position, will learn valuable confidential information, and will not divulge that information to outsiders without the company's express written permission.

If customer lists are at stake, it is helpful to recite that and have the employee expressly acknowledge that he knows customer lists are involved and are considered confidential. If the customer lists are treated as confidential and access to them is limited and the customer information is not generally available from published sources, then recognition of their secrecy by the employee in an agreement will go a long way toward enforcing their confidentiality should a lawsuit later develop.

Restrictive Covenant

Although the law in this area is quite complex (see chapters 5 and 6), it is sufficient to note here that where enforceable (not every state will enforce a restrictive covenant) a restriction against joining a competitor that is reasonable in duration and in geographical area, that does not make it virtually impossible for the employee to continue to work in his field after leaving one company in that field, may prove effective in safeguarding trade secrets. The clause should be carefully drafted—if too extensive, it may backfire. A restrictive covenant can be used with consultants as well as employees. It can be used to prevent suppliers and subcontractors to whom you have given trade secrets from using those trade secrets on behalf of your competitors.

Conflict-of-Interest Policy

It may not be illegal for an officer of a public company to award a major building contract to his brother's construction firm, but public shareholders in the company may well question the propriety of that decision. One question they may ask is whether independent bids were sought; another is whether the company is getting the best job at the lowest possible price.

A conflict-of-interest policy focuses attention on personal relationships with outside suppliers, jobbers, agents, customers, and competitors. It sets forth a code of ethics. Such a policy may prohibit investments (to any significant extent) in companies that compete with or do business with the employer company. Some companies distribute a questionnaire asking employees to disclose financial interests in suppliers, customers, and competitors. That is not an invasion of privacy, assuming the questionnaire goes no further than the legitimate business needs of the company. (A sample conflict-of-interest policy and questionnaire may be found in Appendix 1).

Third-Party Secrecy Agreements

Employees should be discouraged from receiving or accepting any information in confidence, or which is stamped or marked "confidential." To help employees understand the implications of signing secrecy forms and accepting confidential information, informal discussions or in-house seminars may prove beneficial. Many employees are not aware of the law of principal/agent and do not realize the extent to which they bind their companies by their actions.

For example, to protect itself, a company with whom you do business may ask outsiders, suppliers, subcontractors, and even visitors, including your employees, to sign seemingly innocent forms as a condition of entrance on the premises. Those forms often contain a release from liability in the event of an accident, and a confidentiality provision. The latter is very much a secrecy agreement. Employees should be encouraged to avoid signing any secrecy agreements without prior approval. That approval can come from the law department in larger companies, or from an officer of the company who is familiar with the particular situation and has weighed the risks.

Circulation of Confidential Documents

Many a lawsuit seeking to enjoin disclosure of trade secrets has been defeated on this point alone. It is as important as the confidentiality of the information contained in documents. The trouble here is perhaps partially attributable to personality problems. Fear of bruised egos may result in a wider circulation of a confidential document than necessary. Being on the list to receive copies of certain types of information is sometimes regarded as a status symbol. Some executives insist on seeing all memoranda that go to their subordinates. Some even read all incoming mail (except personal mail) addressed to anyone in their departments. At times the excess distribution of documents is deadly to protecting trade secrets. (Note, for example, the discussion of *Motorola* v. *Fairchild* in chapter 7, "Suing the Former Employee." See also Introduction.)

Remember that a trade secret will not be recognized as such unless positive steps are taken to insure confidentiality. When a "trade secret" is widely and freely disseminated throughout the company, and readily accessible to virtually everyone in the company, a court may take that as evidence that the information is not considered of much value, that its ready accessibility permits an employee to conclude that it wasn't really secret. Just stamping a document confidential doesn't make it so, although that can be one step in the right direction.

The flow of documents should be traced, the flow pattern established and then investigated. "Do we really need so many copies?" is a question to be asked time and again. Establish a "need to know" policy. Make every effort to restrict duplication of documents, and record their circulation as well as final disposition.

To make this effort more efficient, establish categories or grades of secrecy. Two or three levels should be sufficient. In practice, when there are three levels, most confidential documents wind up in the middle classification. There seems to be a reluctance to mark something "low priority" or a low-level secret but, by the same token, fewer documents are classified as "top" secret. This permits comfortable control and segregation of those documents marked or graded at the top of the classification scale. Where a company is faced with mountains of paperwork it may be useful to have such a system and to permit a more relaxed system of controls to govern the flow of "medium-level" secret information. But, there has to be some reasonable system applicable to all levels of confidential information, or a court may ignore the classification and rule that the information in question wasn't really being kept secret. It is worth repeating: a secret is not a "trade secret" if reasonable measures are not taken to prevent that secret from becoming public knowledge. Widespread dissemination, beyond distribution among those clearly having a "need to know" is evidence against secrecy. It may not destroy the secrecy entirely, but, as many a company has found to its chagrin and dismay, it certainly may help do so.

Monitoring Copying of Confidential Documents

Overzealous use of the office copying machine may be desirable to the manufacturer of that machine, but it can't help protect trade secrets. A logbook should be kept adjacent to each copier, and anyone using the machine, when copying information that has been designated "confidential"—or information that the writer believes to be confidential—should be required to enter certain control details in that logbook. A chart could look something like this (modified to suit the individual needs of your company):

Date	Name of Person Making Copy	Name of Person for Whom Copy Is Made	Number of Copies	Subject Matter

In addition, some record should be made of where and to whom copies are distributed, although not necessarily in that logbook. It is sufficient if the names of all those receiving copies are written on a cover transmittal sheet or merely kept in the file along with a copy of the document being distributed.

Coding Trade Secrets

When marine biologists study sea life they use tags for identification. When researchers study human physiology they may use a radio-isotope to tag a substance and trace its flow. Tagging for identification purposes is fairly widespread. Its application to the internal processing of trade secrets is relatively simple.

Trade-secret information can be tagged or coded by such obvious means as numbers or colors. Some companies prefer a numbering system on the ground that a color calls attention to the information, thereby inviting the curious and alerting would-be thieves. Others maintain that numbering systems, unless very complicated and changed often, become equally well known to most employees. Color coding highlights the material as sensitive and alerts the person handling it to the need for special treatment— for example, not to leave it lying about on the top of one's desk.

The coding system need not be complicated to be effective. In fact, I recommend a system as simple as common sense dictates for your type of company, depending on such factors as its size, whether it is located in more than one facility, and its type of industry. For example, a small chemical company with only one central location, except for sales offices, and with all marketing plans, research ideas, and other material emanating from people at that central location, would be well served with a single removable plastic clip—perhaps red in color. A red plastic clip of substantial size that can be removed (but not too easily so as to avoid its accidental removal) and that might be stapled to a sheet of paper, may be all that is needed in the case of some smaller companies. Information so identified can be processed separately and maintained in separate files. Because it is physically simpler to remove those red tags, it becomes psychologically easier to declassify information later on. And that is important, to avoid a monstrous situation where information that has long since become public knowledge is maintained alongside secret information.

The purpose of coding is to facilitate the identification of trade secrets by those working with the documents, to facilitate special measures of transmittal and storing. But it's equally important to establish a follow-up system with respect to coded information so that it may be reviewed, at least within a year of its original date and hopefully on an annual basis thereafter, to see if there is any point in continuing to maintain the information as confidential.

Documents that have been designated confidential should be reviewed periodically, and any system that works for your company is fine. Whether those documents are reviewed again by the author, or by the head of a department or section within the company to which that document is most applicable, or by a committee or department secretary is a matter of choice. The larger the company the more difficult it may be to review and declassify information efficiently. But it's important that it be done—even the U.S. government is engaged in periodic declassification of documents. A very large company might well justify hiring one or more individuals to achieve an effective means of declassification and to meet the particular needs of that company.

In the abstract, it's not possible to recommend a complete system for controlling the flow of confidential information, identifying it, storing it, and reviewing it periodically with an eye toward declassification. Much depends on the particular company, the nature of its industry, its size, and how many locations are involved and what departments or functions are represented at each location. But formulating a clear, workable system to meet the needs of most companies requires no more than persistence, patience, and a common-sense analytical approach.

One of the most common coding practices is the use of a "confidential" marker or stamp. But in this context we could as readily speak of the misuse of the "confidential" marker or stamp. True, marking or stamping a document "confidential" gives notice to the would-be trespasser. And notice is an important element in a subsequent lawsuit, to disprove any claim that "I didn't know it was confidential." But if virtually everything is stamped "confidential," if there is no exercise of discrimination, then a court may find that *nothing* was really confidential. That is, if some of the stamped material is really public knowledge and virtually everything is marked "confidential," then the truly confidential information will suffer from the taint of the non-confidential material. Because of the tendency to overuse a "confidential" stamp, I advise companies not to rely on this alone as a coding device.

While confidential information should be designated as such, it should be designated with discrimination, and according to a reasonable plan. Here, too, we can see justification for a classification system. That system need not be as complex as that used by the federal government. Applied with common sense, it may be kept relatively simple and straightforward. Color codings or key words may be used to designate different treatment for different documents. In one major pharmaceutical company, employees are educated to a simple color-coding scheme, whereby, for example, documents having a red strip across the edge of the cover are regarded as primary-source material and extremely important secret information. A blue strip denotes importance but moderate sensitivity. No other codes are used. "Red" and "Blue" data are filed separately and reviewed annually. That way, material can be declassified after it becomes public knowledge (say, through subsequent publication) so that the confidential files do not become cluttered with old and public information.

Screening Publications and Lectures

Inadvertent disclosure is more than a source of occasional embarrassment; it is a serious source of trade-secret leakage. To avoid or at least minimize the risk here, a company should follow a policy of screening all papers and articles, including advance texts of talks —and, in fact, all writings, other than ordinary business mail, intended for "publication." The term "publication" is used here in a generic sense to include every type and manner of publication and regardless of whether the information is to be transmitted in oral or written form.

Some companies appoint screening committees. Others rely on security "readers." It is, of course, possible to establish any reasonable procedure for double-checking publications to weed out information that may be of more help to your competitors than to your company's stock, but let's look at the more commonly accepted methods.

A screening committee may be designated by management to review publications submitted to it before release. The composition of that committee depends upon the nature of the company's business. A company in the toy industry, for example, should have someone on that committee who is familiar with new products and designs that are on the way so that he can read a technical paper or the text of a talk about to be given by, for example, the marketing vice-president, and can know just what information, if any, should be held back. That screening committee should also include someone (not necessarily the company patent lawyer) familiar with the company's patent position, who can determine whether any subject matter that can form the basis of a patent application, or that is contained in a pending application, is about to be disclosed.

There is a misconception about the right to file a patent application after disclosure that is worth clarifying here. Under the U. S. laws, a patent application may be filed within one year from the date of public disclosure of the invention. But under the law as it applies in most of the major industrialized countries of the world, public disclosure before filing in the United States will kill the chance of obtaining effective patent protection in those other countries.

There is a treaty between the United States and many foreign countries whereby the act of filing for a patent application in the United States is accepted as the equivalent of filing in each of the countries that are signatory to the treaty—for the purposes of establishing a "priority date." Application still must be made abroad but, under the terms of the treaty, it now may be filed within one year from the "priority date" established by filing in the United States. That priority date serves to protect the patent owner during the interim period—up to one year from the United States filing date—against forfeiture of patent rights by reason of publication of the invention. But publication *prior to* that priority date, that is, before filing in the United States, may still constitute an absolute bar to patentability in many countries overseas.

Thus, it is important to weed out information from publications or speeches about to be given that would disclose information possibly forming the basis of a patent application. It is also desirable to weed out confidential information that might unwittingly be published or is contained in pending patent applications. Since pending patent applications are confidential and not open to inspection by the public, and since it is entirely possible that at some subsequent date you may decide to abandon your application for patent—to withdraw it from the U.S. Patent Office and to rely, instead, on trade-secret protection—it would be unwise to forfeit that option by disclosing the information contained in a pending application.

In lieu of a formal screening committee, management can designate individual "readers." It is possible for a company to break up its operations into segments and designate different individuals to assume responsibility for screening publications emanating from a particular segment or division of the company. In larger companies where the R&D function can cut across many lines and be quite vast, involving a number of technical and scientific disciplines, it is necessary to select "readers" who are competent to understand the subject matter of the publications and who are security-conscious. Once more, it is useful for them to know both what is pending in the form of patent applications and what inventions have been disclosed to their patent counsel for purposes of preparing a patent application; or those "readers" should coordinate with whoever is responsible for the patent operation of the company to insure that those aspects are not overlooked.

The effectiveness of a screening program is not dependent on whether a screening committee is used or certain individuals designated to review publications prior to release, or whether another means is adopted to attempt to filter out confidential information before it is inadvertently disclosed. A program's effectiveness is actually more a function of its acceptance by management at *all* levels than of the particular screening mechanism chosen. Word that the chief executive or the officers of the company consider themselves above this procedure and will not submit their talks for screening inevitably filters down through the organization and helps create a sense of indifference toward the system. Therefore, it is critical to the effectiveness of any screening program that it be accepted by management at all levels and be applied uniformly. The object should be to adopt a screening program that all personnel in the company can live with. Even if that program does not weave the tightest security web possible, it is still far more effective if it gains acceptance as part of a spirit of cooperativeness than is a more tightly woven security program that various people find justification for bypassing or ignoring.

Clearing Desk Tops

Time once reported an interview with President Kennedy just before his inauguration. He had just visited then President Eisenhower for a post-election "briefing." President-elect Kennedy was asked for his impression. What impressed him most, said Kennedy, was the cleanliness of President Eisenhower's desk. His own desk, according to Kennedy, was always such a mess.

Keeping his desk clean may have been a habit President Eisenhower acquired from his long years in the military—years during which he was doubtless constantly reminded of the need for security precautions. Papers lying about loosely on one's desk can be an invitation to browse—in the minds of some people. Certainly when a salesman is calling on a customer and he notices price quotes from competitors selling the same product, he is provided with a competitive edge. Indeed, whatever he can find out about his competitors and his customer will give him a leg up.

Many security-conscious companies have adopted a rule that employees clear their desks before leaving the office each day. In some instances certain kinds of documents, such as those relating to current R&D or to a current marketing plan, must be locked up. Security guards patrol the hallways and remove business papers from desk tops. The concern here is principally for the thief. It is not uncommon for an "agent" to pose as a cleaning man or woman, for example, and clean away a lot more than dirt.

Use of Shredders

When Jack Anderson, the syndicated Washington columnist, uncovered the Dita Beard memo apparently linking settlement of U.S. antitrust lawsuits against ITT with a financial pledge by that company to San Diego's efforts to attract the 1972 Republican National Convention, sales of shredders, according to *The Wall Street Journal*, suddenly rose. In fact, said the *Journal*, ITT itself subsequently shredded some thirty-two sacks of documents.

Some companies do not discover the shredder until after they have been sued. During the course of "discovery" it is not unusual to learn of some embarrassing documents. Salesmen, for example, may volunteer some of the most interesting information in "call reports" on their customers. In one case, for example, a salesman had called on a customer about installation of a new plating bath involving a new process for depositing "white" gold on jewelry. In his report of that customer call, the salesman wrote words to the effect that "I told 'em all about our white gold bath." That call report was filed away. Subsequently a lawsuit developed, not involving that particular salesman but relating to the white gold plating bath. One of the issues in the case was the secrecy of that bath.

During the discovery stage of that litigation, the stage at which opposing counsel can obtain copies of relevant documents, that salesman's call report was uncovered. Although the salesman who wrote the report, and who was still available, maintained that he spoke to the customer only about the advantages and benefits of the new bath and revealed no confidential information, the written document was clearly damaging. It weakened the company's position and helped create doubt as to how well the company preserved the information it now claimed was a valuable trade secret. There were other factors in the case that contributed to a decision to settle out of court, but that call report was among the more important elements in the decision. After the case was settled, the company invested in a number of shredders and instituted a policy whereby each department would be responsible for reviewing inactive or noncurrent files and shredding those that did not appear to have any permanent value to the company.

Other companies,—Merck, for example—discovered the value of shredders after they learned the real contribution their "trash" made to competitors or industrial spies. Shredding unnecessary documents can also help out in those instances where copies are distributed and find their way into one or more recipients' wastebaskets.

Visitor Pass

It is necessary, at times, to permit outsiders, such as salesmen and servicemen, to enter your plant or office. Technical servicemen, for example, may be needed to repair equipment; technical salesmen may have to know something about your operation to recommend which products among their line of products would be most helpful or suitable to your operation. If there is any possibility that an outsider could gain valuable information—for example, observe methods or techniques or equipment the use of which you regard as confidential—then he should be asked to sign a visitor's pass prior to his admission into your offices or plant.

Many companies follow this procedure right now. Allied Chemical and Monsanto are two examples. Allied's visitor pass contains essentially two types of clauses—not uncommon to visitor passes. One clause provides that the visitor will, in return for being admitted onto the premises, keep confidential any information he learns as a result of his visit. The second clause relates to possible personal injury to the visitor during the visit, and essentially asks for a release from liability for any such injury should it occur.

Now, of course, a visitor pass cannot prohibit a would-be thief from stealing trade secrets. But it serves a number of purposes. For one thing, it constitutes a written record of the visit. For another, it constitutes written notice to the visitor that he will be exposed to confidential information and that he is expected to maintain that confidence. By agreeing to do so, the visitor has essentially entered into a contractual understanding, breach of which exposes him and the company he represents to legal action. A visitor pass can also serve as a psychological impediment to those who might otherwise treat your confidential information in a cavalier manner. Thus, both from the viewpoint of creating civil liability and of creating a sense of responsibility on the part of a visitor, it makes sense to use a visitor pass. That pass should contain a provision regarding responsibility for maintaining in confidence any information acquired as a result of the visit. (Other provisions such as personal liability may be included, but since these are beyond the scope of this book, it is recommended that you discuss their inclusion with your corporate counsel.)

TV Monitors

One way to discourage misappropriation of trade secrets (or pilferage, for that matter) is through the use of closed-circuit TV monitors. Take the experience of a large magazine publishing house, confronted with a mass of mail from people who claimed they had sent in subscription orders with cash yet never received the magazine. When the company installed TV monitors, the problem all but disappeared. Apparently employee pilferage was the problem. The watchful eye of the camera proved to be a powerful inhibitor.

A large department store of the five-and-ten variety ran a test, setting up TV monitors directly over certain cash registers only. A month later it became clear that cash registers that appeared to be monitored, compared with the other registers had relatively few "overrings" or shortages.

True, those situations do not relate directly to trade secrets, but they reflect the powerful inhibiting effect of the TV eye. Perhaps that young girl working on a Saturday at Hoffmann-La Roche would still be alive if TV monitors had been in use. The TV monitor amplifies the effectiveness of even the smallest security guard staff. It permits one man to monitor a multitude of record storage rooms, offices, laboratories, access hallways, and other facilities that might be the target of an industrial spy.

One caveat should be mentioned. The TV camera seems to unnerve some employees to the point where they will bring suit or start a grievance procedure through their unions. In fact, that was done in the first case mentioned, that of the magazine publisher. The employees' union called for arbitration of the dispute created by the TV monitor—and the publisher's contention that the employer has a right to use the TV camera to protect its legitimate interests. A real row was created in Massachusetts in the 1960s over the right of companies to use TV monitors for surveillance. Union pressure on the legislature resulted in a state law banning such use, but the Massachusetts courts ruled that law unconstitutional: if the employer could hire security guards to observe and oversee various segments of its business, then it could legitimately install TV monitors for the same purpose.

Record Keeping—An Inventory of Trade Secrets

"Taking stock of what I have and what I haven't" is more than a line from Irving Berlin's *Annie Get Your Gun*. It is a cardinal principle of doing business. For a business to be run efficiently it must know its inventory. That's accepted as obvious. But try asking the average executive what his inventory is of R&D data, designs, business plans, and/or process formulas, and watch his forehead wrinkle up and his eyebrows begin to come together. And yet, as soon as a key employee leaves and joins a competitor, that same executive knows "beyond a doubt" that his former employee is about to reveal all that valuable and suddenly wonderful "secret" information. That's often true even though a month or so earlier that executive saw no point to taking stock of possible proprietary data.

It's easy to take inventory of what the company considers its proprietary information. It really is. Just think, there are no opposing parties, no court orders involved (assuming inventory is taken before a lawsuit arises), and no one to challenge you as to whether certain information is or is not proprietary. Your guide is common sense. Each department head can take inventory for his or her area of responsibility and simply report to a central coordinator. Each report should define that department's or section's primary function and state whether it utilizes any proprietary or confidential information. If so, then the report should identify the specifics in reasonable detail. Further elaboration may be sought by a committee set up to review the report.

Those coordinating the taking of inventory should follow tight security procedures for receiving and filing each report, carefully controlling and limiting access to the reports on a genuine "need to know" basis. The committee reviewing the reports should see to it that the information is properly indexed and cross-referenced for future use.

The advantage to this inventory taking is twofold: it permits a company to see more clearly what it has and what it hasn't, thus producing a greater sense of perspective for planning purposes; and it is invaluable in the event of a later lawsuit. The mere fact that a company went through this effort helps a court understand the seriousness with which the company treated its information, thereby supporting the thesis that the information is valuable and that the company's employees knew they were being entrusted with confidential information.

Therefore, both from the commercial vantage point of gaining a better grip on one's business to permit better corporate planning, and from a security point of view, it is worthwhile to take inventory of what is considered proprietary and confidential. This should be done approximately once a year, much the same as inventory is taken of other tangible stock. Outside of some security precautions for the handling of such intangible information, which common sense alone will dictate, the inventory process need not differ much from that already in use.

In-house Seminars

One of the most effective ways of resolving any problem is not to let it happen in the first place. One of the most effective ways to prevent lawsuits with employees is to avoid misunderstandings.

At least one large pharmaceutical company in New Jersey has found periodic seminars an effective means of helping to avoid the loss of trade secrets as well as to prevent misunderstandings that could lead to litigation. Employees are invited in relatively small groups (of about thirty to fifty) to discuss problems related to trade secrets—usually along with a discussion of patent rights. At such a meeting employees can be made aware of, or perhaps reminded of, the techniques used by industrial spies and the risks incurred when attending conferences or conventions. (This applies as much to marketing and sales people as to manufacturing and R&D personnel.) Often useful suggestions are made by employees participating in the seminar. But perhaps most important is the participatory feeling itself.

By means of in-house seminars, employees can become conscious of and sensitive to the company's concern for protecting its confidential information. Skillfully handled, these seminars can become a means for enhancing corporate esprit, for providing a cross-fertilization of ideas among members of different departments (this is one reason for not conducting seminars on a departmental basis), and for minimizing turnover in personnel as well as helping to avoid future lawsuits. Employees who have participated in such seminars and have possibly contributed an idea or two are much less likely to disclose confidential information "accidentally" or to fall prey to the industrial spy. Of course, those capable of being bribed would be in any event. But, as noted earlier, industrial spying is quite sophisticated and depends most often on psychology, on manipulating such emotional elements as pride and desire for recognition. A major point of the seminar is to help make an employee who has valuable knowledge aware of techniques used to pry it loose. The "innocent" loss of valuable information can and should be avoided.

It is neither wise nor useful to preclude qualified employees from attending a sales convention or a technical conference. But it is worthwhile to have them armed with an awareness of certain risks they may be exposed to.

Employees who have attended in-house seminars and have discussed problems related to the company's concern for its trade secrets are likely to give greater thought to difficulties that may arise if they join a competitor or establish a competitive company. At the least, they are aware of the company's concern for its trade secrets and that the company is likely to act to protect its position. All too often, a company assumes its employees knew this, only to be told by a judge that it wasn't so. Many if not most employees are not really looking for a lawsuit when they quit a job to go somewhere else. Many if not most lawsuits with employees over trade secrets can be avoided by a clearer understanding by the employee of just what it is that concerns the company.

There is much more to be gained from an in-house seminar besides alerting people to techniques used by industrial spies. Seminars can be used to cover a host of topics not limited to trade secrets. Although a discussion of those topics is beyond the range of this book, it should be apparent that such seminars can be used additionally to foster goodwill, generate cost-saving ideas for the company, and promote a feeling of participation and a sense of belonging among employees.

Unsolicited Ideas Policy

Establishing a "corporate" policy here can be tricky. In order to make it work it must apply uniformly to all levels of management. Therefore it has to be accepted by the top echelons of management. That's true because unsolicited ideas are quite often directly submitted to the president or chief executive of a company by a "friend" or someone introduced by that friend. Initially they meet and talk with the best of intentions.

Take the Dreyfus case, for example. The Dreyfus Sales Corporation is the marketing and distributing organization for the Dreyfus Fund, one of the largest and most successful mutual funds. Harvey Epstein, president of the sales corporation, was approached by a friend of long standing, Herbert Abelow, who told Epstein, of an idea for stimulating sales. Abelow suggested that Dreyfus distribute, free of charge, tape players and cassettes containing educational and promotional material to independent fund salesmen. Abelow would sell the equipment and contents to Dreyfus.

Abelow duly cautioned Epstein that this idea was confidential, that if they didn't reach agreement Dreyfus was not to use it. Epstein apparently agreed to this, assuring Abelow that because of their long friendship there was no need to worry.

During the course of their discussions it was decided that it would be too costly to supply the cassettes free, and that a relatively nominal charge should be imposed. Subsequently disagreement arose over prices Abelow wanted for the hardware and the use of Dreyfus's mailing list, and there was further disagreement on other matters. Dreyfus finally decided not to buy from Abelow but asked Abelow to serve as a consultant. He refused.

A few months later Abelow received a flyer in the mail announcing the "Dreyfus Portable Sales Seminar"—the very name Abelow helped formulate—offering a free tape player plus monthly cassettes at a nominal annual charge. Abelow sued.

The trial was before a jury in New York's Supreme Court. The jury found that Abelow and Epstein never came to an agreement. Abelow also argued that Epstein had essentially stolen his idea. But the New York Supreme Court noted that many other educational tape systems were known, and concluded that the idea involved here was "too flimsy a craft on which to base any recovery."

Thus Dreyfus escaped liability here. But the company came close to owing a lot of money for an idea that was essentially known at the time—the use of cassettes for educational purposes, whose application to sales was obvious.

The Dreyfus case illustrates not only the potential liability for accepting unsolicited ideas in confidence, but shows that the route by which such ideas are introduced is quite often at the top. Therefore, it is important that any policy formulated in this area be one that is accepted by top management. A uniformly applied policy is easier to enforce throughout the company, reduces the risk of inadvertent error, and facilitates a defense against nuisance or crank suits. If it can be shown that the company regularly and consistently follows a uniform procedure in the ordinary course of its business in this area, then a court may accept that "routine" procedure as having been used in the case before it.

For example, the Gillette Company has adopted a uniform corporation-wide policy for handling unsolicited ideas (as have GE, Pet Foods, and other companies). Gillette issues a periodic "policy bulletin" addressed to "All Officers, Department Heads, Executives, and their Secretaries," entitled "Outside Inventions And Ideas." That bulletin advises its reader that Gillette is frequently approached by outsiders with ideas and suggestions. Because Gillette also develops ideas internally and wants to avoid any conflict, the bulletin explains, the company has decided to consider only those ideas submitted on a "non-confidential" basis and on the further condition that the idea be the subject of a patent or patent application.

Gillette has established an office (called the Submitted Ideas Section) for receiving all letters containing ideas or suggestions. All personnel, but particularly secretaries, are instructed to forward all correspondence involving suggestions or ideas to that office, *unread* by the person to whom the letter was addressed. Secretaries are instructed not to make notes or comments. Polite form letters of acknowledgment may be used at the secretaries' discretion, to advise writers that their letters were received but turned over to the director of the Submitted Ideas Section, *unread by the addressee,* in accordance with a company policy designed to avoid conflicts between outside ideas and ideas that the company may be working on or may have already developed.

The objective here is that the secretary act as a filter for the executive. Presumably, the secretary is less likely to understand the idea or fully appreciate its technical and business implications. That point is debatable, but if the idea is highly technical it may have merit. At least it provides some basis for a defense that the company's executives were never informed or aware of the idea that was submitted. Where an executive opens his own mail he obviously incurs a certain risk on behalf of himself and the company—especially if he is involved in a confidential project and a letter from an independent outsider suggests something similar to that project. Gillette's policy is to shield its executives from exposure to unsolicited ideas.

The director of the Submitted Ideas Section retains the original letter, unread, in an appropriate file, and sends the submitter a form letter and pamphlet. (See Appendix 2.) The letter and pamphlet advise the submitter of Gillette's policy and ask the submitter to sign and return a brief submission form. That form appears in duplicate at the back of Gillette's booklet, one form having a serrated edge facilitating its removal. If the form is signed, then the submitter is agreeing to have his or her idea reviewed by Gillette on a nonconfidential basis, and further represents that the idea is part of an issued patent or a patent application. Essentially the submitter is offering Gillette rights under its patent.

If no form is returned, no further action may be called for. Gillette then retains the disclosure in its files, unread, purely as a defensive measure in the event of subsequent litigation. For example, it may help Gillette prove that the idea as actually submitted differs greatly from the product Gillette put on the market. Memories are sometimes based on wishful thinking and the submitter may remember his or her idea with the benefit of hindsight. Thus having the original description of the idea can sometimes be helpful. Of course, if it is similar to the actual product, then Gillette would have to show how the product was independently developed. Here its books and records, minutes of meetings, laboratory notebooks, internal memoranda, and other documents, if properly kept and dated, would serve to prove, for example, that Gillette was already working on the idea at the time it received the outside submission.

It is true a third party has no way of being absolutely sure that no one read the letter, but this is a fact to be established in trial. The point of the Gillette policy is to indicate a standard business procedure and thereby be able to convince a judge and jury. In any trial, Gillette would put the director of its Submitted Ideas Section on the witness stand to testify as to the routine procedure in the office. Gillette will also follow through with many other witnesses familiar with the company's policy, each of whom will testify that *all* such letters are treated uniformly, that no exceptions are made, and that the letter in question was just one of many routinely received, and that it was treated routinely. By establishing an orderly and consistent course of action followed *without exception,* Gillette can create a presumption that any single unsolicited letter was treated in the "usual" manner. That shifts the burden of proof to the complaining party, who now must show some evidence that an exception to company policy was made in the case of his or her letter. Merely proving that Gillette came out with a product incorporating the idea suggested in a letter is not enough to overcome Gillette's presumption based on its consistent policy. Similarity, by itself, may be attributed to coincidence. After all, a good idea doesn't care who owns it or thinks of it first. So by proving a uniform policy consistently applied, Gillette will put the burden on the complaining party actually to prove that the letter in dispute was read, that the idea was stolen.

But note the word *consistently.* Here is often the weakest link in the chain. Although Gillette might be able to prove application of its policy with true consistency, other companies often cannot. And that's the weakness that most lawyers representing a complaining party look for when faced with a "company policy" defense. A couple of exceptions pointed to may be enough to convince a judge and jury that the company's policy isn't always followed and probably wasn't followed in the case under litigation. The point is that the toughest company policy isn't worth a damn unless it is applied uniformly and consistently at all levels, from the chief executive to the custodian.

When Gillette receives a signed submission form it will then evaluate the idea and if it likes the idea it will approach the submitter to acquire patent rights. On the other hand, if Gillette rejects the idea, perhaps for lack of commercial value or unpatentability, or for whatever reason, it will so advise the submitter and return all previously submitted material. At this juncture Gillette has reviewed the idea, and the signed submission form presumably governs Gillette's responsibility to the submitter.

In addition to its general form, Gillette uses special forms when receiving ideas of a business nature, such as ideas from suppliers, where the submitter has no intention of obtaining a patent. Gillette limits its review of such ideas to signed waivers by the submitters of all rights to the ideas submitted. A supplier, for example, might waive rights to an idea in return for consideration as a source of materials should the idea be adopted.

Gillette's policy statement also cautions against receiving ideas orally—for example, by phone. That statement also reads: "Since no one person within the organization could possibly be expected to know the full extent of our store of technical knowledge, the details of our numerous research projects, or the advertising or sales promotion programs which we have investigated or used in the past, no one person could possibly accurately determine whether a newly submitted outside idea is in fact new to us. Therefore, your consideration of outside ideas could quite unwittingly seriously weaken or interfere with our priority rights in the same ideas, and expose the company to needless controversy and litigation."

There are other approaches to a corporate policy for receiving unsolicited ideas. But in general they all ask the submitter to agree to a review of the idea on a non-confidential basis. Some companies go to extremes and simply return all correspondence containing unsolicited ideas, and may even advise senders that they have no wish to review any unsolicited suggestions. Other companies, often small new companies, may welcome unsolicited ideas as a springboard for further growth and will take the risk attendant on receiving them. Most major companies, particularly those that have a substantial investment in R&D, prefer to limit their risks and avoid litigation over claims that they "stole" an unsolicited idea.

Consultants' Agreements

Consultants may offer a degree of expertise and a sense of perspective not otherwise available. In fact, that's often why they are selected. Along with that expertise they bring experience gained on behalf of other clients.

Now that's just fine if they are bringing you the benefit of experience gained elsewhere. But, if after a few years association with you, followed by an amicable separation, they undertake a project on behalf of your competitor and make use of knowledge they acquired from you, their independence takes on a different color.

As an independent professional, a consultant, while working for a new client, is free to utilize whatever information and experience he acquired from past clients. That, of course, does not mean he is at liberty to reveal confidences, but he is free to employ confidential information as an integral part of his experience. By written agreement, however, a consultant may be obliged not to undertake a certain project or type of project for a competitor. A restriction against consulting for a competitor in a designated field is generally regarded as reasonable, if limited in time. The breadth or extent of the restriction, in terms of its duration, its geographic application, and the "field" to which it applies, depends largely on the circumstances.

A consultant who helps a pharmaceutical company develop a heart-lung machine may be, for example, properly precluded from consulting for competitors in the development of heart-lung machines for a couple of years after terminating his relationship with the company. But it is not likely that a court would regard it reasonable to preclude that consultant from working in the pharmaceutical industry entirely, or from consulting on other machinery designed for other purposes, that might use some of the principles developed in conjunction with the heart-lung machine.

Because consultants may lead a nomadic existence, it is wise to enter into a written agreement with them. That is particularly true if you intend to reveal confidences to your consultant about your company's health, as you would to your family physician about your own health. The agreement should spell out the terms of your relationship, namely, what services the consultant is to provide, at what compensation, for how long, how many days or hours he or she is to be available, on what notice, whether the consultant will travel, how often, reimbursement for expenses, and all of the other terms that may apply to your particular relationship.

One provision that should not be neglected is the confidentiality clause. A consultant may be asked to agree that he will respect the confidentiality of information acquired as a result of his relationship with a company, and that he will not disclose it to third parties. In addition, if there is concern—as in the example of the heart-lung machine—that the consultant might help competitors achieve similar products or develop similar machines, a reasonable restrictive clause may be negotiated. (See Appendix 4 for a sample consultant's agreement with an optional restrictive clause.)

Trade Secret Protection In Licenses

When licensing others to use your confidential know-how, it is apparent that you should want to protect that know-how. It is an intangible commodity that loses its value if generally known in the trade.

A difference of opinion sometimes arises during licensing negotiation sessions. The licensor or owner of the know-how will usually take the position that, to ensure safeguarding of the information among the licensee's employees, the licensee should restrict the flow of information received to specific employees, sometimes identified by name or by function. The licensor may ask that a secrecy agreement be signed by each individual employed by the licensee who will come in contact with the licensed know-how.

From the viewpoint of the licensor, the licensee should undertake adequate internal measures to prevent loss of value in the know-how. The licensor wants the licensee to "police" the confidentiality of the licensed information. Thus the licensor may ask for indemnification in the event of disclosure by the licensee's employees. The agreement may even stipulate a specified measure of damages or a formula for measuring damages—for example, a multiple of the minimum or average annual royalties.

Obviously, much depends on the particular circumstances, the nature of the industry, and the bargaining leverage of the parties. The point to be made is that it is important for the licensor to go further than the mere insertion of a standard confidentiality clause from a form book in the license agreement. That standard clause may prove to be meaningless. For example, in one arrangement between two large companies, one in the United States, the other in the United Kingdom, two employees of the licensee collected the information and managed to sell it to a few other, smaller, companies in Europe. The license agreement had simply provided that the licensee would respect the confidentiality of the information it received and not disclose it to third parties. It was a clause similar to that which appears in many form books. But the facts of the case indicate the danger of copying forms blindly.

The case came to court in Britain, and the court ruled that the licensee was not liable. For one thing, noted the court, the information involved was largely a collection of known facts and not true trade secrets. The British lawyer representing the American licensor pointed out that this particular assemblage of facts, known in isolated fashion in several different chemical industries, had not previously been known or applied in waste disposal systems. That the licensee could have independently collected the know-how involved, argued the American company, was beside the point. That effort might have taken years and involved a considerable expenditure. By means of the license the British licensee derived the benefit of the entire package of know-how in a ready-to-use fashion.

That point was well taken, said the court, but the agreement bound the licensee only with respect to confidential information which, by definition, excluded information that was publicly known or available from the published literature. Indeed, most agreements involving trade secrets or know-how will contain a paragraph excluding information that:
  (i)   is already in the public domain;
  (ii) is already known to the recipient;
  (iii) thereafter becomes available either publicly or through independent third parties, without fault or disclosure by the recipient.

The British court also added an ominous footnote to its opinion to the effect that it questioned whether a company can be held liable for the unauthorized acts of employees. Although this case took place in England, the common law applied to the case would probably have been applied in the same manner in the United States.

Clearly hindsight tells us that the confidentiality clause in the agreement should have been spelled out in terms of the know-how conveyed, and specific measures on the flow of that information within the licensee's internal organization should have been set forth, accessibility to all or parts of the know-how thus being limited. Furthermore, the licensee should have been asked to bind those of its employees who would learn the know-how to an appropriate secrecy agreement. Although that may not have helped much in the last instance cited, it often is helpful. At the very least it is an inhibiting factor that makes those employees conscious of their responsibilities. It may also help obtain a court-ordered injunction against third parties getting the know-how from such employees. Thus, the above licensee could have been liable for breach of contract had the agreement spelled out liability in the event the know-how was transmitted to third parties by the licensee's employees.

The licensee, for its part, must decide on the extent of protection it can afford to agree to. The licensee has to think about possible impact on employee morale if employees are not accustomed to restrictive procedures for the handling of data and restrictive employment agreements. The licensee should try to avoid accepting more responsibility for security measures than it reasonably can assume.

Also, from the licensee's point of view, the definition of confidentiality should be as limited as possible. Limitations should be sought with respect to the duration of the licensee's responsibility, as well as to the scope of possible liability. For example, the Warner-Lambert pharmaceutical organization is still paying royalties for the Listerine formula, notwithstanding that it has been a matter of public knowledge for over three decades. When Warner-Lambert sued under its contract to be relieved of further obligation for royalties, the federal court said, essentially, You made your bed, now lie in it. The agreement by which the then-secret formula for Listerine was disclosed to Warner-Lambert contains no provision limiting the duration for which royalties are to be paid. The agreement essentially binds Warner-Lambert in perpetuity—as long, of course, as it sells Listerine.

The licensee should seek to limit its liability in terms of duration or until the occurrence of a specified event, such as publication of the information. The licensee should also seek indemnification in case it is sued by a third party claiming that use of the licensed information violates certain rights—for example, that it infringes a third-party patent. Keep in mind that even when both licensor and licensee agree that certain information is outside the scope of any patent, an alleged patent owner might not agree. An even more likely danger is that neither licensor nor licensee are aware of a third-party patent—perhaps because it is still pending, in secrecy, as an application at the time of the agreement. Imagine the dismay when, a year or two later, after long and hard negotiations resulting in a successful agreement, a third party enters the scene waving a newly issued patent. Because the licensee may have to commit considerable "up-front" capital for the license and for equipment, and even for facilities to get started in the business, he should not only seek indemnification for any damages a court may order paid to the patentee, but preferably insist that the licensor defend at its expense any lawsuit brought against him. That way, the licensee may avoid the sometimes substantial expenses associated with litigation.

The licensee should consider whether he would still want the license if it turns out that the "confidential" information was actually known to him beforehand, or is publicly available to competitors. At times such information might still have value if the licensee was not otherwise aware of its use.

In summary, when entering into any agreement, such as a license involving the transfer or exchange of technology, at least some of which you regard as confidential, beware of relying on simple general statements to protect the continued confidentiality of that information. Give thought to just what is to be protected, for how long, how that protection is to be enforced—that is, what steps are to be taken to avoid disclosure—and the extent of liability in the event of disclosure, including *unauthorized* disclosure by employees.

Consult Prior Employer (with Consent)

Most of the time, a company that is hiring an experienced man or woman is faced with the elementary fact that that person acquired his or her experience working in that same industry and most likely with a competitor. Thus, almost every time a company seeks expertise in a particular field by hiring individuals employed in that field, it can face the prospect of a lawsuit.

One way to minimize that risk is to face the issue squarely in direct discussions with the former employer. Admittedly that is not always practical.

In the early stages of NASA's space program, a space suit had to be designed and developed. International Latex was engaged as a subcontractor to work on the space suit problem for Project Apollo.

International Latex needed some expertise in the field; at that time B. F. Goodrich was the leader in the space-suit field and International Latex was a relative newcomer. It hired Donald Wohlgemuth, former manager of B. F. Goodrich's space-suit department. Goodrich sued. In court, Goodrich pointed to the meticulous detail required in the construction of a space suit "because a failure of a minute part of the finished product would probably result in the loss of the life of the user." Goodrich obtained an injunction to prevent Wohlgemuth from disclosing its secrets.

Goodrich most probably would have been surprised by a call from Latex asking for discussions prior to hiring Wohlgemuth, and perhaps would not have consented. But not all situations present such an extreme set of facts. Keep in mind that Goodrich was concerned about losing out on a major contract. In the ordinary case a company may be reluctant to lose a talented individual, but his or her loss is usually not all that threatening. In many cases it may be possible to avoid litigation as well as checking a prospective employee's credentials by a frank discussion.

There are some industries where employees seem to be on a merry-go-round. In computer sales, for example, programmers and systems analysts, as well as marketing personnel, have exhibited a tendency to rotate among different companies with relative frequency. Where companies are accustomed to losing employees to competitors and acquiring others from their competition, there may be no cause for concern about lawsuits. A call to the former employer may still be worthwhile, as a reference check, if nothing else.

One caveat: calls to a prospective employee's present employer should never be made without the consent of that employee. His current job—the only one he is sure of at present—is on the line. From the employee's point of view, he should not consent unless he is prepared to accept the likely consequences. He should recognize that if he quits to join a competitor and an injunction is subsequently issued, he may be prevented from working for that competitor. If that danger is real, the employee would be wise to ask for a written employment contract assuring him that if the new employer can't use his services in a particular field, he will be engaged—and paid—to work in some professional capacity for at least a couple of years. That economic safeguard may prove essential if trouble brews.

In summary, on reaching an agreement with a prospective employee who is then currently or has recently been employed by a competitor in a field involving sensitive information, an early direct approach just might lead to a negotiated understanding of particular areas where that employee might work without revealing competitive trade secrets. Such an approach is not always advisable and should never be undertaken without the prospective employee's consent. In a ticklish situation, the question should be reviewed with counsel for the company. If a lawsuit appears likely, some attorneys would advise against opening early discussions on the ground that it implies weakness or a sense of guilt. That, of course, is a matter of judgment and depends almost entirely on the particular circumstances. The author has seen cases where a phone call by the president of one company to the president of another avoided a lawsuit, and others where such a phone call resulted in terminating a joint venture and the onset of major litigation.

Exit-Interview Policy

The exit interview is perhaps the last important phase in an internal security program. Here is a golden opportunity not to be overlooked. Now you can find out much about your company that the same person, a few days earlier, would never have revealed. True, you will hear gripes, some undoubtedly not justified, but if you listen effectively you can read between the lines and gain valuable insight into your company's operation.

While the broad subject of how to conduct an exit interview is beyond our scope, the exit interview is an appropriate time to note where the employee is going, and to remind him of his obligations —both contractual and ethical—to your company. Most employees are concerned about their reputation and value a good reference, particularly if they should ever seek employment again. Employees can be reminded that certain information they acquired or processed as part of their jobs is highly confidential. Surprising as it may seem, there are situations where an employee has become so accustomed to dealing with certain facts over a period of years that he simply forgot those facts were not known to most other people. Information can sometimes almost become second nature to you. The exit interview is the time to jolt the employee back into a proper perspective that reminds him that information and techniques that he regards as "old hat" may actually be unknown to competitors.

In addition to reviewing the employee's exposure to confidential information during his employment and reminding him of his obligations under his employment agreement or under the law generally, the exit interviewer should frame questions designed to bring out flaws in the company's existing internal security policy. Since people react differently to the same words, it is important to be sensitive to an individual's personality when framing questions, and to word them accordingly. But in general, the inquiry should be directed to the various steps or procedures carried out to protect trade secrets, to get a reaction as to how effective those steps are. For example:

Interviewer: Mr. Peterson, you've been in charge of product design now for the past twelve years. What do you think of our system for identifying new designs that are confidential?
Mr. Peterson: It's fine.
Interviewer: Can you tell me what specifically is done?

Mr. Peterson might answer by describing the system or he may indicate uncertainty as to the specifics. Any indication of uncertainty indicates a weakness or loophole in the system. No department manager should be unaware of security procedures—not if the procedures are to be enforced.

The interviewer should ask for a reaction to the security system. He may well get a response of annoyance such as: "It's a pain in the neck." That should be followed up to see what measures are causing the "pain." Keep in mind that a system that is too cumbersome will break down eventually because it's too hard or too impractical for busy employees to carry out on a regular and consistent basis. An interviewer should not pass up an opportunity to dig into a remark, even if casually made, reflecting a problem with internal security measures and the company's efforts to protect its proprietary data. By examining criticisms and by asking for suggestions to overcome them, continual improvements can be made.

Thus, an exit interview can be useful to learn about where an employee is going, if you do not already know, to remind him of his obligations, particularly with regard to the disclosure of confidential information, and to gain some insight into your company. As questions phrased in a friendly manner and directed towards the company's procedures for protecting confidential information may indicate weak links in the security chain, so also may an invitation for suggestions actually lead to occasional worthwhile improvements.

Advising New Employer of Restrictions

In addition to an exit interview, you might consider a form letter to be sent to the new employer, advising that employer of certain restrictions applying to your former employee. This assumes certain facts. The most important is that as a result of the exit interview you are not satisfied that the employee can assume his new job without revealing your secrets. Although not essential, if you have an employment contract containing specific provisions that apply, for example, a restrictive covenant (see chapter 6), then it may be worthwhile to write a letter to the new employer advising of the facts and expressing your concern. It may be that the new employer can relieve your anxiety by agreeing to assign that employee to tasks that would not necessitate a disclosure of your trade secrets. A letter can be written in the absence of a previous employment contract, but remember, without a contract, the common law applies and the employee is free to join your competitor. He still cannot, however, reveal your secrets.

But keep in mind that any such letter must be carefully worded to avoid unnecessary accusations or personal inferences. If that letter costs your former employee his new job, he may use it to sue you for defamation of character or slander, and on any other grounds that may be applicable under the circumstances. That's why such a letter should be precisely and objectively worded. It should be kept simple, recite no unnecessary facts, provide no personality characterizations, and express only your legitimate concern.

Preventing Computer Fraud and Embezzlement

There are many reasons for concern with computer security. One, of course, is to prevent the loss of money. Invasion of privacy is an equally important reason. The loss of a business's confidential information, its important technical data, marketing plans, and financial information to its competitors may, in some instances, cause irreparable damage. It may also lead to a spiral of damages that can ultimately eat up company time in litigation and tie up a product to such an extent that it virtually destroys a market for that company. False records, even if unauthorized by company officers, can lead to false information about the company's financial status. Since creditors provide funds to a company based on the accuracy of the financial statements offered and since investors purchase stock on the basis of essentially the same information, there is a positive duty on the part of a company to take measures to see that the information it provides is accurate and secure. There is a well-known Securities and Exchange Commission case—the *Bar Chris* case—which held that a registration statement must disclose every fact about a public company that might influence the decision of the prospective investor. It is for this reason that many knowledgeable SEC lawyers insist that a registration statement must disclose whether a company is using electronic data processing and if so what steps have been taken to prevent embezzlement. Thus aside from the normal desire to prevent the loss of funds and of privacy, the normal desire to prevent others from taking valuable confidential information, whether it be of a financial, technical, or personal nature, there is also the positive obligation imposed on officers of a *public* company to take reasonable measures to prevent computer fraud and embezzlement.

Unfortunately a completely foolproof system has not yet been devised and according to some authorities it may not even be worth the effort. In order to devise a system of controls intelligently it is important that we recognize an axiom of trade-secret practice that has been mentioned elsewhere in this book: people and not inanimate objects disclose trade secrets. Just as preventing the loss of trade secrets depends on a system that traces the flow of information from person to person, from its origin to its end point, just as security depends for its reliability on the controls with respect to the people who process the information at each point, similarly computer security depends for its viability on the ability to oversee the persons who have access to the computer. Since people who handle the information on a computer are really the key to security, let's take a look at the nature of those people.

There are essentially three broad stages of operation with a computer, although each may be further subdivided. The first stage relates to computer input. The second relates to the use or processing of the computer and the third to computer output.

Input may include the programming, establishing a language with which to work the computer and generally setting up a system by means of which the computer is to be operated and provide the desired results. The key to software is really the analysis of *desired* objectives (eventual output) together with the consideration of available input. This first-stage process requires a relatively sophisticated knowledge of the operations of the computer, and the people who are engaged in the input process are generally the more knowledgeable and sophisticated individuals to work with computers.

The second stage relates to the *use* of the computer. This is the stage where technicians and clerical people, the operators of the system, work with the computer, utilizing the system for which it has been programmed. For example, a user may be trained to fill out a punch card properly and feed it correctly to an appropriate slot of the computer. Or a user may be trained to operate a keyboard similar to a typewriter so as to provide instructions to a computer in a manner in which the computer can digest and process.

Once the processing takes place, the information derived from a computer is known as its output. The output may include information about a company's business, its trade secrets, its financial data. Or the output may consist of instructions to other computers such as occurred in the case of Mr. Rifkin when he operated the computers of the Security Pacific National Bank of Los Angeles to transfer illegally $10.2 million through a New York bank to a bank in Zurich, Switzerland.

Who are the people who commit computer fraud-related crimes? In a study by the comptroller general of the United States submitted to Congress in April 1976 (excerpts are reported in an appendix of Thomas Whiteside's book *Computer Capers*) the comptroller general reported that of sixty-nine cases examined, at least fifty were committed by systems users. A Stanford University research report prepared for the government also supports the conclusion that most computer crimes are committed with unsophisticated methods. Moreover, the case histories reported by Whiteside demonstrate that most computer-related crimes are not the sensational ones such as that committed by Rifkin, but rather crimes committed by technicians and other users. The greatest vulnerability appears to be at the user stage. The bank teller who defrauded Union Dime of $1.5 million was a user and had no sophisticated knowledge of computer programming. Whiteside's account of "James Harlowe" is essentially that of an accountant who was a sophisticated user. In this instance it appears that he did have an exceptional understanding of the inner workings of the computer, but the steps he actually took to defraud the company required little more than an intelligent knowledge of computer use. He was not a programmer or systems analyst and the methods he undertook did not require that kind of knowledge.

According to Norma Levy, a former systems analyst, now with Interactive Systems, Los Angeles, engaged in marketing computer software, it is essential to limit access to the physical media on which programs and data are stored and divide the various functions associated with the computer among different people, each of whom has an assigned but independent responsibility.

Let's take a look at accessibility first. Rifkin had to get at a computer terminal of Security Pacific in order to operate it. He ran into the obstacle of a code but overcame that. He was even able to identify himself to the computer with a phony name. The obstacle of accessibility might have been far more difficult to overcome if the terminal had been made inaccessible to any single operator at a time and if the operators (at least two) would have had to identify themselves by fingerprints, voiceprints, or similar means. Requiring the presence of at least two people is simply a recognition of the nature of human behavior and is a standard type of security check. The government Minute Man missile program, for example, requires the coordinated overt acts of pairs of individuals to execute a presidential directive to fire a missile. Each man sits at his own command desk at an opposite end of the control room from the other. Both men must manipulate controls simultaneously in order to launch a missile. This provides a security precaution against the corruption or loss of mental faculty on the part of one person.

The kind of individual who engages in computer fraud, who misuses a computer, is often a "loner." There are not many gangs working in this field. And cooperation among two or more individuals to execute a crime imposes a considerable hurdle, particularly when the crime is of a sophisticated nature and requires a strong degree of mutual trust for an indefinite length of time. That kind of trust is rare among criminals and its requirement among the type of individuals who operate computers is such as to impose a powerful inhibition against committing a crime. The fact that it is not foolproof is irrelevant. There is no perfect or foolproof system. The objective should be to impose significant realistic hurdles in the path of the would-be criminal. And the added cost, when considered against a background where ten million dollars can get lost in a shuffle of twenty billion dollars a week, as reported by *Newsweek* in the Security Pacific case, is relatively nominal.

Norma Levy reports that New York University has adopted a policy of keeping its terminals in rooms that are closed during off hours. The simple measure of locking the door to the terminal to prevent accessibility also imposes a hardship on a would-be thief. The fact is that most computer embezzlers are not given to breaking and entering. The nature of the person involved is such that a simple lock imposes a psychological hurdle with far greater effect than the actual lock and key.

Dividing the various functions associated with the computer is also a powerful inhibiting factor. For example, the authorizing function for the creation of checks should be kept distinct from the distributing function. The story is told of one employee who stole a box of presigned continuous-form checks and after leaving the company wrote himself an undetermined number of checks that did not even have to be forged.

Whiteside describes how a system user, responsible for certifying the eligibility of persons to receive funds under a social benefit program, succeeded in processing a series of fraudulent claims, causing coupons to be sent to accomplices not eligible to receive them. The accomplices redeemed the coupons and apparently no one reviewed the transactions. There was no requirement even to prepare backup source documents to support the fraudulent claim. Whiteside too recommends separating responsibilities so that a system of checks and balances is created. No one individual should have the power to control every stage of the operation or use of the computer. That kind of authority invites misuse.

A system of checks and balances can also be imposed on the input and output stages. An audit system that calls on an independent source to review the input and output is but one illustration. Armand Gazes, a computer systems analyst with Rockefeller University, suggests that periodic tests be made of a given security system to evaluate its integrity. "Lest complacency prove our undoing" says Gazes, "even the cleverest computer security systems should be subject to internal self-testing and auditing as well as manual checks by both the originators of the system and those programmers charged with its maintenance. This can even be accomplished at a low priority level—so long as it is done."

In summary it should be recognized that although no truly fool-proof system exists—it may not even be economically or techni-cally feasible to devise one—there is a real need for computer security. That need is imposed not only by the desire to protect the private information, whether it be trade secrets or other informa-tion of a personal nature, or to protect a company's funds, but also, in the case of a public company, to fulfill a duty to the company's stockholders.

The best way to devise a system of controls is to oversee the individuals with access to the computer. By carefully regulating access in the first place; by imposing a requirement such as the presence of two or more individuals for the operation of a terminal from which particularly sensitive information may be extracted or massive funds transferred; by setting up an identification system that forces an operator to expose himself to identification; and by setting up an audit system for reviewing both input and output, computer theft can be made extremely difficult. Since it is at the user stage that most problems are encountered, emphasis should be placed on dividing the various functions associated with the computer among different people and assigning each an indepen-dent responsibility in such a way that each one's function consti-tutes a form of balance over the function of at least one other person. The mere fact that perfect security cannot be achieved does not excuse indifference. Reasonable precautions can go a long way toward preventing computer fraud and embezzlement.

Conclusion

Coca-Cola's secret formula may be kept in a vault with highly restricted accessibility, but that's just not practical for most compa-nies.

Whether it's a new marketing plan at Procter & Gamble, a new car design at General Motors, or a new toy at Ideal Toys, many minds, often crossing several corporate departments, helped gen-erate the idea for that plan, design, or device. Companies often find it useful to obtain a cross-section of thinking, sometimes de-scribing it as synergistic. And that may well be true. But the price of such synergism is the increased risk of precipitous disclosure.

The use of fences around a plant, security guards, and restrictive employment agreements, and the like may prove to be of limited value to prevent inadvertent disclosure. A good internal security program begins with the information to be protected: identifying it, tracing its flow or accessibility within the organization, and identifying the offices and people through whom the information passes. By examining how the information is conveyed, by whom and through whom, from where and to where, a company can know the extent of its security risk and can act to control that flow of information. In so doing a company not only minimizes its risk of inadvertent disclosure but it also makes its employees more aware of and sensitive to the treatment of confidential information. Also, in the event of a lawsuit, such as in *Motorola* v. *Fairchild* (see chapter 7), it would be more difficult to disprove the existence of trade secrets by the showing of inadequate handling or processing of data within the corporation.

When devising a security system, avoid any tendency to overkill. The measures described in this chapter are not intended to be applied indiscriminately. A paranoid approach may drive away the better employee, whereas a participatory effort will involve him in the process of safeguarding confidential information.

SECURITY GRID

	Employee	Consultant	Visitor	Supplier	Subcontractor	Customer	Licensee	Unsolicited Outsider
Invention assignment								
Confidentiality agreement								
Restrictive covenant								
Conflict-of-interest policy								
Third-party secrecy agreements								
Circulation of confidential documents								
Copying of confidential documents								
Coding trade secrets								
Screening of publications								
Screening of lectures								
Clearing desk tops								
Use of shredder								
Visitor pass								
TV monitors								
Record keeping								
In-house seminars								
Unsolicited ideas policy								
Consultants' agreements								
Trade secret protection in licenses								
Consult prior employer (with consent)								
Exit-interview policy								
Advising new employer (of restrictions)								
Preventing computer fraud								

To analyze your present security system:
1. Check ($\checkmark$) those squares in current use.
2. Cross (X) those squares intentionally not used or not applicable to your business.
3. If any blank squares remain, review your policy with respect to the possible application of the omitted points of protection.

5 □ Anticipating Problems: The Employment Contract

An employment contract is no panacea for every potential employer-employee dispute—that should be understood at the outset. No employment contract can force a talented employee to continue his efforts for an employer—slavery's been abolished. By the same token, no employment contract can compel a company to retain the services of an employee; to pay him perhaps, but not to utilize him. That's one eye-opener Billy Martin of the Yankees, Lee Iacocca of Ford Motor, and Jack Rudman of Cowles Publishing have shared. And as one of Mr. Iacocca's predecessors, Semon "Bunkie" Knudsen, discovered, an employment contract can help insure financial security but does not insure one's position within the company. But, depending on the circumstances, an employment contract may prove valuable to either the employer or the employee or both.

Thomas F. Willers was President of Hooker Chemical Corp. when it was acquired by Occidental Petroleum Corp. As part of the transaction, Willers was given an eight-year employment contract (with an option to extend it to eleven years). He became president of Occidental, and Dr. Armand Hammer agreed to serve as chairman of the board. Not long thereafter a dispute arose and Willers relinquished the presidency in favor of a newly created position as vice-chairman. A new president became the chief operating officer and Dr. Hammer the chief executive officer. Willers, effectively stripped of meaningful authority, eventually left Occidental, having achieved a financial settlement of his employment contract.

Jack Rudman sold his small textbook publishing company to Cowles Communications, Inc., and agreed to stay on, at Cowles' request, as editorial head of a proposed test-book division with the understanding that he would be a "number one man" in his division. Rudman and Cowles signed a five-year employment agreement calling for a base salary plus an annual increase based on sales. Within less than a year, following some internal differences involving Rudman and a divisional editor of Cowles, a new organizational chart was drafted. Rudman now found himself under the supervision of the very editor with whom he had been feuding. He complained, contending that under his employment agreement he should have direct access to a Mr. Mauer, then a vice-president of Cowles' educational division. He argued that he was being placed under lower-level employees. Thereafter Jack Rudman simply refused to take orders from the individuals to whom he was to report. So he was ignored—and later fired.

Rudman sued Cowles, claiming fraud and breach of contract. The case was tried in New York state before a special referee who found that Rudman had been wrongfully discharged. New York's Appellate Division disagreed, reversing the special referee. But New York's highest court, the Court of Appeals, ruled in favor of Jack Rudman. That court said:

> If an employee . . . is engaged to fill a particular position, any material change in his duties, or significant reduction in rank, may constitute a breach of his employment agreement.

As a result of his lawsuit, Rudman achieved a financial award equal to almost three years' salary. There was no question, however, of reinstatement with authority. That would constitute what the law calls "specific performance." And throughout the country courts have uniformly declined to grant specific performance over personal services, which is what is at question when the matter of explicitly defining and enforcing job responsibilities under a contract is raised. Thus, a nightclub that contracts with a famous performer will find that it cannot compel that performer to go on stage. The only legal remedy available is a lawsuit for damages. "Specific performance" is a remedy reserved for such tangible acts as the transfer of rights to property, whether it be the conveyance of a deed or assignment of rights to a patent. Courts will not apply it to "intangibles" such as the performance of personal duties in an employment situation. To do so would open up an enormous area of potential litigation, involvement of the legal system in the too common employer-employee argument as to what may or may not be considered part of a particular job. It also smacks of involuntary servitude. You can't really force someone to work for you, even if he signs a contract. But you can force him to pay you for any financial loss he caused you, and a contract can be helpful in spelling out the damages.

Although an employment contract cannot insure performance of personal services, it can be used to prevent the employee rendering those services to a competitor—at least during the term of the contract. For example, a company engaged a designer to create new toys. He did so but left the company after a while, notwithstanding his employment contract. Although a court would not order him to continue creating toys for his former employer, the New Jersey Chancery Court did rule that, for the remaining three years of his five-year contract, that employee could not invent and design toys for someone else.

When and How to Use

Although there are drawbacks and limitations, an employment contract can be helpful from both the employer's as well as the employee's point of view.

First of all, even in this age of cynicism there are many people who believe in honoring their commitments, who will live up to the terms of contracts they signed as part of their sense of values and ethics. Some are motivated by a concern for their reputation. But regardless of motivation, just as there are people who will stop at a red light at 3:00 AM when there is no traffic—there are a great many people who will honor the terms of a contract they signed. In the ordinary situation most people live up to their contracts without a lawsuit. Most employment agreements are honored by both sides, without ever resorting to the courts.

Of what value is an employment contract? Well, let's look at that:

first from the employer's perspective and then from the employee's. To the employer, the contract represents an opportunity to do more than just recite title and salary. Here is a chance to spell out what is expected of the employee, to make clear that the employee can never say that he wasn't told he would be in a position of confidence, that he would not be entrusted with information that he was expected to maintain in confidence. The contract can refer to corporate policy regarding a host of matters, such as internal security, conflict of interest, and relocation. It can help to prevent future misunderstandings by setting the record straight at the outset. True there are some valuable people who may be turned off, but if exceptions are going to be made for them, the best time to do so is before they are hired, before the company invests significant sums in relocation and in possible training. At the least, an adjustment period is necessary whenever an employee is hired—and the more talented the individual, the more responsibility assigned to him, the more time may be involved in "adjusting." For example, when Thomas Willers left Occidental he joined Champion International as its president. He spent virtually all of his first year visiting all plant sites and familiarizing himself with that company's worldwide facilities, resources, and people. Most people, of course, are not hired as presidents, but some time for adjustment is almost always necessary. That time can be costly, costly not only in terms of the employee's salary but in terms of the company's business and productivity. Thus, if an executive doesn't work out, the impact to the company can be much more serious than only the salary and relocation expenses paid out.

A small company hired an executive to take charge of its equipment manufacturing division. He appeared to be functioning effectively until a labor dispute arose. He refused to attend any evening meetings, arguing that he worked hard enough during the day. But those meetings were essential at that time. Others in the company found it difficult to substitute for him, not only because as operating head of that division he was most familiar with its day-to-day needs and problems, but also because some of the antagonism was directed toward him. The lack of continuous discussion was clearly hampering an effective settlement—and proving costly in terms of productivity.

By happenstance someone discovered that this particular executive owned a restaurant that he operated in the evenings. When confronted with this fact he maintained that he did nothing wrong, that the restaurant was simply an investment on his part, many others in the company had investments in real estate, securities, and the like. But, said the company, operating the restaurant was more than an investment—it was moonlighting and conflicted with the company's policy against moonlighting. The executive claimed he was unaware of any "moonlighting" policy, and that if it was the policy an exception should be made. In this case the matter was resolved privately, following a frank and open discussion. An exception was made because of a desire to keep an otherwise effective manager, but the employee signed an agreement that his first responsibility was to the company and that in the event of a conflict in demand for his time, including evenings and weekends if necessary, he would be available. Quite obviously, not all such cases have a happy ending. Much depends on the desirability of keeping the employee. But the point is that an employment agreement at the outset that referred to the company's policy against moonlighting just might have avoided the problem in the first place.

An employer finds another advantage to a contract in that it can serve as a basis for tying up a talented or creative individual in a highly competitive field. The employee can't be forced to work for any employer, but he can be barred from working for one's competitors, so long as the bar is reasonable. (*Reasonable,* as we have seen, is a term of art in the law, best defined in terms of some actual cases. This point is discussed more fully below.)

In addition to affording an employer an opportunity at the outset to prevent and avoid misunderstandings with a prospective employee, and to make certain that the employee is aware of the company's regard for its confidential information, the employment contract can serve to override the common law regarding title to inventions. According to the common law, the employer owns an invention of his employee only when the latter is "hired to invent." However, the question of whether a given employee was actually hired to invent or to make a particular invention is often subjective and leads to disputes.

An employment contract can avoid the "hired to invent" dispute by stating in unequivocal terms that any invention made by the employee belongs to the employer. By contract, an employer can avoid disputes over whether the invention relates to company business, was made on the job or with company equipment, or was facilitated by other ideas generated first at the company. By contract, the employer can avoid being limited to a shop right in his employee's inventions. Thus, by appropriate use of employment contracts an employer can secure his capital investment in his business, secure title to improvements and discoveries made by employees, and help secure his trade secrets.

From the vantage point of an employee, an employment contract can secure income for a definite term or it can provide safeguards against loss of income in event of termination. Many executives prefer a termination clause to a stated term of employment. That clause provides that, regardless of the cause of separation, salary payments will continue for a specified period of time, usually one or two years.

Aside from securing income, the employment contract can be used to spell out the employee's level of responsibility. Thus, if the company later decreases your level of authority, as Cowles Publishing apparently did to Jack Rudman, then the company has breached its agreement. The company will sometimes be legally required to reinstate the employee in the position of authority disputed, but if not, a claim for damages may be warranted.

A prospective employee should not hesitate to ask whether he will be required to sign *any* agreement as a condition of employment. All too often employees in middle management, including particularly scientists and engineers, find that after accepting a job, on the first day of work, they are faced with what are euphemistically called "forms" to be signed. Among those forms is something many companies call an "invention assignment". Some companies seem to have persuaded themselves that an invention assignment is not an employment contract, that it is just some silly form their patent counsel worked out in the middle of a nightmare. An invention assignment, however, is most definitely an employment contract. But it is a limited contract in that it relates only or primarily to inventions and possibly ideas and discoveries made by employees. Most of those agreements also relate to confidential information and impose obligations of secrecy on the part of the employee. If you are considering employment you should ask about any "forms" you will be required to sign, ask for copies in advance, and read them carefully.

In more than one case known to the author, prospective employees have objected to terms in a form and have succeeded in obtaining modifications. For example, one chemist challenged a clause on the ground that it covered not only any company-related inventions but her cooking recipes as well. That clause was modified. In another case the form specified that the company would own inventions made for two years after the employee left the company. After the employee's objection on the ground that this would make him unemployable during that time, the company agreed to limit the time span to six months and further agreed to limit that clause to inventions related to the company's business and actually conceived prior to the date of separation.

Many middle-level management employees mistakenly assume they have no bargaining leverage and that a company will not change its forms for them. This is by no means entirely so. Much depends on the level of management the prospective employee is dealing with. Do not underestimate the power of a department head or manager who seriously wants to hire a competent man or woman. While drastic changes may not be obtained, at least not in the usual situation, relatively modest changes are possible. Most company lawyers are sensitive to the need for talent and will work with a department head who expresses a strong interest in hiring a skilled individual and wants to resolve reasonable objections to the terms of an employment agreement, even if it's an invention assignment form. Do not be too quick to accept the argument that "everybody else signed it," and therefore you should too. Companies are run by people and even the largest companies are malleable in policy, if the approach is made correctly and the change sought is reasonable under the circumstance.

Generally speaking, an employee's bargaining position is better before he is hired and it is therefore most often to his advantage to iron things out ahead of time. If you are considering joining a company that has certain policies you find objectionable, the best time to air any objections is before you accept the position. If you know the company expects its employees to sign an agreement (a form) containing a restrictive covenant (a clause prohibiting you from joining a competitor), do not expect to find support afterwards from the department head or executive who hired you if you did not object before you were hired. It's usually not easy to get a company to waive a restrictive covenant. The company will have to want you more than you want them, and the people who want you will need an opportunity to go to bat for you.

An employment contract, while not a panacea for a company or an employee, can be of positive value to both. It can help set the record straight for both at the outset and thereby reduce or avoid future problems. It can put the employee on notice of what is expected of him, of what rights he is giving up, of corporate policies affecting his time and income, and of who will own his future creations, inventions, and discoveries. It can provide an employee on the executive level with a clear understanding of his level of authority, and with financial security either in terms of a fixed period of employment or by means of a termination clause. It can, of course, provide for payment in forms other than cash, such as stock or stock options, deferred compensation, bonus incentive tied to performance, and retirement and health benefits. But for the purposes of this book, we will concentrate on only two aspects of employment agreements; the two most commonly found in the so-called invention-assignment forms, namely, who owns the rights to future inventions and under what conditions, and what obligations are imposed relating to trade secrets. We will, however, incidentally discuss related clauses that frequently appear in contracts or forms to be signed by key employees.

Defining Which Employees Should Be Covered, and the Different Forms of Agreement

Quite obviously, certain levels of top management are accustomed to contracts, and if your company has been around awhile it has established some track record of experience in this area. You may have a formalized company-wide policy established relating to employment contracts. If not, you should consider one. At the upper management level all employees should be under some kind of contract. It may be a simple memorandum or a multi-page document resembling an insurance policy. Both can be equally effective.

From the employer's standpoint, the short memorandum agreement or the simple exchange of letters describing the terms of employment might be more effective than a long-winded, highly detailed 'instrument' full of legal jargon. An executive who signs one of those highly stylized contracts without benefit of legal counsel may later claim that he never really understood what that contract said. People almost never read their insurance policies, and most of the time judges take that into account when deciding cases involving claims against insurance companies. (Some people suggest that judges themselves can't understand their own insurance policies.) In any case, an executive can't hide behind a shield of complexity, behind a cry that the contract was drafted by the company lawyer and is too abstruse to be understood, if what he signed was a letter or memorandum spelling out the terms of employment in plain and simple words. An informal agreement is also better from the employee's point of view—it gets to the point more quickly and is easier to grasp.

Virtually all members of upper-level management are likely to learn or at least be exposed to all or almost all of the company's proprietary data. A top-level executive is exposed to the full complement of a company's business; its customer lists, its marketing and production techniques, its buying sources, its financial condition (in the more intimate sense of an "insider"—with all due respect to the public disclosure requirements of the SEC), and its technical position—the status of various R&D projects and whatever details about those projects the executive cares to learn. That kind of intimate information can be used—potentially—to the severe detriment of a company.

Since most men or women who have reached the top echelon of corporate management are likely to want or even insist on written agreements, a company is not likely to run into any opposition to the concept of an agreement. But at this level be prepared to throw away your forms. Each agreement is negotiable and quite often individually negotiated. The types of clauses that appear in some agreements may be unheard of by over 90 percent of management —and probably beyond their reach, in the absence of some very special negotiating leverage.

In general most company employees below the level of upper management can be divided into two categories: technical and nontechnical. Those categories may be subdivided into professionals/executives in middle to lower levels of management and the nonmanagement level. Those employees who are union members, whether laborers or clerical, are governed by their labor union contracts with the company. (Incidentally, it is worth keeping in mind that many unions have come to acknowledge and accept clauses in their contracts whereby trade secrets such as production data or manufacturing processes are protected and inventions assigned to the company. In at least one instance, the union agreed to an invention assignment clause with the stipulation that the employee involved would be paid one hundred dollars for each such assignment. That is not at all unreasonable.)

Those who fall within the nontechnical category—those who have no technical, scientific, or engineering background or who are simply not hired to invent—may still be creative and may still be exposed to sensitive confidential information. Novel marketing programs can be as valuable as any invention. Powerful advertising copy can be extremely valuable. Therefore agreements with nontechnical employees should cover the protection of confidential information, nondisclosure to third parties, the rights to new designs and to sales and advertising literature. Under the new copyright laws the company would own advertising copy written for it as a "work for hire," but there is no harm in spelling this out in an employment agreement. Sometimes even a redundant statement is justified if it might later avoid a lawsuit.

Agreements are not ordinarily necessary with nontechnical, nonmanagement personnel. But if the company is a pure research company or is engaged extensively in government contracting, then a confidentiality agreement calling attention to the sensitive nature of the company's business may be justified for all employees.

Agreements of some sort are necessary for all technical employees, regardless of rank. Even a technician in a laboratory is sufficiently trained to understand research projects that may be highly sensitive. Furthermore, anyone with a technical background —including education acquired primarily through experience— should be regarded as capable of coming up with an invention. For example, a small Long Island electronics manufacturer hired a largely self-taught individual as its production chief. The company was engaged as a subcontractor to manufacture noise-reducing devices. Since the production chief had no formal education in electronics, no consideration was given to offering him a contract or asking him to agree in advance to assign any inventions he might make. In fact, no one at the company gave the matter any thought until the new production chief, within several months of the time he was hired, came up with an improved noise filter. The company was quite dismayed to learn that it did not own the invention but had only a shop right.

That production chief suddenly found himself with considerable bargaining leverage in that company, enough to negotiate a healthy stock option as part of a favorable contract. And the company suddenly woke up to the need for written agreements with their employees, particularly agreements providing for the assignment to the company of all rights to any inventions and discoveries made by employees. Some form of agreement, covering at least inventions and confidential information, should be considered for *all* employees in the technical category, from technicians, laboratory assistants, draftsmen, production or manufacturing foremen or supervisors, on up the management ranks.

When acquiring a company, employment contracts may serve as a useful inducement to retain key employees. Experience shows that acquisitions often instill fear among employees of the company being acquired. When certain employees are considered highly desirable, an offer of an employment contract for a few years may help stabilize the situation. It may also serve, perhaps indirectly, to prevent "followers" of those key employees from leaving their company. A rapid turnover in an acquired company in the first year of acquisition, before the company has been fully integrated into the parent organization, can be very costly.

There is a point worth noting here relating to the concept of consideration. This applies particularly in the case of acquisitions. To illustrate: when Giant Company acquires Tiny Company, can Giant insist that all of Tiny's employees sign a new agreement—Giant's standard "form" agreement—as a condition of continued employment? The law seems to be divided here, with some cases holding that continued employment is adequate "consideration" for such a new agreement and others that some new or "fresh" consideration to the employee is necessary to sustain the validity of such a contract. Employees of Tiny may well argue that any

agreement signed with Giant, without any additional consideration
or benefit to them—such as increased salary or change in position
—was signed out of fear and under coercion and is therefore
unenforceable. Whether such an argument would hold up depends on the state where the case is tried and possibly the attitude
of the judge before whom it is tried. Precisely because the law is
unsettled here, it's worthwhile to give this matter some thought
before acting. Some acquiring companies have held back, applying
their "form" agreements only to new employees hired after the
acquisition and to existing employees at the time of a favorable
salary review or promotion. That salary raise or promotion might
serve as "fresh" consideration. The last point is not absolute but
it furnishes a reasonable argument in favor of the agreement and
may help enforce it, if necessary. But this topic, relating to the
acquired employee, suggests another which should be explored,
namely:

The Right to Require/Refuse Such Agreements

There are two stages at which an employment agreement is
entered into:
a. prior to hiring as a condition of employment;
b. during term of employment as a condition of continued employment.
An acquisition does not actually present a third stage, but rather
creates a situation that lends itself to interpretation—whether the
acquired employee is being freshly hired or merely continuing in
his employment.
When a company offers a position to an individual, there is no
question but that it may attach certain conditions to its offer. A
company may and indeed should advise a prospective employee of
its policies relating to conflict of interest as well as other policies
that may affect that employee. Aside from legal considerations; it
is ethically wrong to confront an employee with company policy
only after he is hired. And sometimes that is carelessly done by
companies that have been around long enough to know better.
When an employee is offered a position, it is reasonable to
condition the offer on the employee's acceptance of company pol-

icy—including acceptance of an employment agreement governing such matters as ownership of inventions, designs, and plans, and the protection of confidential information. The agreement may go further, including, for example, ownership of inventions made subsequent to termination of employment, or the right to join competitors, or to set up a competitive business. At this stage an employee who is fully aware of the implications in the terms of the offer can simply reject the offer if he finds it unacceptable. (It may be worth noting that many people disagree with this line of reasoning. They argue that the average scientist/engineer has little bargaining leverage. A number of professional organizations have lobbied for legislation that would protect employees against "one-sided" agreements imposed by some companies as a condition of employment.) Fair or unfair, a company may write its own contract governing conditions of employment, and whether describing it as a "form" or not, the company may lawfully impose it, prior to hiring an individual, as a condition of employment.

When a company decides to adopt a policy affecting *existing* employees and asks existing or present employees to sign something that governs their employment, problems may arise. That is not, however, always true or necessary. IBM has revised its policy in this area several times and asked existing employees to sign their successive new form agreements along with new employees. But an examination of those successive agreements shows that each is somewhat more lenient or favorable to the employee. Thus, existing employees were never really asked to surrender meaningful rights during the course of their employment.

The problem arises, however, when a company wants to adopt a more restrictive agreement or perhaps even to adopt any kind of agreement where no agreements exist. Take the case of that small Long Island electronics firm that actually had no agreements with any of its employees. It certainly wished it did after its production chief made an invention and it discovered it didn't own that invention. Clearly, had an agreement been imposed retroactively, that production chief would have left the company. But suppose the company asked all existing employees to sign away their rights to their discoveries as a condition of continued employment? Would such agreements be enforceable? Remember that in the absence of a written agreement the common law says that an employee owns the invention unless he was "hired to invent" and, from the case law, hired to make that invention or to invent in that particular field: in other words, that invention was part of the employee's assignment.

To carry the illustration a bit further, assume that the company wants to impose restrictions on present employees to prevent them from joining a competitor or setting up a competitive business. Clearly those present employees can quit. But in doing so they give up their jobs, their family's principal sources of income, their pension rights. Thus, to say that the average employee has the right to refuse to sign an agreement presented as a condition of continued employment is to stretch the literal truth beyond reality. As a practical matter, the ordinary middle- or lower-level management employee, the average researcher, engineer, marketing or sales executive would simply accept a new agreement. Refusal to do so, while a legal right, is not, in most instances, a practical or realistic alternative. The question then raised is whether such a contract, offered to an employee in midstream of employment, as a condition of continued employment, will be enforced by the courts.

Up to about World War II, and even through the 1940s, the law seemed pretty clear on this point. If the employer was not originally bound to keep the employee, and in return for not being fired the employee signed a contract, that contract was enforceable (assuming, of course, that the contract did not contain other clauses that were illegal). The law viewed private contracts of this nature to have a certain sanctity. Let's take a brief look at why this was so.

Article I, Section 10 of the United States Constitution provides that "no state shall . . . pass any law . . . impairing the obligation of contracts." In 1885 the New York Court of Appeals ruled that a state law designed to end sweatshop factory conditions in the cigar industry violated the right of the workers to contract for services. The fact that those workers were working in apartments in multi-family tenement housing, under cramped conditions, with poor lighting and little ventilation was not as important to the Court of Appeals, from a legal viewpoint, as the alleged fact that the law deprived the worker of his freedom to contract for his services. In 1905, in *Lochner* v. *New York*, the U.S. Supreme Court overturned a law limiting bakers to ten hours of work a day. The

Court characterized such a law as an arbitrary interference with the bakers' right to contract to work longer hours, if they pleased. On May 27, 1933, a day many legal historians refer to as "Black Monday"—the same day the Supreme Court nearly destroyed Roosevelt's New Deal by holding the National Industrial Recovery Act unconstitutional—the Court also ruled unconstitutional a federal law providing relief to farmers threatened by mortgage foreclosures, because that law interfered with the right to contract. "Black Monday" was the trigger for an onslaught of anti-New Deal cases that eventually led to the famous Roosevelt "court-packing" plan in 1937. Although that plan never succeeded, some changes did occur. On March 29, 1937, the Supreme Court reversed itself and upheld a Washington state statute providing minimum wages for women. It also approved an amended law easing the plight of farmers unable to meet mortgage payments. On April 12, 1937, the Court upheld the National Labor Relations Act and on May 24, 1937, the Court upheld the Social Security Act, thus breathing life into the two most dominating pieces of social legislation in this century. It is important to recognize that the Constitution had not changed, but that the judicial interpretation of it was changing. That change had a profound impact on employment agreements.

In 1934, in Connecticut, Carl Roessler, a manufacturer of delicatessen products, sued a former employee, Wayne Burwell, for breaching an agreement that he would not call on Roessler's customers for one year after leaving. Burwell had left voluntarily. He argued that he had signed the agreement after having worked for Roessler for three years, that he was not guaranteed any minimum period of employment nor given anything he did not have before, and therefore, according to Burwell, he received no consideration for the agreement.

In law, a contract, to be valid, requires "consideration." The form that consideration takes is irrelevant. Whether it is money, property, personal services, the doing of an act, or simply the "not doing" of an act, all represent consideration. A contract can be bilateral or unilateral. It is said to be bilateral if both parties agree to something, such as an exchange of property, cash payment for services—or if they agree to refrain from doing something. It is bilateral if one party agrees to refrain from doing something in return for something else, such as cash, property, or simply the promise by the other party to refrain from a similar act. "I won't sue you and you won't sue me" is bilateral. A contract is unilateral if it is contingent on an act or event. "I'll pay you x dollars if you fix the roof" or "if you assign your patent to me." The point is that you did not absolutely agree to fix the roof or assign your patent, and you are not bound to do so. But if you do, the contract becomes enforceable.

The preparation of a magazine article on speculation is an example of a unilateral contract situation. The editor says, in effect, "We'll pay you for a good piece on this subject," usually specifying something of the focus and the desired length. The author prepares the piece with the understanding that if it is accepted he or she will be paid the agreed-upon fee. Both parties are clear that any binding obligation is contingent on acceptance of the piece for publication.

"I'll pay you x dollars if you don't join a competitor for a year after leaving this job" is a similar type of promise, and if the promise is fulfilled it becomes a unilateral contract. Keep in mind that an act can be negative as well as positive—"I'll pay you x dollars *not* to build within one hundred yards of my property" is a unilateral offer and acceptance takes place by the act of not doing something. But if you and your neighbor sign a contract that he won't build within a certain distance of your property line, in return for some consideration (act or money or whatever) then the contract is bilateral. It is now a promise for a promise, where both parties have undertaken future commitments to one another, as opposed to a promise conditioned on the other party doing something. In the latter unilateral situation, the party making the promise or commitment is not bound unless and until the act, on which the promise is conditioned, is performed. Similarly the other side is not bound to perform the act. Only when the act is performed does the commitment or promise become an enforceable contract.

Note that in the case of bilateral contracts, with both parties committing themselves to do something, the consideration is each party's promise or obligation to the other. In the case of unilateral contracts, the consideration is the event, the act of doing or refraining from doing something, for the promise.

In the Connecticut case of *Roessler* v. *Burwell*, Roessler approached Burwell, after employing him as a salesman for three years without any written agreement, and offered him employment "indefinitely" at a weekly salary as "mutually agreed upon," and Burwell would agree, in return, if Roessler should discharge him "for any cause whatsoever," not to compete for a year. Burwell, as noted earlier, was not discharged but left voluntarily. The Connecticut court said the agreement was enforceable. It said that Burwell had continued to work for Roessler under the agreement for four more years and had accepted the benefits of the agreement. Therefore, said the Connecticut court, Burwell having voluntarily left, he should not be able to disregard his obligation. Note particularly two points. One is that the court seemed to take particular note of the fact that Burwell quit as opposed to being discharged. The other point is that the agreement called for a promise by Roessler to continue Burwell in his employ but for no definite period. Therefore Roessler could have rejected the agreement at any time. But Burwell essentially agreed that in return for continued employment, he would not compete for a year. Having accepted the benefit of Roessler's "act," namely, that Roessler did not discharge Burwell was now, in the eyes of the law, bound to fulfill his commitment not to compete. Burwell's argument that he was already employed by Roessler; that he was receiving the same weekly salary; that he had worked for three years before the contract under essentially the same conditions he worked during the four years after the agreement; that he really had no choice but to sign because of the scarcity of jobs (remember this was the 1930s); and that he actually got nothing for signing but gave away something; all this fell on the ears of an unsympathetic court.

Similar decisions were handed down time and time again, with few exceptions, throughout the country in the 1930s and 1940s. For example, the Missouri appellate court ruled, in 1933, that a salesman of ice, coal, and fuel oil in St. Louis, who had first signed an agreement midstream of his employment, promising not to compete in his sales territory for a year after leaving "voluntarily or involuntarily," was bound by that agreement. McKee, the salesman, had also left voluntarily. He made the same argument about having to sign and about lack of consideration. But the Missouri appellate court said: "Attacks on such contracts have been made on various grounds, but it is now well established by the decisions of our Supreme Court and appellate courts that contracts similar to the one in this case are based upon a sufficient consideration, namely, the mutual promises of the parties." It's interesting to observe that the contract in question was said to be based on mutual promises when there was no requirement that City Ice & Fuel Co. continue to employ McKee. Apparently that kind of sloppiness in judicial reasoning was due to a casual indifference to the realities of the transaction. After all, if a baker can agree to work more than ten hours a day under adverse working conditions because—as the Supreme Court said—that's part of his freedom to contract, then why can't the ice salesman agree to stay away from his sales territory for a while, in return for not being fired?

About the same time Connecticut decided *Roessler* v. *Burwell* and Missouri, *City Ice & Fuel Co.* v. *McKee,* New Jersey's Chancery Court, and courts in Pennsylvania, Texas, and Vermont were arriving at similar conclusions. That the employer refrained from discharging the employee was repeatedly held a sufficient consideration for the employment contract, even though it was offered after employment had begun, with no new benefits to the employee aside from not being fired. In almost all instances the contract was required because of a "concern" by the employer that the employee might go out and compete or work for a competitor.

While the great majority of cases ruled in favor of the employer, a few courts took exception. The state of Washington, for example, in 1934, in *Schneller* v. *Hayes,* decided that such an agreement, signed midstream of employment, was not really "a contract of employment" but an "ancillary unilateral engagement"—a legal euphemism for an offer outside the employment relationship. Hayes was an optometrist/optician who signed an agreement some time after he was hired that, in consideration of continued employment, he would not thereafter enter into business "either as owner or part owner of optometry and optician in the city or within one mile of the corporate limits thereof." The Washington court refused to enforce the agreement, and denied a request for an injunction by Schneller. The appellate court took note of the relationship saying: "Upon the question of consideration it is apparent from the language of the contract itself that Hayes was already employed by [Schneller]. His employment was by the week. August 24, the date of the contract, was in the middle of the week. Appellant [Schneller] was bound to respondent [Hayes] for that week's employment. The contract didn't promise any additional employment. . . . It promised respondent [Hayes] nothing in the way of future employment and stipulated nothing as to wages. Courts will not ordinarily undertake to weigh the adequacy of consideration. The parties, being competent . . . are permitted to make their own contract . . . But in this case the contract is wholly lacking in consideration moving to respondent [Hayes]."

One of the more vigorous opinions written on behalf of the employee was handed down in 1944 by a state court in North Carolina. In *Kadis* v. *Britt,* Britt had been employed for several years, according to the court's opinion, when he was required to sign a contract "not to divulge information" obtained in his employment, and "not to engage in other employment in a similar business for two years after the cessation of his employment" with Kadis. The North Carolina court said the contract was "exacted" from the employee without adding anything to the employee that he did not already have, in return. As to the argument that Kadis, the employer, had refrained from firing Britt, that court said: " . . . continued employment must be understood to mean further continuance in employment, which more than implies the threat of immediate discharge. A consideration cannot be constituted out of something that is given and taken in the same breath—of an employment which need not last longer than the ink is dry upon the signature of the employee, and where the performance of the promise is under the definite threat of discharge. Unemployment at a future time is disturbing—its immediacy is formidable."

In 1949, a case was decided in the Pennsylvania Superior Court relative to companies that "acquire" employees through acquisitions. That case, *Markson Bros.* v. *Redick,* involved the sale of a retail clothing store. Redick had been employed by the store as a buyer when it was acquired by Markson Brothers. Redick was retained as general manager of the same store. About six months later, Redick signed an employment contract agreeing not to compete with her new employer or to work for a competitor for a year after leaving. Nearly six months later Redick decided to quit and start her own retailing business nearby, in competition with Markson Brothers. Her employers sued and obtained an injunction prohibiting Redick from engaging in competition with them in violation of her employment agreement. On appeal, the Superior Court reversed and dismissed the case. In doing so, it observed that Redick had been employed in the same store prior to its sale to Markson Brothers and that even after its sale she had been employed under an oral understanding for several months prior to signing the employment contract. The court then added a new wrinkle avoided by courts in the past. It said that the covenant not to compete was in partial restraint of trade. In order for it to be enforceable it had to be based on sufficient consideration. The court said Redick actually received no consideration because her salary remained the same and she was not assured of any definite term of employment.

Oregon is another state that has said that mere continued employment is not sufficient consideration for an employment contract. *Phillip N. McCombs* v. *Ruth L. McLelland* was decided by the Supreme Court of Oregon in 1960. McLelland had been employed by a press-clipping service for about six and a half years when she was asked to sign a contract promising not to join a competitor later on. She was not threatened with discharge if she didn't sign and all the employer ever said to her was, "Here it is, sign it if you want to." And she did, and she continued to be employed for a couple of years until she quit and joined a competitor. The Oregon court refused to enforce the restrictive covenant, saying that it was not supported by any promise of continued employment or other good consideration.

Court opinions in this area of the law have been changing slowly. But courts have become increasingly conscious of social reality and their written opinions reflect it. In 1969, in *James L. Leoscher* v. *Robert A. Polcky,* the Supreme Court of South Dakota ruled against the employee but went out of its way to point out that the employee, Loescher, a veterinarian, knew about the contract and agreed to accept it before he was hired—even though he didn't actually sign it until a few months later. The contract was held to be enforceable.

What does happen when an employee refuses to sign and hands in his resignation? That actually happened in the case of an engineer by the name of Kenneth Pankow.

Pankow was hired by Engineering Assoc., Inc. in 1962 as a project engineer. In June of 1966 he was asked to sign a contract agreeing not to join a competitor if he should leave Engineering

Assoc. Inc. He refused and was promptly told he could pick up his check. He resigned and did join a competitor. Engineering Assoc. sued for an injunction to prevent Pankow from working for the competitor, on the grounds that he had learned trade secrets as to the methods and designs of Engineering Assoc., Inc. The Supreme Court of North Carolina denied the request for an injunction and added the comment that even if Pankow had signed the employment agreement it would have been unenforceable for lack of consideration.

South Carolina has followed North Carolina's position, refusing to enforce employment contracts entered into during the course of employment for lack of consideration. But recent cases in Alabama, Georgia, and Florida have held continued employment to be adequate consideration although signed subsequent to employment. The Alabama case, *Doughtry* v. *Capital Gas Co. Inc.,* involved a contract that contained a clause calling for a minimum term of employment of three months and for two weeks' notice in case of termination, which was something the employee did not have before. Thus some "fresh" consideration was added.

By this time it should be clear that the law is evolving in this area and that the trend is toward an increasingly pragmatic view of the facts of a case. Although on the basis of numbers of cases it would still appear that the majority favor the employer, many practicing lawyers today would argue otherwise. There is a growing tendency of courts to show a concern for an employee's actual situation, as opposed to his theoretical rights. Because of conflicting court opinions and an ever-growing trend toward concern for the employee, a company would be well advised not to require current employees to sign employment contracts. In addition to legal reasons, there are problems of morale to consider. Employees, particularly the more competent ones and therefore the employees you most want to keep, are likely to resent having to sign an agreement just because it's part of a new company policy. And calling it a "form" is not likely to make it any more digestible.

Well, what can a company do with respect to its employees when it finds it has not adequately protected itself? As to prospective employees, they should be informed of company policy before being hired and offered contracts, or asked to sign certain agreements at the outset as a condition of the offer of employment. As to present employees, any attempt to alter their terms of employment, which involves their surrendering a right, is best made in conjunction with some additional consideration. A reasonable minimum term of employment that the employee did not have before, a promotion, a raise, or special training are all examples of what courts have found to serve as additional or "fresh" consideration to sustain agreements entered into during the course of employment. Employees acquired with the acquisition of a company are best regarded as present employees. The fact that they are permitted to stay on while the acquired company is dissolved is not really the same as an offer of employment. Acquired employees are not truly changing jobs. The temptation to have all such newly acquired employees adapt to company policy and sign new company agreements, as would be asked of them if they were just hired, should be resisted. Although this practice is still conducted today, it is not a wise one. An individualized approach to newly acquired employees may take some patience, but in the long run it will provide not only a more enforceable legal position but improve employee relations.

The Form an Agreement Can Take

1. Oral or written

An agreement can be oral as well as written. But if oral—watch out! Proof can be difficult. If it is based purely on testimony, then it can become a question of the employee's word against the employer's. Furthermore, there is a natural tendency to remember facts as you understood them. Quite often people will shake hands on a deal and when the time comes to carry it out find that some misunderstandings remained to be ironed out. A written agreement has the advantage of permitting any confusion to surface early, so that the parties clearly understand the commitment each is making.

Oral agreements have other shortcomings, aside from problems of proof. For example, when Housebow Hotels acquired the Emmory Motel near Kansas City, the hotel chain owners summoned the Emmory's manager, Jack Gilder, into their office. According to the testimony at a subsequent trial, the owners told Gilder they wanted him to continue as manager for "at least five years." When

Gilder was dismissed within a few months he sued claiming $68,534 damages for breach of contract and $100,000 punitive damages. But the Supreme Court of Missouri dismissed Gilder's case on the ground that any agreement for more than one year must be in writing. A five-year oral contract simply cannot be enforced. Thus, if you intend the agreement to last longer than a year, or if it may be carried out some time beyond a year from the date it becomes effective, then be sure it is in writing.

2. The letter/memorandum and the formal contract

According to his testimony, William P. Hillman, Jr., wasn't at all sure he got the job after the interview. He told his wife, when he got home, that he was keeping his fingers crossed. The next day he was pleasantly surprised to receive the following letter:

> This will confirm my conversation with you today. Hodag Chemical Corporation of Skokie, Illinois, will employ you to perform such functions as assigned for two years minimum and at $15,400.00 per year. This employment begins today.
>
> Very truly yours,
>
> Hodag Chemical Corporation
> (signed) Sheldon E. Kent, President

> Agreed:
> William P. Hillman, Jr.

Hillman signed and returned the original, retaining a copy. He went to work for Hodag but, unfortunately, things soured after awhile. In fact the job didn't last more than a few months before Hodag fired Hillman.

Hillman sued Hodag for breach of contract. Hodag said that Hillman's claim was nonsense, that the letter sent Hillman wasn't a contract, it was merely notification to Hillman that he was being offered the job. But the Appellate Court of Illinois disagreed. The court said that whether the document involved was a letter or a more formal agreement was irrelevant. What counts is whether the writing is definite: whether it clearly states the terms of the understanding, and is agreed to by both parties. The letter met all the criteria for a contract, it was definite in its terms, consideration (in the form of salary) was spelled out, it was signed by both parties, and therefore was just as enforceable as a more formal document.

Let's look at another case involving a letter. There's a case that has been dubbed the "Candyman" case. In that case, a letter became the basis of a lifetime contract. It started when Joseph Pridmore, president of Hollywood Brands, was looking for an experienced production man to run a new candy manufacturing plant in Texas. He wanted someone who not only knew how to run a plant but who knew the candy business. He found someone, a career man with the Curtiss Candy Company, C. D. Ward. It was perfectly understandable that after twenty-five years with Curtiss, having reached the position of general superintendent of manufacturing and shipping for three Curtiss plants in Illinois, Ward was reluctant to leave. Ward was concerned about giving up fringe benefits he had accumulated over the years, including his retirement benefits.

Pridmore sent Ward a letter offering a salary of eighteen thousand plus an annual bonus of up to 50 percent of salary, tied to the performance of his division. The letter also said that Ward would not be forced into retirement. Ward's responsibility would be reduced to that of a consultant at ten thousand per year. Pridmore ended his letter to Ward with the statement: "of course, this is based on performance. Frankly, I hope you are around until you are at least 83."

Thereafter Ward and his family picked up their belongings in Chicago and moved to Sulphur Springs, Texas. As with any new plant, there were a host of startup problems—equipment, design of the building, hiring personnel, and clearance by FDA inspectors. At first the plant was in the red but by year's end it appeared that it might soon turn the corner into profitability. But Ward's champion in the company, Pridmore, died in an automobile accident.

Within a few months the new president of Hollywood Brands fired Ward—eight days before he was to get his bonus for 1970—because things still weren't going well at the plant. Ward sued for breach of contract. The Texas Court of Civil Appeals reversed a lower-court ruling for the employer and sent the case back to the trial court. The Court of Civil Appeals found that the letter established an employment contract for life, subject only to termination for good cause, and that whether there was good cause for Ward's dismissal was a factual question for the jury to decide. This order for a retrial led to a settlement. But the point of the case is clear. A seemingly innocent letter can be the basis of a serious contract, even a lifetime contract. A letter offering a position to an employee can be, depending on just how you word it, an employment contract.

Whether you use a letter or an informal memo or draft, a multipage formal contract is more a matter of style than law. All three are subject to the same rules of interpretation. So long as there is an offer of employment for a specified salary and it is accepted, there is a contract. True, that contract can be terminated by either party "at will" if no definite or minimum term is provided, but until it is terminated, the employee is entitled to the salary specified. Thus, in the case of bankruptcy, the employee has a clear claim— there is no ambiguity as to what is owed him for his labors.

3. The agreement to agree

Sometimes a formidable legal document that you think is an employment contract really isn't. Take the case of H. L. Scott, for example. He sold his manufacturing business to Ingle Bros. and, as part of the sale, he and Ingle Bros. agreed, or so Scott thought, to a five-year employment contract at a specific salary. In fact, the legal document covering the sale of Scott's business read:

> (5) An Employment Agreement has been prepared, wherein H. L. Scott will manage the business for a minimum of five years at an annual salary of $15,000, payable monthly, with a $3,000 increase after the first year, providing annual gross sales exceed $200,000.00.

That was back in 1969. But in 1971 Ingle fired Scott and Scott sued. Here the Texas Court of Civil Appeals reversed a lower court ruling in favor of Scott. The trouble with that contract, said the Texas court, was that no separate employment agreement was ever prepared. That paragraph in the agreement covering the sale of Scott's business really states only an intention to enter into an employment agreement, but a promise to agree is not enforceable. In other words you can't just agree to agree. Once more we see the pitfalls of employment contract law. Surely Scott thought he had a contract—or must have thought so, since he never asked for a separate employment agreement. Scott apparently thought the contract of sale for his business took care of it all. It could have, had it been worded a little differently. A positive statement, such as: "An Employment Agreement is hereby entered into . . ." instead of the reference to another agreement would probably have done the trick for Scott in that case. Thus, whether writing a letter, a memorandum, or a formal agreement, watch your wording. When offering employment in a letter, try to avoid gratuitous remarks such as the "hope you are around until you are at least 83" comment in the "Candyman" case unless you mean to hire the man until he is 83. Say what you mean, no more and no less.

Federal and State Laws and Their Impact on Employment Agreements

Several states have enacted laws prohibiting contracts restraining a person from engaging in a lawful business, profession or trade. Their objective is to prevent the restrictive covenant, that is, to prevent the employer, in the ordinary or normal employment relationship, from imposing a requirement in an employment agreement on the employee so that after termination, the employee cannot compete with the employer. Among the states involved are: Alabama, California, Florida, Indiana, Louisiana, Michigan, Minnesota, Montana, North Dakota, Oklahoma, and South Dakota, and Wisconsin.

Similar legislation has been proposed in other states and, therefore, in each instance when a restrictive covenant is considered, it is essential to review the laws of the state in which the contract is made or signed, as well as the laws of the jurisdiction which is to govern the contract according to its terms. In addition, the laws of the state in which the employee is to work should be checked, because some courts will decline to apply the conflicts-of-law policy. There is a conflicts-of-law policy that applies most of the time. Although the subject has filled the pages of many a treatise, its objective is simply to resolve differences between the laws of different jurisdictions. For example, when a contract is signed in one state and it is the subject of a lawsuit in another, the usual conflicts-of-law rule is that the court sitting in the state in which the lawsuit is pending will apply the law of the state in which the contract was signed. But there are many exceptions, and one involves the matter of public policy. Therefore, a court may decline to apply the conflicts-of-law rule in a dispute where, in its opinion, to do so would violate the public policy of the state in which that court sits. Thus there is a need to consider the laws of the jurisdiction where the employee will be working because it is entirely possible a lawsuit will have to be brought there.

In addition to specific statutory legislation, it is worthwhile to recognize that in some states the courts have, by interpretation, ruled that it is against their public policy to enforce a restraint on trade and, therefore, have simply declined to enforce restrictive covenants, notwithstanding the conflicts-of-law principle. Texas, for example, has declined to enforce restrictive covenants in certain cases where the court concluded that enforcing such a provision would violate their antitrust laws.

Several states have begun enacting laws governing rights to employee inventions. Minnesota, for example, has passed a law to the effect that an employer cannot compel an employee to assign all of his inventions made during the period of employment without regard to their subject matter. California has followed suit at least to the extent that the California Assembly passed a law— which, as of this writing, is pending before the state senate— providing that if an employee develops an invention *not related* to the employer's business and on his own time with his own resources, it is the employee's own invention. It will be recalled that in the absence of such legislation it is possible for an employer to provide in the agreement that all inventions, whether related to the employer's business or not, and whether made on the employer's time or not, will belong to the employer. The law in Minnesota is substantially the same as that passed by the California Assembly. Thus in Minnesota an employer cannot insist upon taking rights to inventions that are unrelated to the employer's business and not made on the employer's time utilizing the employer's resources.

On the federal scene, there have been many bills introduced from time to time seeking to alter the equation between the rights of employer and employee. The Brown bill, introduced by Congressman George E. Brown, Jr. (D.–Cal.), and later the Moss bill, introduced by Congressman John E. Moss (D.–Cal.), have both sought to protect the employee in contractual situations. The Brown bill tried to return the status quo to the common law by providing that the employer cannot, by contract, take title to inventions from an employee who was not hired to invent. Under the Brown bill the employer would have got a shop right to inventions utilizing the employer's time and resources, but not title. The Brown bill is not too different from, although it would go further than, the Minnesota law.

Congressman Moss has repeatedly introduced a bill that seeks to simulate the law governing rights to inventions in West Germany. Although that law will be described a bit more fully in chapter 9, it is worthwhile noting here that in West Germany a system of compensation exists whereby the employee shares in any profits made on his invention. Furthermore, the employer must return title to the employee in the event that the invention is not used within a certain specified period of time. At present, some companies in the United States—Exxon, for example—have a policy whereby they will return to the inventor all patent rights to inventions that remain unused after a specified period of time. The Moss bill has found many critics in industry because it would involve a form of governmental arbitration of disputes with respect to just how much the inventor is to be paid. (Further discussion of the Moss bill may be found in conjunction with the description of West German law in chapter 9.)

It is of more than passing interest that the engineering profession has increasingly tended to mobilize in the direction of vocal and politically active professional associations. Among the natural consequences of such activities is the lobbying for legislation that will be beneficial to the engineer or scientist. Therefore, it is to be expected that we will see more bills along the lines of the Moss and Brown bills and that we will, in the course of time, see some legislation which affects and perhaps limits the rights that may be transferred or acquired by contract from an employee in the normal employment relationship.

6 □ Anatomy of an Employment Contract

We have already seen that the simplest-sounding letter can be a binding contract. Indeed, it may be more effective than the most formal document, from a legal as well as a morale viewpoint. It's not always necessary to cross all the "t's" and dot all the "i's." And you can probably cite many happy employment relationships based on a handshake or something written on a scrap of paper at a restaurant or bar. We've all heard of cases like that. There's something to be said for them. But in today's mobile society, where talent often seeks its highest bidder, and where loyalty, either by the corporation to the employee or vice versa, seems to have a price tag associated with it, there's something to be said for crossing all "t's" and dotting all "i's" too.

If we assume an arm's-length transaction between a company and an executive it wants to hire, and if we assume both are interested in formalizing their understanding, what are the standard terms found in most such agreements, and what are some of the more important points for each party to look for? Let's look at how an employment agreement is structured.

Basic General Provisions

Defining the parties

The opening paragraph conventionally identifies the parties, typically by name and address—except that if a party is a corporation it should indicate the state of incorporation. (Every corporation owes its status as a legal entity, and its right to contract, to its charter, which can vary from state to state; thus the state of incorporation is a useful as well as customary means of identifying corporate bodies.) Failure properly to identify the parties in the agreement is not necessarily fatal, but keep in mind that the whole point of the agreement is to reduce an oral understanding to an enforceable writing. The less fuzziness there is in the agreement, the less chance there will be of a future misunderstanding. This principle should be applied from the first paragraph through the last.

A typical opening paragraph may read:

> THIS AGREEMENT, entered into this ___ day of _____, 19___, between ABC CORPORATION, a corporation of (state of incorporation), having its principal office at _____, (hereinafter called "ABC") and JOHN H. SMITH, whose address is ___ _____, (hereinafter called "Smith") . . .

The "WHEREAS" clauses

These clauses are customary in the more formal agreements, but not necessary to the validity of the agreement. Their purpose is to set the stage, recite the background or intent of the parties, and provide a sense of perspective for the agreement. In the event of subsequent litigation, a judge may find it helpful to refer to the "whereas" clauses to interpret a clause or phrase in the body of the agreement that is otherwise ambiguous.

Ordinarily the "whereas" clauses can be dispensed with. They may say nothing more than:

> WHEREAS, ABC wants to hire Smith; and WHEREAS, Smith wants a job with ABC; NOW, THEREFORE . . .

But, if Smith is being hired as part of a special arrangement, or if the circumstances are unusual, then pay attention to the "whereas" clauses. They might make a difference later on. For example, if ABC is acquiring the Magic Balloon Company and if Smith is a key employee who knows all the trade secrets about making magic balloons and the value of the company depends greatly on Smith sticking with ABC after the acquisition, then the "whereas" clauses might be used to set forth the intent of the parties (although, once more, these clauses are not necessary). An example of the latter would be:

> WHEREAS, Smith is presently employed by the Magic Balloon Company and acknowledges he is a "key" employee thereof, occupying a position of mutual trust and confidence, and in such capacity is privy to confidential information related to the manufacture of magic balloons; and
>
> WHEREAS, ABC is negotiating for the acquisition of the Magic Balloon Company; and
>
> WHEREAS, ABC desires to retain the services of Smith in the event of said acquisition, and
>
> WHEREAS, Smith desires to remain with the Magic Balloon Company in the event of its sale to ABC, but only as the chief operating officer of said Magic Balloon Company, with a title appropriate to that position; and . . .

It may be evident that the above "whereas" clauses have set the stage for the agreement. In the event of a dispute, should there be any ambiguity in the rest of the agreement, reference to the purpose of the agreement may help clear it up.

Definitions of terms

Not all agreements have a special section devoted to defining terms, but in a lengthy or complex agreement such a section is usually invaluable. Defining terms at the outset eliminates the need for doing so in the main text, thus reduces the size and verbiage of the rest of the agreement. This technique helps increase the readability, and therefore the clarity, of the rest of the agreement.

What terms are defined? Any terms that come up more than once and that have special meaning to the parties involved. For example, when a consultant is hired and asked not to consult for a conflicting organization, the latter should be defined. Is an organization "conflicting" if it sells a similar product but based on a different technical principle—say, mechanical versus digital watches? That probably would depend upon whether the consultant is a manufacturing engineer whose experience is specific to one type of product, or a marketing consultant who is being engaged to help increase the sale of watches.

The definitions section can be used to define what the parties mean by "confidential information," "inventions," the company's "bonus" or "management incentive" system, or any terms of art that either party believes may be misunderstood or possible of more than one interpretation. Some of the agreements in the appendix of this book contain definition sections.

The "operative" clauses

At the heart of virtually any agreement are the operative clauses. After all, that's what it's all about.

The operative clauses say, essentially, "I give this in return for that." Or, in terms of ABC and Smith, the operative clauses recite point blank what commitment ABC is making to Smith and vice versa.

For example:

ABC hereby employs Smith, and Smith hereby accepts employment by ABC, effective with and contingent on ABC's acquisition of the Magic Balloon Company, subject to the terms and conditions hereof.

The operative clauses then go on to provide:

(a) *The term of employment.* Once the agreement becomes effective it should specify how long it lasts. (Note that the date the agreement is signed is not always the effective date. In the case of ABC and Smith, their agreement becomes effective on the date of the acquisition and is contingent on that event, but the parties can specify any effective date. If they don't, then the date the agreement was signed would be presumed to be the effective date. Even that presumption, however, can be rebutted by evidence that another time was intended—a typical example of how a seemingly minor point can become a source of friction and litigation.)

The date employment is to begin and end, conditions under which it is to begin or end, and any conditions under which it can be terminated sooner than the term specified, are all important facts. The way an agreement is normally constructed is first to set forth the term of employment, say, five years from the effective date of the agreement (or until some specific date). Later in the agreement, in a paragraph relating to termination, conditions are set forth under which the agreement can terminate sooner than the "term" that was specified earlier—such as for "cause." From the employee's point of view, the term "cause" should be defined as specifically as possible. But most employers will object, because from their point of view "cause" should be open-ended so as to include virtually any act, conduct, or failure to act that is considered inimical to the company's best interests. Any definition here necessarily restricts the employer's latitude for action, while simultaneously benefiting the employee. In practice, it is only the exceptional employee who wins on this point.

In addition, earlier termination conditions are sometimes built into other paragraphs—disability provisions, for example. The original term itself may recite that it is subject to certain limitations, such as meeting certain quotas of production or sales volume. The author has found it helpful, when reviewing a formal employment agreement, to chart or tabulate all paragraphs that have any effect on the length of the employment, the "capacity" or role that the employee is to serve, and anything bearing on compensation.

(b) *Capacity.* In what capacity is the employee to serve? Most executives who have reached a significant level of responsibility are presumably as much concerned with their role in any new position they undertake as with their compensation. In our hypothetical case, Smith is agreeing to stay on with ABC because, at least in part, he wants to manage the Magic Balloon Company and he is being given an opportunity to do so.

From the employer's viewpoint it is best either to omit any commitment regarding capacity or to retain the option to vary the position of the employee. Language such as the following is desirable:

> ABC hereby employs Smith, and Smith agrees to serve, in such employment capacity as may be determined, and with such powers and duties as may be conferred upon him, by the Board of Directors of ABC, from time to time.

From the viewpoint of the employee, however, the commitment as to the role he will play and authority he will have, should be as strong and specific as he can negotiate. In Smith's eyes, the following language would be desirable:

> ABC hereby employs Smith and Smith agrees to serve as President and Chief Operating Officer of the Magic Balloon Company with full authority and responsibility for the day-to-day management of said Magic Balloon Company, including the right to make all decisions affecting personnel, purchasing, and manufacturing and production, sales and marketing, subject only to corporate-wide policy decisions, long-range planning and capital expenditure commitments established by the Board of Directors of ABC and applying uniformly to all ABC divisions and subsidiaries.

The above clause is not often seen in an employment agreement. In practice, ABC would be unlikely to delegate its management prerogatives to such an extent, even if it meant losing Smith and possibly forfeiting the acquisition. That kind of clause is generally reserved for an employment agreement in a close corporation, a family-controlled corporation, or where a single individual owns a controlling interest—and then that individual probably doesn't need the contract, except for tax and estate planning purposes. But it is something a key employee can bargain for, anyway.

A realistic compromise that might be arrived at would be to recite the role contemplated for the employee, to recite the title and function intended for him, and to indicate he will be given that title and function initially, subject, however, to certain constraints. The company may reserve the right to delegate duties and responsibilities including the right to make changes, from time to time. But any material change would constitute a breach of the agreement. (Remember the case of Jack Rudman and Cowles Publishing, where Rudman expected to head up the company he sold to Cowles, and as a result of an organizational change found himself too far down the management rung, stripped of authority to make any meaningful decisions. That was a material change and a breach of the agreement. Cowles had to pay Rudman damages.) The agreement can provide for certain payments to be made to the employee in the event his role is changed in a manner inconsistent with the role initially intended or designated. That way the employer can reserve its management prerogatives, while the employee can get off the hook if he is dissatisfied with any organizational changes—and still be compensated according to terms spelled out in the agreement.

For example:

> ABC hereby agrees that Smith shall be promptly given the title of _____, with the responsibility, duty and authority commensurate with that title, subject to the right of ABC to make such changes in said responsibility, duty and authority, from time to time, as it deems necessary in its best interest and further subject to the right of Smith, upon the occurrence of each such change, in the event he deems his level of responsibility, duty and authority to have been materially reduced, to elect to terminate this Agreement in accordance with the termination provisions set forth in Paragraph____.

That termination paragraph would, of course, set forth certain terms of payment to Smith in the event he elects to quit because his duties were changed.

(c) *Salary.* Another of the most important elements of the operative clauses is, of course, compensation. Salary is but one form of compensation. Bonus or management incentive plans, retirement, health, disability benefits, commissions, stock options, salary deferred schemes, and the like are all forms of compensation. They need not be recited in detail. And usually they aren't. The compensation clause most often recites a base salary, indicates that the employee will participate in the same benefit plans generally applied to employees in a similar management level or capacity, and may recite any special payments to be made, such as reimbursement for expenses or a one-shot bonus to induce him to join the company.

Where the employee cannot join a company plan—if, say, the employee is ineligible for the retirement plan because of his age, and it is contemplated that certain payments will be made to a special fund to be established in lieu of a pension—then that, too, is to be spelled out. Note that sometimes, instead of a retirement plan, a company hiring a mature executive because of his special talents may arrange a consultancy to go into effect when the employee reaches a designated age. That was done in the "Candy-

man" case referred to earlier. The consulting agreement can provide for a monthly stipend in return for a certain number of hours'
consultation. It can also provide for a flat payment to the employee's family or widow in the event of his death before the
natural termination date of the agreement.

Note the compensation clauses in the consultant's agreement in
Appendix 3. They can be applied after normal retirement.

(d) *Disability*—From the employer's viewpoint, it is important to
link the compensation clause to performance. This does not just
refer to a scale, such as a commission or bonus based on production or profitability. Those arrangements vary greatly based on the
nature of the industry and its customs, as well as what the parties
negotiate. Those terms should be spelled out, of course, but the
performance link referred to is the physical ability to perform.
Therefore, the employer should seek a disability clause in the
agreement, linked to and limiting the obligation to continue paying the employee.

To the employee a disability clause is not necessarily a one-way
street. Drafted properly, it will serve to protect both employer and
employee. It may call for disability insurance, usually at the employer's expense, thereby providing the employee with a continued source of income in the event that he is physically unable
to continue working.

In some agreements the disability clause will be found in the
body of the agreement soon after the salary or compensation
clause. In others it may be found in a section or article marked
"Termination" as one of the conditions for terminating the agreement. Where you locate the clause is optional so long as you are
aware of its effect and intend that effect. A disability clause may be
grounds for termination even if not located in the termination
section, so long as the clause, regardless of where located, recites
that it is intended to have that effect.

It is wise to define the term "disability," preferably in the section
reserved for definitions, early in the agreement. Most often "disability" is defined in terms of an illness or injury that precludes the
employee from working for a certain consecutive period of time,
say, six months. The definition can be adapted from that found in
insurance contracts. Sometimes the disability clause is defined in
terms of mental as well as physical impairment. There should be

criteria for determining the existence of the impairment as well as its duration. For example:

> The term "disability" as used herein shall mean Smith's inability by reason of physical illness or injury or mental impairment for a period of not less than 180 consecutive days to perform the services which are the subject of this agreement; and such condition shall be deemed to exist or no longer exist when so certified in writing by a disinterested licensed physician or psychiatrist selected by ABC, or at the election of Smith, by two out of three such physicians or psychiatrists selected by ABC, or when determined to exist or not exist by a court of competent jurisdiction. Smith hereby agrees to submit to examination and diagnosis by such physician(s) or psychiatrist(s) selected by ABC or by such court.
>
> In the event of such a determination of disability, this agreement shall terminate.
>
> or shall remain in effect except that in lieu of compensation, Smith shall receive only those benefits normally provided by ABC to its employees.
>
> or Smith shall continue to receive his salary along with any bonuses due him for a period of one year thereafter in lieu of any benefits or rights which Smith may otherwise have.*

Other variations are or will become apparent, particularly if you get into serious negotiations. The employer should check to see that termination does not relieve the employee of his obligation to keep trade secrets confidential. The employee should check to see that the determination of disability cannot be arbitrary and that in the event of genuine disability, his right to receive whatever benefits or payments are set forth in the agreement is not contingent on further events or conditions.

The agreement may anticipate the death of the employee and recite the specific benefits or payments to be made to the surviving spouse. This clause is often found in agreements made with principals of a company being acquired. Those principal or key employees are rightfully concerned with protecting their estates and the agreement should recite whatever obligations or promises were made for the benefit of the employee's family in the event of the employee's death.

*Only one of these alternatives should be selected, the choice dependent on preferred policy or negotiated agreement.

Responsibilities and Obligations with Regard to
Confidential Information

"But I was never told I would have to keep anything I learned confidential" is a theme often recurring in employer-employee lawsuits. When an employer seeks to protect confidential information in court, it strives for a preliminary injunction as a first measure—to get a court order enjoining disclosure before the horse gets out of the barn. This is usually done as soon as a problem surfaces, for the price of hesitation may be the reality of a loss of trade secrets. Once disclosed, secrets are obviously lost and the only remedy left is an award of damages, which may not be entirely satisfactory. Furthermore, proof of the extent of damages can be delicate and difficult.

The employment contract can serve as a powerful tool to help obtain an injunction—assuming, of course, that it contains a written promise not to disclose confidential information. That written promise also serves as an acknowledgment of the nature of the relationship. In other words, it is an admission by the employee that he expected to receive information in confidence and agreed to maintain that information confidential.

You may recall from an earlier discussion of the right of the parties that a contract is not needed to establish a confidential relationship between an employer and employee. That is true. But a contract can help *prove* that relationship. Even more, it can specify the obligation and responsibility of each party. It can provide protection for information that is not normally recognized by the law as a trade secret, but which the employer still considers proprietary. Know-how, for example, may involve much detailed information that is generally available to the public—assuming one knew where to look, and what, specifically, to look for. That kind of information is not normally protected by injunction in the absence of a written agreement covering it. The difficulty with protecting know-how is essentially a problem of proof—proving it is confidential. Quite often the information involved is little more than a collection of details, which, on hindsight, may seem quite obvious, particularly to a judge in a courtroom who is unfamiliar with the problems of the industry and who is trying to resolve conflicting testimony. In that kind of situation, faced with a morass of conflicting technical details, a judge may understandably throw his hands up in despair and deny an injunction.

A preliminary injunction is granted to preserve the status quo, to prevent either party from upsetting the apple cart before trial. If it appears to a judge that an employee is about to do something that would irreparably alter the status quo before a full trial of the issues, that judge will likely grant an injunction. Where there is no contract, no written promise, the common law takes over. The common law imposes its will on both employer and employee, generally requiring the high-level employee to respect his employer's confidences, and generally speaking, requiring the employer to show that he did, in fact, have information that was confidential in the first place and that he entrusted it to his employee. Implicit is the understanding that the employee knew he was receiving certain information in confidence, knew just what that information was, and thus knew what he was obligated not to reveal. As you can imagine, the chain of proof is complex. A contract can help simplify matters. For example, if the contract recites that the employee is hired to work on a particular project, say, the development of a zinc-chlorine battery, and all information related thereto is agreed to be proprietary to the company, then any situation where disclosure is likely is more readily seen as threatening the status quo.

With a contract you have an additional cause of action: breach of the agreement itself. The contract, in a sense, substitutes for the common law because courts do permit parties to arrive at their own understanding and, unless some law or public policy would be violated, courts will enforce that understanding. Thus, all information of a confidential nature, including know-how, can be protected by agreement. That know-how may include such information as who the most reliable suppliers are, which will furnish supplies at the lowest price, which supplies should be inventoried, and to what extent—the kind of day-to-day business knowledge that can be obtained through experience and is in a literal sense "publicly available" but may take months, if not longer, to accumulate. Meanwhile considerable profit may be lost. That kind of information is often the reason a company buys a "turn-key" operation as opposed to merely taking a license or buying individual hardware. Know-how is the software that binds the hardware together and makes the most efficient use of it. Since it can be obtained publicly, in the sense that the information can be pieced together from published sources and experienced individuals in the trade or field, it does not technically qualify for trade-secret protection under the common law. However, it can be protected by contract.

The wording of the confidentiality clause depends, of course, on what it is that you are trying to protect. In some agreements, the terms do little more than put on paper what the common law imposes anyway. There is nothing wrong with that—provided it is what both parties intend. Other agreements are quite elaborate in spelling out just what the term "confidential information" is to cover, whether it is intended to embrace know-how, and what the obligations are with respect to the use or disclosure of that information.

In its simplest form the agreement may recite:

> Smith hereby agrees that except as required by his duties to ABC, he shall not use or disclose any information acquired in confidence from ABC.

That clause essentially recites Smith's obligation to ABC under the common law. It would be imposed by the law in the absence of a written contract. Thus, it is a condition implied by law in that relationship. But writing still has at least one advantage to ABC. It is recognition by Smith that he may expect to receive confidential information.

A more complex version will define what the parties mean by "confidential information." For example:

> The term "Confidential Information" as used herein means information disclosed to Smith or learned by Smith during or as a result of his employment by ABC, and as used by ABC not generally known in the trade or industry in which ABC is engaged and relating to:
> the business of ABC.
> or the magic balloon project or industry.
> or ABC products, processes, equipment, services, manufacturing, purchasing, marketing, merchandising and selling

data and know-how, as well as all ABC financial, data processing, research and development and engineering information.*

The employee should be concerned to impose reasonable time
limits on his obligations so as not to remain bound forever. Certainly the employee's obligation to maintain confidentiality of a
trade secret should expire once the secret becomes publicly
known.

The Supreme Court stated in *Aronson* v. *Quick Point Pencil Co.* that
a contract providing for the payment of royalties *indefinitely* so long
as sales of an unpatented keyholder were made was a valid, enforceable agreement. This was so even though the keyholder became public knowledge once it went on sale. The court noted that
the parties could have provided for a limited term for the payment
of royalties, but since no limit was specified, Quick Point had to
keep making payments to Aronson as long as it sold the keyholder.

The point is that unless a time limit is specified, either based on
a set number of years or upon public disclosure of the information,
it is conceivable that an employee could be bound by contract
indefinitely, although practical circumstances may make it difficult
for an employer to enforce such obligations. The employee should
also be concerned with any restrictions on his freedom to utilize
experience and continue to work in his field if the job doesn't work
out or last. (See also chapter 2.)

Defining Rights to Inventions, Ideas, and Discoveries

What happens quite often in employment agreements or in form
agreements called "invention assignment forms" is that the company seeks title to *any* invention the employee comes up with, and
to *all* of his ideas and discoveries. This is true whether or not the
invention, idea, or discovery relates to the work the employee is
doing, that is, his assigned work, or even to the employer's business. For example, an electrical engineer working on communications devices might tinker a bit at home and come up with something that relates to digital computers. If the engineer has signed
an agreement to the effect that he will assign all inventions that he

*The definition in the agreement would use any one of these alternatives.

comes up with during the period of his employment to his employer, then the employer takes title, even though the invention was made off-hours and is not related to his employer's business. Because this point is essential to our discussions, it may be worth reviewing common-law concepts of ownership and shop right. That way it is easier to understand what the contract is designed to do.

Under the common law, in the absence of a contract, the employer takes title only to those inventions that are made by an employee who was hired to invent, and only when the invention is within the scope of his employment. Essentially, the employee must be paid to do a job and to come up with inventions (or to do a job where it is understood that he may reasonably be expected to come up with inventions). In that circumstance, his pay is the consideration for the company's or employer's gaining title to the invention. Where the employee is not hired to invent, or where an employee is hired to invent but comes up with an invention that is outside the scope of his employment but if some use is made of the employer's facilities, then the employer gains a *shop right*. The shop right is *not* ownership. It is simply the equivalent of a nonexclusive, royalty-free, noncancellable, nonassignable indefinite *license* to use the invention. In addition, under the common law, the employer has no right to inventions made by his employee that are outside the scope of the employer's business even where the employee makes some use of the employer's facilities. Furthermore, under the common law, the employer has no right to any invention that is made subsequent to the time that the employment relationship ends.

By contract, however, the employer can take title to all inventions, all ideas, and all discoveries regardless of whether the employee was hired to invent or not, and regardless of whether the idea or discovery is within the employer's scope of business. The employer gains title rights simply by stating clearly in the contract signed by the employee that as a condition of employment, in consideration of salary, the employee agrees to transfer those rights. (Because most employees are simply not in a position to bargain for their common-law rights, professional organizations have got together and lobbied legislators to oblige a closer adherence to the common law principles.)

The agreements in Appendix 4 contain sample clauses that illustrate the contract provisions used quite commonly in industry as part of an invention assignment form and which call for the assignment to the employer of all rights, all title, and all interest to inventions, ideas, and discoveries by the employee as a condition of employment. It may be of interest to note that contracts with major executives contain no such clauses. Of course, it is questionable what kind of inventions or discoveries they would come up with, if any. Quite often contracts with major executives do contain clauses to the effect that the executive will abide by corporate policies relating to conflict of interest, and some incorporate, by reference, agreements that are customarily signed by management employees. In such situations, those agreements should be attached as an appendix to the main contract, and the executive would be well advised to review them carefully before signing the contract. Agreements such as invention assignment forms, which are referred to in a contract and incorporated merely by reference, are as much a part of the contract as if they were originally set out in the agreement. The employee should review an agreement carefully and if it refers to any documents beyond the four corners of what he has in front of him, it is smart to insist on seeing every form and every document referred to. Those silent forms and documents can really sting if not reviewed ahead of time. Furthermore, since they were referred to in the original agreement and the employee was advised of them, he would not have the argument of lack of consideration referred to earlier. When you are advised of a term in an agreement, and that term refers to something else, then it becomes *your* obligation to check that "something else."

One of the more important aspects of an employment contract that has been mentioned before and deserves mentioning again here is that it supersedes the common law. Without a clause in an agreement that determines rights to inventions, ideas, and discoveries, the common-law determination governs. In other words, without an agreement, an employee will own the rights to his inventions, ideas, and discoveries unless he was hired to make that particular invention, or to come up with that idea or discovery, in which case ownership goes to the employer. Since very often as a practical matter it is quite difficult to prove that someone was specifically hired to invent a particular invention, or to come up with a particular idea, an employment contract can prevent a lot of hassle. It can prevent misunderstanding. From the viewpoint of the employee, of course, it would be better not to have that agreement, or to let the agreement remain silent as to ownership of rights to inventions and discoveries. In an agreement the employee should be concerned about surrendering rights, especially to inventions actually outside the scope of employment.

The Question of Post-Employment Inventions

Post-employment inventions are simply inventions, ideas, and discoveries made subsequent to the time when the employment relationship ends. The concern here is with the employee who quits and, low and behold, files an application for a patent—a brilliant idea—which just happens to be similar to the very idea that he was working on during the period of his employment. Companies have become increasingly concerned with this possibility.

In *Jamesbury Corporation* v. *Worcester Valve Company,* decided in 1971 by the Federal Court of Appeals sitting in Massachusetts, the issue presented was that of ownership of patent rights. At stake was a patent to a double-seal ball valve that was a significant improvement over previously known single-seal ball valves for the control of the flow of fluid. Prior valves tended to leak. The inventor was Howard G. Freeman, president of Jamesbury Corporation.

It appears that Freeman had worked for the Rockwood Sprinkler Company from 1940 to January 1954. He had signed an employment contract with Rockwood agreeing "to give to Rockwood the full benefit and enjoyment of any and all inventions or improvements" which he might make while in the employ of Rockwood "relating to methods, apparatus, chemical substances, or methods of producing which are being used, manufactured or developed by Rockwood, or the use, manufacture and development of which was at the time of said invention or inventions in contemplation by Rockwood, and all inventions which are made or worked out on the time and at the expense of Rockwood."

Freeman also agreed as part of his contract that he would promptly disclose to Rockwood any and all inventions or improvements that he made while in the employ of Rockwood. The contract was silent as to post-employment inventions. During the time that Freeman worked for Rockwood, he was a prolific inventor and was responsible for the grant of nineteen patents in his name, which were assigned to Rockwood. Freeman had risen to become director of Rockwood's research at the time that he left. The evidence seemed to indicate that by the fall of 1953 Freeman had the confidence that he could develop a double-seal ball valve and profitably market it through a company of his own. Freeman raised funds for a new company and asked investors to postdate their checks to February 2, 1954. He left Rockwood on January 25, 1954, and held an organizational meeting of his new corporation on January 29.

It further appears that it was not before February 1 or 2 that Freeman had begun to make drawings or sketches of the double-seal ball valve concept.

After Freeman left Rockwood and set up his own company, Rockwood was sold to a new company called E. W. Bliss. When Bliss heard that Freeman, through his new company, Jamesbury Corporation, held a patent on the double-seal valve and was asserting that patent, claiming infringement by the Worcester Valve Company, Bliss intervened in the lawsuit, claiming to be the true owner of the patent.

The Federal Court of Appeals for Massachusetts stated that the essential issue in the case was the interpretation of the word "invention" as used in the 1940 employment contract between Freeman and Rockwood. If the word "invention" was construed as including conceptions or ideas, then the patent would belong to Rockwood and in turn, to Bliss. But the court noted that an idea does not become an invention until put to practice or embodied in some tangible form. It recognized that "before an idea becomes a workable reality, there often lie severe and long continued labor and repeated failures, and that success is not always achieved by the one who first strikes out the idea." The evidence in the case indicated that when Freeman left Rockwood, he did not have a tangible invention. He had an idea that he put to paper in the form of drawings or sketches in February of 1954, approximately a week after leaving Rockwood. The inference that the idea was conceived while employed by Rockwood was extremely strong, and it was an inference that the court drew. But the court said that having had the idea was simply not enough. The evidence indicated that the idea was not reduced to practice—that is, a tangible embodiment of the idea was not actually made nor was a patent application filed until after Freeman had left Rockwood.

The court referred to the arguments by Bliss that Freeman had acted in bad faith and that the court's decision should serve to frustrate the success of such bad faith. "Perhaps so," said the court, "but the contract could easily have provided that Rockwood was entitled to any inventions, patented by Freeman and relating to Rockwood's business, within a specified number of years after termination of employment." The court said that it did not want to be put in the position of having to "read inventors' minds in order to determine when the essential idea behind an invention was conceived."

In arriving at its decision, the court referred to some other cases and particularly noted that in one such case, *New Jersey Zinc Co.* v. *Singmaster,* an employee conceived the idea in dispute in July, disclosed it to others in September, made a written description in November, and left his job the following April. In that case it was ruled that the invention had been conceived ten months before the employee left work and belonged to the former employer. But in that case the contract involved an assignment of "ideas" to the former employer. That is, the employee had agreed that he would assign all *ideas* that he came up with during the term of his employment to his employer. The trouble with the contract between Freeman and Rockwood was that it applied only to *inventions* made while Freeman was employed by Rockwood, and not to inventions conceived of or ideas conceived of by Freeman during his employment by Rockwood. Had the latter been true, it is pretty clear that the case would have gone against Freeman.

As a result of cases like that involving Freeman and Rockwood, companies have modified their employment contracts or invention assignment forms to specify that they cover *ideas* conceived of by the employee during the term of his employment as well as *inventions* actually made while employed. Companies have also been adding clauses to their agreements relating to inventions made after the employee leaves the company—clauses that are referred to as "trailer clauses." Those clauses apply immediately after the employment relationship ends. The most common type of provision is one where the company asserts title to inventions, ideas, and discoveries made or conceived of within a limited period of time, perhaps the first six months or the first year after the employee leaves the company. Generally those clauses are limited to inventions that fall within the scope of the company's business. Some companies seek longer trailer provisions, lasting perhaps two or more years. It is questionable whether those lengthier trailer provisions can be enforced.

If he has any bargaining leverage at all, the employee should beware of a trailer clause. For one thing, it affects his ability to take a job afterwards. If you quit a company and there is a trailer clause in your agreement and you want to get a job in your field, then the new employer can be justifiably concerned that you will be getting paid to come up with inventions that will belong to your former employer. A trailer clause can have the impact of making it difficult to get a job in the same field, especially with a competitor.

Courts have come to recognize this, and for that reason they tend to look at a post-employment restriction or a trailer clause the same way they look at other restrictive covenants, and they have increasingly applied the laws against restraint of trade to those clauses. But they continue to be enforced in most states, and they continue to be commonly used. In 1965 the National Industrial Conference Board published a study of eighty-six major companies in the United States, twenty-one reporting that they used "trailer" clauses. The period of restriction ran from three months to two years. Ten of the twenty-one companies imposed a one-year restriction and eight a six-month restriction. The language generally used applied to inventions conceived or reduced to practice by the employee (alone or jointly with others) during any term of his employment by the company and for a certain number of months immediately thereafter. The restriction on post-employment inventions was generally related to discoveries or inventions pertaining to the company's business. Those restrictions were generally imposed irrespective of whether the employee quit or was fired. At least the clauses were so worded that the restriction would apply regardless of how the employment relationship was terminated.

Some of the agreements referred to by the NICB study sought to shift the burden of proof to the employee. That is, they sought to set up an assumption that inventions made within a certain period of time after termination of employment, say the first six months, were presumed to have been an outgrowth of the employment with the company and, therefore, were presumed to be the company's property unless the employee could prove that the inventions were actually made after the employment relationship ended.

Courts have enforced trailer clauses. One case referred to by the NICB in its 1965 study was *Universal Winding Company* v. *Clarke,* in which a federal district court enforced a one-year restriction. The contract with the employee stated that the employee agreed that all inventions or improvements "heretofore or hereafter made or invented by me at any time during my employment by the company, *or within one year from the termination of such employment,* and relating to the subject matter of my employment or to any subject matter or problems which I have or shall become informed by reason of my said employment . . . shall be the sole and exclusive property of the company." The former employee who had signed that agreement designed a coil-winding machine for a competitor within a year after he had left his former employer. The court awarded the invention to the former employer, saying that the restriction was reasonable and that it applied within a well-defined field of manufacturing, and therefore, was quite specific.

When the contract is open-ended, however, it is not likely to be enforced. For example, in the case of *Guth* v. *Minnesota Mining & Manufacturing Company,* a federal district court refused to enforce a trailer clause that applied to all inventions which the employee made or conceived "at any time hereafter." But it is clear that a reasonable post-employment restriction, limited in time and reasonably related as to subject matter, is likely to be enforced.

It is advisable for an employer to use a trailer clause to avoid the risk of loss that might result if an employee hired to invent, comes up with the invention, conceals it, and quits. In most cases it is sufficient if the trailer clause is applied for a year and is limited solely to those inventions related to the work that the employee was doing for the company just before leaving. That way there can be no quarrel as to the specificity of the restriction. The trailer clause should not be open-ended and should not be vague or indefinite.

While it is advisable for the employer to seek a trailer clause, it is preferable for the employee to avoid any clause that limits his freedom after his employment terminates. Often the employee does not have adequate bargaining leverage and that is simply a fact of life. Where possible, however, the employee should seek to negotiate that clause, as well as any other clause that would apply subsequent to the termination of employment. Any post-employment restriction automatically restricts the employee's ability to work for a competitor or to set up a competitive business. Remember that the common law expressly permits an employee to quit his job and set up a competitive operation or work for a competitor. Remember too that if you are representing the employee or if you are the employee, that it is desirable to leave the door open to obtain employment with another firm or company in the same field, and to continue to engage in work in which you are best qualified and in which you have acquired the most experience.

Although an employer is justified in seeking maximum protection, an employee is equally justified in seeking maximum freedom of movement once the employment relationship ends. The problem with trailer clauses is that they can, if not carefully applied, serve to mortgage an employee's mind. If anything that an employee conceives of, any idea he comes up with after the employment ends still belongs to the former employer, then for that period of time the employee's mind has, in effect, been mortgaged. The true objective of a trailer clause is to avoid fraud and to make life difficult for the would-be thief who might otherwise conceal his ideas until after he quits. It is difficult to strike a fair balance here because any compromise depends on a knowledge of the circumstances surrounding a particular employment and the particular industry. In some circumstances sensitivity to the loss of secret information may justify trailer clauses, particularly where the entire business is built up around a novel product or process. A post-employment clause such as the following might be considered reasonable:

> In the event of termination of employment, and for a period of one year thereafter, Smith agrees to assign to ABC any and all inventions, improvements or discoveries made, and any and all patent applications filed during said year, whether made individually or jointly, which relate to the subject matter of Smith's employment on

behalf of ABC during the twelve-month period immediately preceding termination of said employment.

The above paragraph speaks of inventions, improvements, and discoveries but it does not speak of ideas or concepts. An idea, such as a solution to a problem, marketing plan, concept for a new product, process, machine, or composition of matter, may be of a general nature, and reducing it to a practical form may be a long way off. An invention, improvement, or discovery implies something further along the road than just the conceptualization of something. It implies some practical embodiment of the idea. (Lawyers, particularly patent lawyers, love to discourse over the meaning of these terms. Indeed one judge, Giles S. Rich, who is highly respected at the patent bar, has written reams about the term *invention* and, because of its vagueness, recommends doing away with it altogether.) The purpose of the clause above is to capture any inventions that may have been made as a result of Smith's work while still employed by ABC and which he may be withholding from ABC. But it leaves Smith free to own ideas he comes up with *after* he leaves his job with ABC. If the above clause included the term *ideas,* then it would apply to concepts that Smith first thinks of after leaving ABC. Although some companies use this term in their trailer clauses, it does go a bit far. Unless the circumstances of Smith's employment justify an attempt to own ideas conceived of by Smith after termination of employment, that attempt is likely to be considered unreasonable. But the terms *ideas* and *concepts* should be included in the clause that applies to the period of time *during which* Smith is working for ABC. ABC should benefit from Smith's ideas while they employ him.

The point of the trailer clause is not to retain rights to Smith's brain after he leaves the company, but to get the full benefit of what Smith came up with while still an employee. A trailer clause can put an end to the bickering over when the employee came up with the idea or discovery. The clause above resolves that dispute by saying that if Smith "makes" something—that is, reduces a concept to some practical form—within one year after leaving ABC then it belongs to ABC. The objective is to insure getting the benefit of ideas or concepts of the employee that formed while he was still employed but that were reduced to some practical form soon after he left his job.

If we look back once more to the facts of the case involving Freeman and Rockwood, we note that Freeman came up with the idea while employed by Rockwood but did not reduce it to practice and "make his invention" until after he left Rockwood. There are two periods of time involved here. If a contract is made to apply to inventions, ideas, and discoveries as well as improvements made during the course of employment (first time period), and if the post-employment clause is limited to inventions that have been reduced to practice, as well as to patent applications filed during the year after termination (second time period), then the Freeman situation would be avoided. That is, any idea conceived during employment would become the property of the employer. Then if an invention is made in the sense that it is reduced to practice, or if a patent application is filed on it immediately after the employee quits, it automatically becomes the property of the former employer. At the same time, however, the clause does not prohibit the employee from coming up with new ideas, meaning original ideas conceived of subsequent to termination of the employment. That way, the employee is left with the reasonable possibility of working for a new employer and generally coming up with new ideas that can be assigned to the new employer. That kind of a post-employment restriction is more likely to be enforced and to be considered reasonable although neither its reasonableness nor its enforceability can be judged out of context. Much depends on the circumstances surrounding any particular employment relationship.

Further General Provisions

Best-efforts clause

Often when an employee is hired, the expectations may exceed reality. Company releases about their new personnel generally describe the new employees in glowing terms. The fact is that that very same employee may just have left a job under circumstances where his efforts were considered in less than glowing terms. The contrast of the expectations held of that individual in his new position as opposed to performance on the prior job may very well be striking. But high expectations are the rule, not the exception.

Just what is expected of an executive can, of course, be defined in a written agreement. But if the agreement fails to spell out in crystal-clear language the precise performance expected, then the law imposes a standard governing that individual's obligation. For example, Ed Gaines was hired in October 1969 by C. W. Jones and the Jones Investment Company to assist as well as manage purchases, sales, and development of real property. He had been recommended to Jones by Jones's attorney, Sylvanus Felix, as a suitable person to manage Jones's real estate operation. Felix had written a letter to Jones about Gaines and had described him as having had "considerable experience in all phases of real estate activities . . . But there are a lot of things that he would have to have guidance in . . ."

Jones hired Gaines and they signed an employment contract that provided for Gaines to render certain services. Those services were defined in the agreement. The agreement called for Gaines to assist C. W. Jones in evaluating and negotiating the purchase of real property, negotiating and handling sales of properties, supervising the development of property including construction and renting, and finally the performance of "all other things directed by [C. W. Jones] relating to the duties set forth above."

When things didn't work out to Jones's satisfaction and Gaines was not successful in his attempts to secure financing for an apartment project that was contemplated, he was dismissed. Jones asserted that Gaines "was not competent to handle loan negotiations for a multi-million-dollar project and generally failed in his performance." Gaines, however, said that he did everything that was requested of him and that he performed under the contract as written.

The court said that all that the law required of Gaines was that he prove "he substantially performed his part of the contract up to the time he was prevented from doing so by [C. W. Jones]." Judge Donald P. Lay, in his opinion on behalf of the United States Court of Appeals for the Eighth Circuit, that heard the case on appeal in September 1973, decided that "the evidence demonstrates substantial performance . . ." Accordingly the court awarded Gaines the $75,000 that the contract had provided as liquidated damages for his dismissal prior to the expiration of the agreement.

Sales executives will sometimes be hired on the basis of their earnings, at least in part, being contingent on the sales volume. The formula depends on the business involved and the nature of the industry, and can be any formula that the parties agree to. The point is simply that if a formula is agreed to—that is, if the written agreement specifies that the sales executive is to get X dollars in the way of a base salary, for example, and then a percentage of sales based on sales volume in accordance with a specified sales table or chart—then the courts will enforce that agreement and the formula agreed on will govern the extent of that sales executive's earnings under the contract. But sales and marketing people are not always hired according to some specific formula. For example, when Karr Manufacturing Company hired Richard Ralph as its sales management and marketing consultant to help boost sales, it gave him a contract that called for Ralph to "put forth his best efforts." The contract also provided that Ralph was supposed to "increase car sales . . ." It appears that after a year, Karr Manufacturing became disenchanted with Mr Ralph's activities on its behalf and dismissed him. When Ralph sued, Karr contended that Ralph had contractually obligated himself to "increase" sales. But the appellate court in Illinois that heard the case said that "there was no requirement that there be an increase in sales solely from his [Ralph's] efforts." The court noted that essentially the contract called for Ralph to put forth his best efforts and it appeared that he had done so. He had become active in conducting marketing surveys and establishing a sales control program, lining up manufacturers' representatives, and helping to prepare promotional material. The obligation undertaken by the employee was not one calling for a guarantee of success, nor was he obligated to meet certain specific goals with respect to an increase in sales, but rather to use his best efforts in a diligent manner to help his employer increase sales.

The point in both the examples given is that the law implies only a "best efforts" requirement on the part of the employee unless the contract *specifies* more. An employee should look twice at an obligation committing him to meet specific goals without qualification, as opposed to using his best efforts. Where specific goals are set forth and not met, then the employee can lose out on the agreement. An obligation to keep certain information confidential, for example, with no time limits and no criteria for determining confidentiality, can expose the employee to an indefinite burden, possibly outlasting the secret. Take the case of Warner-Lambert and its royalty obligation on Listerine as noted in chapter 4. Although the "secret" of Listerine has been public knowledge for quite some time, a federal court ruled in 1959 that the royalty obligation remained. Nothing in Warner-Lambert's agreement on Listerine provided any relief from an obligation to pay royalties once the secret formula became public knowledge. This is but one illustration of an unqualified specific commitment. Unqualified restrictions on activities after a job ends—calling on the same customers or using your skills (including newly acquired skills and information) in a competitive way—should make the employee wary.

In the marketing area, where an executive enters into a contract setting forth specific sales goals and tying income to those sales goals, the employee should consider insisting on language in the agreement to the effect that failure to meet those goals will not constitute a breach of the agreement but will merely affect the extent of income. Furthermore, the employee should try to negotiate for at least a pro rata payment so that if the goals are met in part, the employee gets commensurate payment. Moreover, as most sales executives have learned, it is most essential to provide for an adequate base salary along with repayment of expenses. In addition, the sales executive signing a contract of employment should avoid a situation where he can be dismissed for failing to meet his goals *in any one year.* Indeed, failure to meet sales goals should simply be a factor measuring the total extent of income, but unless the sales are below an extremely low minimum for a consecutive period of at least two or three years, the employee should not be at the mercy of the employer in terms of dismissal. The point is that the executive should be able to ride out at least one or two years, and the agreement should be sufficiently flexible so that aside from a proportionate reduction in income during those one or two bad years, the executive can continue in the job and hopefully recoup those losses in subsequent years. The employee should check the agreement and make sure that he can't be dismissed arbitrarily—that the failure to meet a specified goal over a short range will not serve as a basis for his dismissal.

The agreement referring to the formula involved should be so worded that it is specifically confined to the income of the executive as opposed to other rights, including the right of dismissal. Note, for example, Richard Ralph's case mentioned earlier. It appears that Ralph could justify an argument that in creating a force of manufacturers' representatives and in conducting marketing surveys and preparing promotional material, he was laying the groundwork for an increase in sales that would eventually appear. The sales and marketing consultant may need more than one year to lay the foundation for the improvement in sales that the company expects.

In summary, where the agreement is specific with respect to the expectations of the employee, the agreement governs and will be enforced. Where there is uncertainty or vagueness in the agreement, then the courts will apply a standard that generally calls for substantial performance by the employee with good faith and with reasonable diligence. In other words, the law expects the employee, essentially, to put forth his best efforts.

Termination clause

As a practical matter today, executives are increasingly turning to the use of a so-called "termination contract" as opposed to the more formal employment contract. Actually, a termination contract is nothing more than a written provision requiring the employer to pay the employee a certain stipulated amount in the event that the employee is terminated.

The objective of a termination contract or a termination clause in an employment contract is to substitute for a specified term of employment. That is, instead of a contract for *x* years, whereby the employee is obligated to provide certain services, whether described generally or specifically, and to receive certain payment during those *x* years, the employment contract can simply be reduced to a memorandum stating that the employer can dismiss the employee at any time from the time that he is hired but that in doing so he will have to pay the employee *y* dollars.

Many key executives shy away from contracts calling for them to perform for a period of, say, five years and obligating the company to make payment for that period of time. And many companies prefer the termination provision or contract to govern the relationship, because it gives the company greater flexibility. The parties both know in advance that the employee is hired at will, that he can be dismissed at any time and that his obligations are essentially to perform a generally understood task but with no specific goals. In the event of any disagreement or dispute, the employer can at any time dismiss the employee without further liability or obligation than the obligation specified in the termination agreement. The agreement usually states that in the event of termination a certain amount—perhaps six months' salary, perhaps six years' salary (but usually the practice runs more to about one year's salary)—will be paid to the employee.

The amount of payment can be whatever the parties agree to. Whatever terms are agreed on, the parties should be aware of the consequences. Unless otherwise stated in the agreement, the termination provision will become operative regardless of whether the employee is dismissed the next day or the next year. In other words, if the termination agreement provides for the payment of, say, one year's salary on termination, then the employee is entitled to that one year's pay even if he is dismissed the next day. The fact is that a dispute can arise at any time. Therefore, the employer would be well advised to try to negotiate an agreement that would prorate the termination payment in the event that the employee is terminated within the first year of his employment. In practice, some agreements call for a prorated payment based on the length of the termination payment. That is, if the termination payment is for six months' salary, then it may be partially offset in the event the employee is dismissed within the first six months. But if the termination payment is a year's salary or longer, then it is prorated in the event that dismissal takes place within the first year of employment.

The executive should be careful to avoid a complete pro rata formula because it may destroy the whole point of the termination clause. The objective on the part of the executive is obviously to protect himself in the event of termination so as to give him some flexibility. While it may be legitimate for the employer to want to avoid payment of a full year's salary in the event that termination occurs within the first week or two after the employee is hired, nonetheless it would be foolish for the employee to leave himself open to the payment of only one or two weeks' salary in the event of such premature dismissal. That would simply be a self-defeating measure. Keep in mind that from the executive's point of view, the termination agreement is being accepted in lieu of a contract calling for a minimum period of employment. Thus, the executive may be justified in seeking a minimum payment that may be equivalent to a certain number of months' salary regardless of when termination occurs—even if it is the day after being hired. A compromise that has sometimes worked is an agreement by the executive to accept half of the full termination payment in the event that the agreement is terminated within less than half of the period of time that is equivalent to the salary for the termination payment. Take the case of a termination agreement calling for the payment of a year's salary on termination. It can provide, for example, that if termination occurs for any reason whatever, for cause or without cause (and this is a point worth noting for the executive: the termination payment should be so structured that it is payable regardless of whether termination occurs with or without cause), the executive employee will be paid a year's salary, with the understanding, however, that if termination occurs within the first six months, then the payment will be reduced to one-half the minimum or six months' salary. Under the latter arrangement, the employee would be entitled to the full termination payment of one year's salary beginning with six months plus one day on the job.

But note that this increasingly popular variation on an employment contract has no direct bearing on confidentiality or ownership of ideas or inventions. Therefore it is still necessary to consider whether you intend to have the common law apply in that context or whether you want the agreements to override the common law. Remember that silence as to confidentiality or ownership of rights means essentially that you accept common-law rules. Any departure from the common law should be spelled out in writing, whether or not you choose to use a termination contract or clause.

The termination clause can, of course, be part of a standard employment contract, or it may form the basis of a separate contract. It can reduce an otherwise complex understanding to a simple one-page memorandum that gives the parties considerable flexibility in terms of their operations and specifies a fixed measure of liability on the part of the employer in the event that things don't work out.

The arbitration clause—arbitrating employment agreements

Arbitration is often a sensitive subject. It is a term frequently used in labor negotiations and it has overtones of labor disputes that carry over into the commercial sphere. Those overtones cast such a shadow on arbitration that many businessmen tend to shy away from it. Some executives see it as beneath their dignity because they are not unionized employees. Some consider it unprofessional, and others, including especially members of management, look at it as a possible infringement on their prerogatives. In any case there is a tendency either to love it or hate it, but few feel complete indifference towards arbitration. That's unfortunate, because arbitration is a useful tool when considered objectively, and when one does not permit past experiences in other fields to color the value of arbitration in the area of resolving employment disputes.

Arbitration can be quite useful as a means of resolving private disputes out of the public's eye and minimizing litigation expenses as well as possible embarrassing public relations. This is particularly true in agreements with key executives. The experience of some companies with arbitration, particularly in the labor field, has sometimes been negative, because of a feeling generated among members of management that the arbitrator tended to favor compromise as opposed to determining and separating right from wrong and insisting on compliance with legal obligations. True, many arbitrators find themselves in the role of compromiser. Arbitrators have been likened to King Solomon, attempting to split the baby in half.

One story about arbitration may be worth repeating here: Two men came before an arbitrator, both fighting over a claim to land. The first argued quite vigorously that the entire stretch of land was rightfully his. The second conceded that half the land did belong to the first. But, he said, the other half actually belonged to him. The arbitrator listened to the arguments and pronounced judgment. As to the first half of the land, the half conceded to belong to the first party, there was no issue and, therefore, the first party received an award of that half. But as to the second half, the half that was in issue, the arbitrator decided to split that in half. Thus the first party wound up with three quarters of the land. The moral of this fable is supposedly that when arguing before an arbitrator, seek as much as possible on the theory that you will get about half of what you ask.

That story, of course, is fiction. But regrettably, the thought that all arbitration involves compromise and that all parties to an arbitration will get at least something of what they ask is more often than not fact. It is simply a statement of experience that arbitration will result, in most but not all cases, in a decision that reflects a compromise between the demands of the parties. The American Arbitration Association, however, has taken a policy stand against arbitration serving as a mere form of compromise. Today, arbitrators are increasingly looking to the merits of a situation, and more and more arbitrators are rendering decisions that attempt to reflect the merits of the situation and that will result in a decision entirely in favor of one side to the dispute.

Indeed, the crowded courtroom calendar is such that very often judges attempt to serve as mediators in the hope of encouraging parties to resolve their disputes without the necessity of going to trial. As a result, judges will sometimes pressure opposing counsel into agreeing to a compromise that they would not otherwise like, and which neither party finds truly acceptable. Thanks to crowded courtroom calendars, many litigated cases are being settled in a compromise resembling the result that is characteristic of what is expected from an arbitration as opposed to a lawsuit. Traditionally, one anticipates that in a lawsuit a decision will be rendered that finds in favor of one of the parties—that there is a right separated from a wrong based on the merits of the case, and one side is the victor and the other the loser. When an individual feels strongly that he is right, it is sometimes difficult to accept a compromise. That has been one source of resentment toward arbitration in the past. But it should be recognized that with a crowded court calendar, there is some justification for the desire of many judges to strongly encourage a settlement.

Thus arbitration, even in the form of compromise, is still a worthwhile consideration. It can be effective as a tool resolving a dispute with an executive employee. Provided that the parties agree that the arbitration will be conducted privately and that neither party will issue public statements concerning it, then binding arbitration can achieve a quiet, usually more rapid, and less expensive resolution of a dispute with an employee. The fact that it can take the dispute out of the public eye can be of value to the employer. That it may be less expensive is of value to both sides. That there probably is a greater chance of compromise as opposed to a technical and literal enforcement of the agreement which, at least in theory, could be obtained from a courtroom, tends to work in favor of the employee most of the time—but not always. One thing that arbitration can do that a lawsuit almost never can accomplish is permit a quiet and quick resolution of a dispute, and permit the employment relationship to continue afterward. It is rare that an employment dispute finds its way into a courtroom and winds up with the parties continuing to speak with one another and able to function in a normal employment relationship.

There are some advantages to arbitration even after an employee has left the company. Arbitration can be conducted in a more intimate and informal setting, without the usual pretrial hassle over interrogatories (written questions) and discovery (pretrial examination of witnesses), and with a more relaxed attitude toward hearsay and other rules of evidence. In the context of such a setting the parties are more likely to come to terms in the form of a mutually agreeable settlement. There is the advantage, too, of greater "privacy." Although protective orders can be used effectively in a lawsuit to protect a trade secret, the fact of the lawsuit itself—the actual complaint—is almost always a matter of public record. But the fact of the arbitration proceeding may itself be kept confidential.

Arbitration is inadvisable if the employee will not agree to hold off using or disclosing alleged confidential information until the arbitration is decided. Then an injunction is called for. Also, once the horse is out of the barn, so to speak, the courtroom is more likely to be of benefit to the employer. But whether to arbitrate or litigate is a strategic decision to be made in the context of a particular set of circumstances and with the advice of counsel. Sometimes a major corporation will not want its "dirty linen" aired in public, not even with protective orders. The factors of informality, economy, and a prompter decision may warrant going the route of arbitration, or the private settlement possible via arbitration may still be considered desirable.

When the agreement contains a covenant not to compete and

the employer is concerned about competition from the employee, it is important that the agreement provide that during arbitration the employee not compete or set up a competitive operation. On the other hand, the employee would be well advised to avoid such a restriction because it completely ties his hands pending the arbitration proceeding. It is true that an injunction would have the same effect, but presumably the employee would be in a position to argue that an injunction is unwarranted for any of several reasons. This point is discussed in greater detail in the next chapter relating to lawsuits with former employees, but it is important to note here that the employee should think carefully before agreeing to waive his right to compete pending the outcome of an arbitration proceeding.

When drafting an arbitration clause the employer should consider whether he may need the instrument for an injunction, and if so he may be well advised to insist on the right to seek an injunction apart from the arbitration proceeding. An alternative is an agreement by the parties that either one has the right to institute an arbitration proceeding but that once instituted, it will operate as the equivalent of an injunction, and that pending the outcome of the arbitration, neither party will alter the status quo. More specifically, the employer should be concerned about the employee setting up a competitive operation and competing during the arbitration proceeding. In a dispute of this sort it is essential that the employer be able to seek an injunction promptly; if too much time has to be lost, it may be impossible to obtain adequate relief afterwards.

Defining jurisdiction

This is a point sometimes overlooked, particularly by the parties involved. Indeed, there are times when even attorneys overlook the significance of this aspect of the agreement. Attorneys who become familiar with the law in their state will sometimes insist strongly that the agreement provide it will be governed by and interpreted in accordance with the laws of the state in which they practice. That does have some merit. But regrettably it ignores the possibility that the law in another state may be more favorable to their client.

Not only is it important to know the law as it governs the employment relationship in all jurisdictions; it is probably of greater importance to be able to control the jurisdiction in which any lawsuit involving the contract will be brought. And the latter is a point very often ignored. Rarely does the employment contract expressly provide that any lawsuit involving that agreement will be brought in a specific jurisdiction or before certain specific courts. And yet, it is entirely possible for the agreement to provide that any lawsuit will be brought, for example, before the courts of the state in which the employer has his principal place of business or in which the business is incorporated, or in the state in which the employee resides at the time the suit is initiated. The latter can be important, especially to an employee in terms of defending the suit.

If an arbitration clause is agreed to, the provision relating to arbitration should stipulate that the arbitrator's award can be entered by either party as a consent judgment in an appropriate court that would have jurisdiction over the parties. The significance of this is simply that to enforce an arbitrator's award it may be necessary to use the powers of a court. One cannot levy execution on the basis of an arbitrator's award. The parties must voluntarily comply with the award. A judgment, however, carries with it the power of the court to cite a party for contempt. That is a fairly powerful weapon. Contempt of court can bring harsh penalties in terms of fines and prison sentences. Thus it is advisable to incorporate the power to convert an arbitrator's award into a judgment.

When considering the question of jurisdiction, it is essential that the laws of the states involved be considered. A number of states have enacted laws prohibiting the enforcement of restrictive covenants in employment agreements. Thus any agreement which contains such a restrictive covenant should also provide carefully for the jurisdiction in which the agreement is to be enforced, so as to exclude those jurisdictions that will not enforce such covenants. Where the suit will be brought can have a definite and strong impact on the outcome. And from the point of view of convenience alone, the employee especially is usually better off fighting such a lawsuit in his home state than out of state.

"Boiler plate" clauses

The term "boiler plate" is an unfortunate one. The clauses often regarded as "boiler plate" are not unimportant. It is just that they are generally included and tend to apply relatively uniformly, regardless of the particular parties involved. It is because of their possible universal application that they may be considered "form-type" clauses and simply applied to the agreement without consideration of the specific issues or parties. But such conformance can be dangerous.

For example, there is a clause relating to successors and assigns, which typically provides that the agreement will inure to the benefit of and be binding upon the employer, the company, and all their successors and assigns. That could mean that the employee would find himself bound to a company that he would not have gone to work for in the first place, had his company not been sold to the new company. It could also mean that the company would be bound to the administrators and legal representatives of the employee in the event of his death. Now there is nothing wrong with those obligations—just so long as they are justified by the circumstances. Frankly, in most cases, the circumstances will justify a successors-and-assigns clause. And such a clause should also spell out that the agreement will become the obligation of any company acquiring all or substantially all of the assets of the business of the employer, and that the employer will be bound to the heirs, executors, administrators, and legal representatives of the employee. But the parties should be advised of the significance of this clause. It should not be treated with indifference and its applicability under the particular circumstances involved should be thoroughly considered and reviewed.

Other clauses that are often characterized as "boiler-plate" clauses include a "provision for notice," that is, a requirement that any notice by either party to the other under the agreement will be set forth in writing and mailed by registered or certified mail. If this provision is used, then there should be a specific address given and a provision made for changing that address. Specific parties to receive the notice should be mentioned. The concern here is that years after the agreement is signed, a letter will be sent by registered mail to a given address but, in fact, that letter may not be received.

Another clause that is sometimes described as "boiler plate" is one to the effect that the document being executed represents the entire agreement between the parties, that there is no other agreement, and that the agreement cannot be modified except by a written amendment signed by both parties. That type of clause is frequently applicable, but once more its implications should be considered. All too often the employee signs an agreement with a handshake understanding on the side to the effect that he will be given certain responsibilities or accorded a certain measure of influence. Or other promises may be applicable. A promise that the employee will not be relocated; will be brought up for eligibility for certain stock options; will be made part of a profit-sharing plan; or will be considered for election to the board of directors within a year—those are all understandings that have often formed the basis of a handshake and have not been included in the agreement. When the employee is actually on the job and that handshake agreement is not literally followed—sometimes because of a genuine misunderstanding as to what was intended—hard feelings may surface. And lawsuits often follow on the heels of those hard feelings. Either party, the employer or the employee, may find himself dismayed with the written document, particularly when there is a clause saying that the document represents the "entire understanding" and that no other understanding applies unless it is in writing signed by both parties. All those handshakes and oral understandings suddenly fall by the side. The danger here is readily apparent in the case of trade secrets and possible subsequent competition if the employer relies on an informal, oral agreement to protect interests that a court may be reluctant to characterize as trade secrets.

The point to be made, and it is a genuinely important point, is that none of the terms of the employment agreement should be ignored, and that those provisions often referred to as standard or "boiler plate" provisions should always be reviewed with an eye toward their applicability under the particular circumstances involved.

7 □ Suing the Former Employee

In the musical, *Fiddler on the Roof,* the character Tevye has a number of unique qualities. Among them is the ability to argue with himself, simultaneously taking both sides of a given issue. If Tevye were presented with the problem of whether to sue a former employee, his reasoning would likely be: On the one hand, it is necessary to file a suit to prevent loss of trade secrets by disclosure to third parties. After all, if I do not act quickly, my former employee may make the information public, and once made public, that trade secret vanishes forever. Of course, it may be possible to obtain some money as a result of a lawsuit, but if I were looking for money, I would have licensed my competitors a long time ago.

On the other hand, bringing an action against a former employee has certain risks. For example, more than one company has brought suit against a former employee, only to learn that the employee did not know as much as it thought he knew. The lawsuit, however, served to educate that former employee to the significance of certain facts and details that he had not previously appreciated. In one case, a respected company in the pharmaceutical industry learned the hard way, through a suit against a former employee, that the employee, although intimately involved in production, was ignorant of certain details and did not appreciate some key aspects of technique that were fundamental to a successful, commercial process. During the course of litigation, as the result of discovery (pretrial examination of witnesses and relevant

191

documents) and the questions asked of the former employee, the company became painfully aware of the employee's ignorance. The word "painfully" is appropriate, because the former employee was sufficiently talented and knowledgeable to recognize what it was that he had missed or forgotten.

In the course of trade-secret litigation against a former employee, both sides are likely to take depositions by way of discovery and the former employee can be expected to press hard for a specific disclosure of just what his employer claims to be secret. The burden is on the party alleging secrecy to establish, at least prima facie, the existence of trade secrets. Although "in camera" proceedings (closed to the public) can be requested, and while copies of confidential information are kept apart from public files and are not generally available to the public, still the former employee, as a party to the suit, will be informed of just what his former employer is claiming as a trade secret.

And yet, on the other hand, to continue reasoning like Tevye, a lawsuit against a former employee can sometimes serve to establish a precedent in the firm, and to establish an image. The lawsuit may prove to be useful as a deterrent to other employees. While an overly aggressive policy may backfire, a lackadaisical policy may prove equally inadequate to protect trade secrets and discourage mishandling or abuse by former employees.

And yet again, if the court finds the absence of any trade secrets, it may decide to publish the information in its opinion as part of its analysis of the facts, and explain why it concluded that there were no trade secrets. While the court may well be correct, as a matter of law, still, if your competitors were guessing—if they were somewhat unsure of what you were doing—they no longer need guess: they can now read about it.

A lot of factors have to be weighed when considering suit against an ex-employee. There are perfectly valid and justifiable reasons for suing a former employee, but one thing to realize from the outset is that emotion is not one of them. All too often, the decision to sue stems mainly from the emotional context of the relationship between the former employer and the employee instead of being the calculated, deliberate decision it should be. This is particularly true in paternalistic companies where employees are vested with a large degree of "trust" and are sometimes considered "part of the family."

There is a theory, sometimes called the "blinder theory," which runs something like this: Most individuals—and particularly technically trained specialists such as engineers and scientists—tend to compartmentalize their work and to sub-specialize. This is often true because of the practical problems of keeping up with new developments, the limitations of time, and the demands of one's job and one's outside interests. The net result is that an individual over the course of years may learn a piece of a puzzle, if we may use that analogy, exceptionally well. He probably understands, in a general sense, how the piece he is responsible for fits in the overall puzzle, but perhaps not in sufficient detail to be able to produce the entire answer. Thus, it is necessary to assess the knowledge of a former employee against the perspective of how his work fits into the entire scheme of things, what his plans are for the future, just who he will be associated with or working for, and the likelihood of his actually being able to damage the company he left.

One of the first considerations that should be made is to determine, as precisely as possible, the full extent of the former employee's knowledge—not just the amount of knowledge that he appears to have had based on the nature of his former job, but the knowledge that he, in fact, did possess. Often conversations with the former employee's associates at work will reveal much about the extent of that former employee's true knowledge. This is particularly true if the exploration with those associates is handled properly. For example, by inquiring into the extent of the knowledge possessed by those associates, one can extrapolate to learn the extent of knowledge that the former employee had. Ignorance of certain key elements on the part of other employees charged with similar or related responsibilities may indicate similar ignorance on the part of the former employee.

After making that evaluation on as objective a basis as the circumstances permit, and assuming a lawsuit is justified, then the key word is *speed.* It is essential to act fast.

Quick action is important for several reasons. One of them, the prevention of disclosure and loss of trade-secret status, has already been mentioned. Another reason is to avoid creating an impression—which will most surely be seized upon and emphasized to the court by counsel for the former employee—that the trade secret is not really important: otherwise why would you hesitate so long? You may have waited before deciding to assert your rights for perfectly legitimate reasons but, nonetheless, you are put on the defensive in having to offer an explanation. And as any good lawyer knows, it is far better strategy to keep your adversary on the defensive. You lose valuable time and money in having to "excuse" conduct that may be justifiable but weakens your position in the justifying. And, more important, it serves to divert the court's attention from the issues you would like it to concentrate on.

A further reason for acting promptly is to prevent a substantial investment in your alleged trade secret by the ex-employee or his new employer—or else you may find yourself with a fait accompli. This is because the law applies equitable principles of estoppel and laches* where, because of your delay, the ex-employee or his new employer justifiably assumes that you will take no action (or perhaps, that you have concluded you have no cause of action) and proceeds to invest heavily in reliance on that assumption. By analogy, if your neighbor builds his house partly on your property (just over the property line) and you know he is trespassing but deliberately wait until he is finished, you may well find that you can no longer get a court to order him to tear down his house. (You may still, however, be allowed reasonable compensation for the trespass.)

If the delay in asserting your rights is significant, if the circumstances reasonably justify the ex-employee's assumption that you will not or cannot take action, then you may well find the principle of estoppel applied against you. That does not necessarily mean you forfeit all your rights, but your remedy may be limited and you may forfeit your right to an injunction. In trade-secret cases against a former employee, an injunction is generally the most valuable and important remedy. As in the analogy of the house built partly on your property, you may be entitled to reasonable compensation in the form of damages. But this is tantamount to a compulsory license of your trade se-

Laches in law refers to undue delay in asserting a right, or in claiming or asking for a privilege.

cret. Thus, while it is important to investigate the facts surrounding an employee's departure thoroughly, it is equally important to do so in a quick and efficient manner.

The rules of practice in the federal courts and in many state courts permit you to move for a temporary restraining order on the basis of affidavits, and a limited notice to the opponent (often less than a day, sometimes only an hour or two). The court may issue a ten-day restraining order and schedule a hearing for a preliminary injunction. Trade-secret cases are often won or lost at this early stage of the litigation.

If a temporary restraining order is granted, then the parties will be encouraged to take depositions before the hearing on the preliminary injunction. Quite often, cases are settled at the time of depositions. Furthermore, you learn a lot more through those depositions. And your views on the knowledge that the former employee possesses—as well as the extent of harm he is most likely to create—can and frequently do become clearer. With increased knowledge, you may alter your views or position with respect to litigation, or perhaps alter your strategy in the litigation itself.

It is worthwhile to keep in mind that the purpose of the restraining order and the preliminary injunction is to maintain the status quo and to prevent the defendant, or ex-employee, from divulging the secret information and thereby obtaining an unfair competitive advantage. When it is denied, the ex-employee can compete and possibly divulge the information before a trial. In many cases, courts have held that the mere public sale of products made with the utilization of a trade secret constitutes a public use of that trade secret. In one such case, the use of a lady's undergarment—the wearing of a girdle under a dress, obviously not in public display—constituted a public use. The point is that the defendant's, or ex-employee's, use of the information can destroy its trade-secret status prior to the time that an actual trial is held, and from that point on *all you can hope to recover is damages.* You cannot enjoin an act or event that has already occurred.

The Supreme Court, as Karl F. Jorda points out, has yet to resolve the status of a trade-secret owner who suddenly finds that someone else has come up with the same idea independently and patented it. Jorda, corporate patent counsel to Ciba-Geigy, the international Swiss pharmaceutical firm, has made an extensive investigation into this topic. He has urged legislation that would resolve the issue by providing the prior trade-secret owner a personal right of continued use. As things stand now, the law depends partly on the court before which a lawsuit is brought. Some courts have held that the patent is invalid, even though the trade-secret owner never publicly disclosed the information. In *Dunlop Holdings Ltd.* v. *Ram Golf Corporation,* the United States Court of Appeals in Illinois said that a secret golf ball cover designed to resist cutting was not so much a secret use as a "non-informing" use. The golf ball cover was used publicly even though the originator had not disclosed the nature of its material (a new duPont synthetic, Surlyn). So a subsequent patent claim was invalid.

To obtain a preliminary injunction, it is essential to persuade the court of at least three conclusions:
    (1) The likelihood of success on your part at a subsequent trial;
    (2) the likelihood of disclosure in the absence of an injunction; and
    (3) the inadequacy of monetary damages as a remedy.

The Likelihood of Success in a Subsequent Trial

Likelihood of success at the trial stage is an important factor because the court is reluctant to grant an injunction, even on a temporary basis, that can prevent the former employee from engaging in an otherwise perfectly lawful business or occupation, and particularly because, as a practical matter, a delay of any significant time may prevent an effective startup of a competitive business altogether. In addition, as a matter of public policy, courts are reluctant to encourage any restraint on trade. Therefore, it is essential to satisfy the court that you have not only a prima facie case, but that there is sufficient substance to your case for you to succeed in the event of trial. Thus, in a sense, courts often weigh the probable value of the evidence you have and subjectively predetermine the likely outcome.

But, keep in mind that likelihood of success is not the only factor. For notwithstanding all the proof in the world of likelihood of success, should a court find that under the circumstances disclosure before trial is not likely, or that monetary damages are an adequate form of compensation, then it will not issue a preliminary injunction.

Likelihood of success is proven by establishing the following three key elements:

A) the existence of an enforceable trade secret;
B) an obligation of confidentiality on the part of the former employee;
C) the fact that disclosure would damage your business.

Let's look at each element separately.

A. Is there an enforceable trade secret?

The criteria employed by most courts in determining whether they will enforce a trade secret is as follows:

1. The extent to which the information is known outside the employer's business.

To evaluate this you should first determine whether the information has been included (perhaps inadvertently) in publications or patents, or in public talks delivered at technical symposia, professional meetings, or sales conventions. A slip of the pen or tongue is not uncommon. In addition, a search of the literature and prior patents should be undertaken.

2. The extent to which it is known by employees and others involved in the business.

Aside from examining published information, examine your own employees to see how close the competition really is. Your own employees are often a good source of information, within this sphere of activity or expertise, as to what is known in the trade or field, what competitors are offering, and the differences between products or services available in the field. One caveat, however, is worth noting. After years of specialization, people sometimes look at differences between their work and/or products and that of competitors and see the differences with a degree of magnitude many times that with which a lay judge will view those same differences. Thus a slight difference in temperature conditions, type of controls, or in the raw materials may be important to one who works in the field, but to a judge those distinctions may appear as just so much minutiae. Therefore, when gathering such information, it is worthwhile to think in terms of an ultimate presentation to a judge unfamiliar with the small details of your work. Gather information that will support your estimate of the importance of the distinctions you wish to make. It is helpful to think in terms of the *results* brought about by the distinctions you refer to and why those results are important. For example, a slight shift in one raw material, which may be similar to that used by competitors, may well give rise to a much less costly and more efficient process. The difference between what you and your competitors are doing may appear small, but in terms of *results* that difference may loom quite large. Focusing a judge's attention on those results will probably have more effect than focusing it on the element of difference in the processes alone.

3. The extent of measures taken by the employer to guard the secrecy of the information.

If we had to choose one point or area of maximum vulnerability on the part of most employers, this would be it. The case law is rampant with instances of failure by an employer to enforce a trade-secret claim because of the way the information was treated internally. For example, when Motorola lost a suit against several of its former employees and Fairchild Camera and Instrument Corp., the court stated: ". . . plaintiff's [Motorola's] trade-secret claims must fail because as to those in issue at trial *no real effort was made* by plaintiff prior to trial *to keep them secret.* They were also either revealed in the marketed product; fully disclosed by issued patents; generally known to those skilled in the industry or trade; or consisted of information easily acquired by persons in the industry from patents, literature, or known processes fully available. . . ."*

Motorola v. *Fairchild* demonstrates that it is important for the employer to segregate confidential information from general information and to be sure to make every effort to maintain that information in confidence. It is helpful to identify properly confidential information, limit its distribution to those having a "need to know," and restrict access to it. There should be no question in the minds of employees as to just what information they are handling is confidential and what is not.

4. The value of the information to the employer and to his competitors.

*Emphasis added. Author.

That the trade secret was obtained at great expense is generally an important fact. It tends to impress on a court the significance of the case, the seriousness of the harm. It also serves as evidence of the likelihood of disclosure of the trade secret because of its desirability to competitors. Whether you are using the information and whether it is providing you with a "competitive advantage" are important criteria to which most courts look in deciding whether to accord information trade-secret status—or at least whether to issue a temporary injunction pending determination of trade-secret status.

5. The amount of effort or money expended by the employer in developing the information.

This factor is indicative of possible unjust enrichment on the part of the former employee or his new employer. They, presumably, are being spared the expense, effort, and time of learning the information independently, through experience or research and development. They are spared the need to purchase or license valuable know-how. The time factor, in some cases, may be the most important from a commercial or marketing viewpoint. The lead time in many businesses, particularly in those in high-technology areas, can sometimes be critical to the success of the business and is often, at the very least, an important component of profitability. Having to acquire know-how through independent trial and error or research can not only be costly but time-consuming.

6. The ease or difficulty with which the information could be properly acquired or duplicated by others.

The law permits competitors to copy unpatented products through reverse engineering and chemical analysis. Just so long as your competitor does not attempt to trade on your goodwill by "palming off" his product as being yours, so long as he avoids any misrepresentation of the source or origin of the product in such areas as labeling and appearance, he is free to reproduce an unpatented product and sell it. A court looks at the ease or difficulty with which a trade secret—through reverse engineering or chemical analysis—may be obtained by competitors, to help it determine whether the information is truly "enforceable" as a trade secret. If its intrinsic nature is such that the secret may be readily perceived, a court would deny it trade-secret status. To do otherwise would be to engage in a useless act.

For example, in *Wesley-Jessen Inc.* v. *Reynolds* the federal district court in northern Illinois denied relief to ex-employer Wesley-Jessen in a case alleging ex-employee Reynolds's violation of a confidentiality agreement in constructing a competitive camera for use by optometrists. Among other things, the camera, used to help reveal the shape of the human cornea for the purpose of fitting contact lenses, had been sold and leased publicly and regularly. And the court found that in a couple of days of study the camera could be "reverse-engineered" to reveal its secret. Although, in that case, there was also evidence of disclosure of "secret" information in publications and promotional literature, it is nonetheless extremely unlikely that the court would have accorded trade-secret status to information that could have been obtained simply by a study of the publicly available camera. The district court also said it would not enforce a covenant not to compete that was based on a "secret" that was not really secret.

B. Is there an obligation of confidentiality on the part of the former employee?

It is necessary to establish that the former employee not only knew of the information but also knew of its confidentiality and that it was entrusted to him in confidence. Proof of knowledge need not be absolute but can be implied from the circumstances. For example, proof of access to where the information was stored, the capability to understand and appreciate the true significance of the information, and the opportunity to read and copy the information are all indicative of possible knowledge. Combined with other evidence indicating the desirability of taking such information—for example, that the employee suddenly set up a competitive business that inherently utilizes that information—a prima facie case of knowledge can be made.

More often, the evidence of knowledge is much stronger. Usually the employee not only had access to, but received copies of the information, his name appeared on copies of documents, and some of the documents may have been addressed directly to him with copies to others. That former employee may well have been a key man, if not the key man, in a product line or segment of the business. Thus, actual knowledge of the information or data can often be established.

That the employee had knowledge of the information or data is still not adequate, because it is necessary to show that the employee also knew of its confidential or trade-secret status. Here, as mentioned earlier, the manner in which the information is treated internally, whether it is marked confidential, segregated from non-confidential information or data, filed separately, and whether access to the information is limited, are all key factors. It is not enough to show that someone "told" the former employee that the particular information was secret. If, in fact, that information was not treated as a secret, but was widely disseminated and generally accessible, copies being available in general files open to most employees, then the information in question cannot be enforced as a trade secret.

Would this be so even if an employment contract specified confidentiality but internal evidence showed information was not treated as a secret? Usually yes, because confidentiality is not generally defined in terms of specific information but in terms of itself. Most employment contracts require the employee to maintain in confidence that which is given to him in confidence. Therefore, if the information is widespread and not confidential in the first place, the restriction doesn't apply. In the rare circumstance when a specific secret is disclosed and the agreement expressly identifies that information, then the restriction would apply. In cases such as this, however, a fairly negotiated agreement would contain a proviso that the obligation to maintain secrecy expires once the information becomes public.

The law recognizes, and, indeed, imposes a special duty on "key" or high-level employees. That obligation, as previously noted, is often characterized as "fiduciary": that is, the high-level employee is deemed to hold a position of trust and the standard of conduct expected of him as fiduciary is different than that normally expected. This common-law principle is derived from "master-servant" law developed first during the Middle Ages in England and brought here on the *Mayflower*. Although the law of master-servant, as we have seen, has been considerably modified, there are some basic notions that remain, and the concept of fiduciary responsibility is one of them.

For the wheels of commerce to turn smoothly, it is essential that an organization be able to trust its key or high-level employees.

The law does not recognize an arm's-length relationship between an employer and his employee, particularly if that employee holds an important position exposing him to and entrusting him with the employer's secrets. Thus, an employment contract is not a prerequisite to a successful lawsuit against a former employee and, indeed, may even be a hindrance. That is, an improperly drafted contract may be the basis for dismissing a lawsuit, particularly in those jurisdictions that decline to "blue-pencil" a contract they regard as unenforceable. Some courts will limit the scope of contractual employee restrictions considered to be against public policy or in violation of a statute, but others will simply find the contract unenforceable as written and dismiss the complaint.

A contract provides an additional basis for a lawsuit. An enforceable employment contract with a well-drawn confidentiality clause is, of course, positive evidence of the employee's obligation. Presumably, in that contract, the employee recognizes that he will be entrusted with confidential information and agrees to maintain its confidentiality. In that respect a contract can facilitate proof of an obligation of confidentiality; it can facilitate proof that disclosure would constitute a breach of confidence. But note that a contract does not prove that the employee actually knew of the information in question nor that he knew it was confidential. It does, however, serve as part of the surrounding circumstances and can help an employer establish that the employee was in a position to know the information and knew what was expected of him as to the treatment of that information. In short, a contract may give rise to an inference that the employee had reason to know or determine that certain information was confidential and was not to be disclosed. It provides a basis for a breach-of-contract claim in addition to claims based on common-law principles.

C. Would disclosure damage your business?

The element of damage is significant for several reasons. For one thing, courts are loath to entertain lawsuits between private parties to allay fear, suspicion, or to correct a breach of principle where no real harm is at stake. Further, the prevention of damage is part of what a preliminary injunction is all about: without damages, there is no reason for a court to issue an injunction—no purpose would be served. Moreover, a strong indication of severe damages tends to impress a sense of urgency on the court.

Take a close look at the value of the information or data. How much did it cost you to acquire? How long did it take? When calculating cost, keep in mind such factors as salaries, benefits, and overhead in research and development, and also costs of supporting services, general administrative costs (which can be allocated pro rata), materials and parts costs, fees for consultants' services, and other expenses reasonably related to learning the information or data in question. In some instances, of course, the information may have been acquired by sale or license from a third party. The cost, however, is not necessarily limited by the purchase price or royalty payments. There may have been significant expenditures preliminary and subsequent to the sale or license—in evaluating the information, determining its desirability, in negotiations (including travel and entertainment), counselling fees, in adopting the information to conform to your particular business, and in modifications or improvements.

Don't overlook the importance and value of "lead" time or the time it takes to get a head start. If the information takes time to learn or develop independently, then the sooner that information is acquired, the sooner one can start in business. A fair measure of the lead time is the time it took to develop the information in the first place. The burden then shifts to the former employee to establish that less time is needed because of other published advances in technology or possible reverse engineering. But whatever lead time is established, courts tend to permit recovery for lost sales or lost profits during the interval they see between the time the trade-secret information was misappropriated and the time it would take to reproduce or independently acquire that information.

As a practical matter, at the outset of a trade-secrets case it is difficult to measure "lost sales." At the time a motion for a preliminary injunction is brought, courts tend to view evidence of lost sales as speculative, and unless you are selling a major item such as jet aircraft, where the loss of one sale is substantial, it is ordinarily difficult to predict future losses. Thus, in most cases, particularly in the early stages, it is important to focus primarily on the cost of the information to you. That cost, in terms of time and money, should be emphasized to the court.

Among other factors important to the assessment of damages is loss of market position—to the extent it can be attributed to the entrance of new or cheaper products by competitors benefiting from the misappropriation of your trade secrets. The loss of licensing revenue, both in terms of actual or potential licenses, also forms a measure of damages. But note that the existence of licenses tends to weaken a request for a preliminary injunction on the theory that since the information has been disseminated to others, damages (equivalent to royalties) would serve as an adequate recovery. There is no requirement for compulsory licensing, although some representatives of the Justice Department have informally expressed their personal views in favor of such a requirement, but a court may assess damages that approximate a reasonable royalty. Thus, it is important to show the court why a license or its equivalent, having been granted to others, is inappropriate here. Although, technically speaking, the mere fact that you just don't want to grant another license usually is enough reason for *you* to refuse a request for license, it is sometimes inadequate when you are requesting a court of equity to issue an injunction. The fact that you may have granted an "exclusive" or "sole" license; commercial considerations making it anticompetitive to dilute the marketplace further; or such low profit margins that another licensee would drive existing licensees out of business, are all relevant considerations to the inadequacy of monetary damages and may help persuade a court of the need for an injunction.

The loss of other gains and advantages enjoyed by the proprietor of a trade secret should also be pleaded. This is somewhat of a catch-all category that may encompass economic advantages that are unique to a particular situation and may be lost on loss of the trade secret.

Punitive damages and attorneys' fees may form part of your plea for damages and may be recovered after trial, particularly in aggravated cases where the evidence points to a wilful disregard of the employee's obligations and an intentional misappropriation of the employer's trade secrets. Although this is not really an issue at the time of a motion for preliminary injunction, it is noted here because, if applicable, it should form part of the initial pleadings, and evidence of predatory conduct may influence the court to issue the preliminary injunction.

Is Disclosure Likely in the Absence of an Injunction?

If we keep in mind that the purpose of a preliminary injunction is to maintain the status quo during litigation, then it is easy to perceive why a court must look to the likelihood of disclosure in terms of whether the status quo is about to be upset in the absence of an injunction. The courts have a tendency to talk about likelihood of disclosure in terms of its "imminency" or "inevitability."

When duPont brought suit against American Potash and Chemical Corp. and Donald E. Hirsch, over the hiring of former employee Hirsch, who, duPont alleged, was its second most knowledgeable employee as to the manufacture of titanium dioxide by the chloride process, the court issued a preliminary restraining order barring Hirsch from engaging in any work with American Potash in connection with or related to the operation and development of that process. In denying a motion for summary judgment on behalf of defendants, American Potash and Hirsch, the court left the restraining order standing pending the trial of the case. In its opinion the court described a series of events leading up to the motion before it. Those events included a description of aborted efforts by American Potash to acquire the know-how from duPont through a license; American Potash's efforts to get into the business, including its recruitment of personnel for a plant it was designing in California for the manufacture of titanium dioxide; and its recruitment of Donald Hirsch through advertisements in a newspaper in Wilmington, Delaware, where duPont's plant was located. Although the issue before the court did not require a direct ruling on the issue of imminency of disclosure, that issue was indirectly presented to the court by American Potash in its argument that in the absence of an "imminent" threat of disclosure there was no factual basis in the record before the court to continue the case, and therefore summary judgment should be granted. DuPont argued that disclosure by Hirsch in the event he worked on the titanium dioxide process for American Potash, was "inevitable." In denying the motion for summary judgment by American Potash and Hirsch, the court noted and let stand the restraining order pending the trial and observed, in its opinion:

... the trial court is entitled to consider, in judging whether an abuse of confidence is involved, the degree to which disclosure of plaintiff's trade secrets is likely to result from the circumstances surrounding Hirsch's employment by Potash. The defendants say that a finding of "inevitability" would be no more than a "prophecy" here. Nonetheless, in the context of determining whether a threat of disclosure exists, it is but a finding as to the probable future consequences of a course of voluntary action undertaken by the defendants. Courts are frequently called upon to draw such conclusions based on a weighing of the probabilities, and *while a conclusion that a certain result will probably follow may not ultimately be vindicated, courts are nonetheless entitled to decide or "predict" the likely consequences arising from a given set of facts and to grant legal remedies on that basis.* I am satisfied that the degree of probability of disclosure, whether amounting to an inevitability or not, is a relevant factor to be considered in determining whether a "threat" of disclosure exists.*

The requirement for "imminency" has been phrased in various ways. In the case of *Jackson* v. *Walton* the Louisiana court said:

> There must be at least a reasonable probability that the injury will be done if no injunction is granted, and not a mere fear or apprehension.

It is interesting to contrast the *duPont* v. *Potash & Hirsch* case with that of *Standard Brands, Inc.* v. *Zumpe*. The latter case relates to the issuance of a permanent injunction after trial. In denying the request for an injunction the court noted:

> Absent imminence of disclosure, an injunction shall not issue. Disclosure has not been shown to be either imminent or eventually inevitable.

Walter T. Zumpe had been a plant manager for Standard's Chase & Sanborn Product Division in New Orleans before resigning to join William B. Reily & Company, Inc. The Reily company operated a plant in New Orleans just a few hundred yards away from Standard's plant. Reily made a coffee blended with chicory marketed under the trade name "Luzianne." Zumpe was hired as Reily's vice-president and general manager in charge of produc-

*Emphasis added. Author.

tion. Standard operated a pilot plant engaged in testing and improving its coffee and tea products. Since Zumpe, as Standard's plant manager, had access to and had received much technical information, including trade secrets, Standard sought an injunction to prevent him from working for Reily. Among other points, Standard contended that Zumpe could not discharge his duties for Reily without "inevitably" disclosing Standard's trade secrets.

The court disagreed, noting that Reily had an existing plant for the manufacture of coffee (American Potash was just getting into the business) and did not need know-how or secrets from Standard (American Potash had tried to license know-how from duPont). Furthermore, the nature of Reily's business was somewhat different and there was no evidence of an intention by Reily to "market a new dry coffee concentration in the foreseeable future" (Potash intended to manufacture and market in direct competition with duPont). Thus, the court concluded:

> It is doubtless true that Zumpe may be tempted to use his confidential information to Reily's benefit, but, because of the nature of Reily's business, it does not follow that disclosure is inevitable.

The Inadequacy of Money Damages as a Remedy

Ordinarily a court will deny a request for a preliminary injunction if it considers the matter essentially rectifiable at the time the case is tried. Although a lawsuit can remain pending for months and even years before trial, most courts prefer that a trial judge, who has the benefit of a full presentation of the facts at trial, issue whatever orders are appropriate. Thus, if it appears that a matter can reasonably wait until trial, and any damage done be remedied then, a court will usually not issue a preliminary injunction. Hence it is essential to demonstrate to the court the consequences of permitting the former employee or his new employer to make use of the trade secrets pending the outcome of a trial.

Unlike many commercial transactions, including patent disputes, trade secrets constitute a unique property right. What other right vanishes on disclosure? In a lawsuit over patent infringement, for example, the trial court can decide to issue a permanent injunction to prevent future infringement and can assess damages for past infringement. The patent remains intact. Therefore, in most patent infringement suits, courts tend to deny motions for preliminary injunctions. But in a lawsuit over a trade secret, a trial judge may not be able to decide on issuing a meaningful injunction. Obviously no court can enjoin disclosure once made—a secret depends on no disclosure being made at all. And since trade secrets often represent the kind of know-how that disappears into a manufacturing process or a product, it may no longer be practical to attempt to enjoin the "use" of that trade secret. And a court is not about to halt the operation of a plant or the manufacture of a product unless the trade secret is essentially synonomous with the manufacturing process or product. There have been some such instances. One occurred in *Head Ski Co.* v. *Kam Ski Co.* in 1958 where the court found that the defendants, former employees of Head Ski, would not have had the idea of making a metal ski but for their work for Head Ski. The court attributed essentially all of their ski making operation to the know-how acquired during their employment by Head Ski. The court stated:

> In the instant case . . . defendants' entire operation has been built upon plaintiff's techniques, methods, materials and design. In such a case, an injunction against manufacture of the product is appropriate.

In the ordinary case, however, a trade secret may disappear into existing processes and product lines and not be clearly distinguishable. Moreover, the knowledge, once possessed by the marketplace, cannot be erased. Therefore, assuming the facts so indicate, it is necessary to impress on the court, at the time a request for a preliminary injunction is made, that a trial court may be stripped of the power to issue a meaningful injunction, no matter how warranted, because of intermittent events or acts, unless those events or acts are enjoined pending the trial.

In the absence of an injunction, you must rely on monetary damages. But the contribution of the secret information to a competitor's products or processes may not be measurable in dollars and cents. Unless, as in *Head Ski* v. *Kam Ski,* the entire product can be attributed to the trade-secret information, it may simply not be possible to determine which portion of a given process or product is utilizing a trade secret and how much contribution that trade secret is making to the profitability of any particular product, as opposed, say, to increased advertising, a reorganized or stronger marketing program, or other modifications to the process or product. Where the facts permit such isolation of a trade secret's contribution to a process or product line, then its further use may be enjoined at trial and damages assessed. But where the trade secret is fungible,—its use in a process is not readily visible—then an after-the-fact assessment becomes extremely difficult. It is in the latter instance that a court will most likely issue a preliminary injunction.

As noted earlier, a preliminary injunction is important in a trade-secret case, not only because it prevents disclosure and further damage pending trial, but because it can also serve as an indicator of the ultimate outcome of the case. Having obtained a preliminary injunction, it is reasonable to conclude that the court was satisfied that you at least have a prima facie case and probably can prevail at trial. However, failure to issue a preliminary injunction does not necessarily mean that the court has decided you are not likely to prevail at trial (although this, of course, may well be true). The court may simply not have been persuaded of the urgent need for an intermittent remedy. The court may have felt that the circumstances were such as to justify waiting for a trial, and perhaps that disclosure was not likely or that adequate relief could be had then.

A trade secret case follows the normal pattern of litigation, although, as we have seen, the early stages take on heightened importance and sometimes can be decisive. After the preliminary injunction stage, further discovery through written interrogatories and oral depositions may be had. Considerable time may elapse while that discovery takes place, additional motions are filed, and, perhaps, settlement discussions are held. In a trade-secret case, time, in the absence of a preliminary injunction, is usually on the side of the former employee and his new company or employer.

Motions for summary judgment, such as that made in *duPont* v. *American Potash,* rest on the premise that there are no issues of fact in dispute. If that is true, and only issues of law have to be resolved, then a trial is pointless and a court should resolve the issues of law on such a motion. But it should be recalled that in the case cited, the court denied American Potash's motion for summary judgment because it could not reach a conclusion from the facts before it.

Pretrial conferences with the judge assigned to the case may give rise to a basis for settlement, but otherwise a trial date will be assigned. The evidence at the trial will essentially constitute a more elaborate presentation of the same points noted earlier with respect to proof of the existence of a trade secret. During the trial, counsel for the employer will emphasize the extent of damages to maximize recovery. Where it appears that the former employee has done well and that success can be attributed to the trade secrets, then the former employer will seek recovery of those profits. But where the former employee, perhaps due to startup problems, has not fared well, the former employer will probably concentrate on his own losses as the measure of damages, arguing that the former employee's inability to make a high profit initially was attributable to a high initial capital investment or to early management or marketing mistakes. The former employer will attempt to show that loss of the trade secret resulted in loss of a marketing position, loss of market share, loss of ability to influence market price for his product, and, if applicable, loss of possible licensing revenue.

If the former employer is successful, the trial will end with an award of damages and a permanent injunction. If the former employee is successful, it may end with a judgment in his favor and, depending on the existence of counterclaims (for matters outside the scope of trade secrets), an award of damages or other relief, depending on the nature of those counterclaims.

8 □ Hiring Your Competitor's Employee

So far we have concentrated on the rights of the individual, particularly vis-à-vis the rights of his employer. But what of the third party, the company that employs an individual who worked for a competitor and who may possess valuable information? When you come right down to it, are you as a third party exposed to any liability for hiring your competitor's employees? Or, from the other side, can you sue your competitor for hiring one or more of your trusted employees? The answer is: it depends. Let's take a look at just what it depends on.

The law in this area can be traced back to the Ordinance of Labours (23 Edw. III st 1) enacted in England in 1349. That ordinance imposed a penalty on anyone who received and retained the services of a laborer who had run away from his employer. The law at that time sought to protect the customary seven-year period of indenture. In addition to, or perhaps as a result of, that ordinance, the law began to recognize the right of one master to sue another for enticing away and harboring his servant.

But as we have seen, in the course of time the master-servant concept has been altered to reflect contemporary attitudes. Today an employee is not considered a servant, at least not in the sense in which that term was used in the Middle Ages. There is no system of indenture. An employee is no longer regarded by the law as property but rather as an individual. As such, he has a right of mobility, a right to take employment when and wherever desired.

211

That right is now recognized by the law and zealously guarded. Therefore, as a general rule, since an employee has a right to elect to pick up and leave and take a new job—and in the absence of a contract his employer can fire him at will—his new employer (the third party) has a right, equally recognized by the law, to retain the services of that employee. So on the face of it, it seems quite simple. But in reality it turns out to be more complex.

The complexity stems from the competing principle of law that seeks to protect trade secrets and to protect an individual or company from unfair competition. It is considered unfair competition, for example, to raid a competitor to hire its employees for the purposes of damaging its business, or for the purpose of acquiring its trade secrets. And it is those competing interests on which we will now focus our attention.

The most concise statement of the law in this area is found in the Restatement of Torts. The Restatement is not a law enacted by any legislature, but rather an attempt by legal scholars to formulate principles and define them. The Restatement reflects an analysis of literally thousands of cases. It restates the law based on an analysis of judicial decisions that go back over a century in the United States and which, in turn, are derived from or founded on law that was decided in England over previous centuries. Although not having the force of law itself, the Restatement is almost always cited by judges writing opinions in this area, and it is almost always looked to for guidance by judges, serving as a yardstick by which to measure the facts of the individual case. Thus the Restatement should not be taken lightly.

Section 766 of the Restatement of Torts says ". . . one who, without privilege to do so, induces or otherwise purposely causes a third person not to (a) perform a contract with another, or (b) enter into or continue a business relation with another is liable to the other for the harm caused thereby." Those words state the basic principle by which the liability of a third party is determined.

Let's now apply that Restatement to situations as they ordinarily occur. For example, you receive a résumé from an employee of your competitor, and that employee seems to have the qualifications that you have been looking for to fill a certain vacancy that exists in your company. What risks do you run if you hire him?

Assuming that the opening is a legitimate one (not artificially created), that your interest in the employee is based on the ability to fill that opening, and that there is no preconceived plan involved to acquire trade secrets from or to injure your competitor, then there is no liability. Some companies, perhaps to be on the safe side, actually require new employees to sign a statement to the effect that they are not under any obligation to their former employer and that they will not reveal any trade secrets in their new employment. The signing of such a statement does *not,* however, always help. For example, in *duPont* v. *American Potash,* cited above, Donald Hirsch had signed an agreement with American Potash not to divulge his former employer's proprietary information or trade secrets. American Potash cited in support of its claim that it had no intention of obtaining duPont's trade secrets from Hirsch. But the injunction duPont sought was granted and the court refused to lift it. The key element there was simply the fact that Donald Hirsch was instrumental in duPont's manufacture of titanium dioxide by the chloride process and if he worked in the same technology for American Potash, it appeared likely or probable that he would reveal information he had gained in confidence from duPont.

By contrast, when Operations Research, Inc. sued Davidson & Talbert, Inc. in 1966, the Maryland court took special note of the fact that Davidson & Talbert did not solicit employees of Operations Research, but that those employees voluntarily left and in fact sought out Davidson & Talbert and asked for work. There were no facts to indicate that the employees of Operations Research had been recruited, or offered special bonuses or particularly high salaries. Even so, the mere fact that a competitor, or someone acting in his behalf, actually offers a job to someone else's employee does not, in and of itself, give rise to liability. For example, in *Triangle Film Corporation* v. *Artcraft Pictures Corporation,* Judge Learned Hand, writing for the New York Court of Appeals, said that in the absence of some monopolistic purpose everyone has the right to offer better terms to another's employee, so long as that employee is free to leave. In that case, actor William S. Hart had agreed to work for Triangle, but his agreement was to work under the direction of Thomas H. Ince. When Ince left Triangle to go with Artcraft, Hart also left Triangle and went to Artcraft. Triangle complained, among other things, that Artcraft made no effort to dissuade Hart from leaving Triangle. But the New York Court of Appeals said that there was no reason for Artcraft to have made any effort to dissuade him. The court said that the object of the law was not to put an end to competition or to prevent employees from bettering themselves. There is no evidence in the case that Artcraft had schemed or plotted to hire Hart or other Triangle employees in breach of any agreement with Triangle or for the purpose of damaging Triangle. Judge Hand wrote that to preclude Hart from joining Artcraft "would be intolerable, both to such employers as could use the employee more effectively and to such employees as might receive added pay. It would put an end to any kind of competition."

Thus you are free to hire your competitor's employees, particularly when they approach you and your objective is simply to fill a legitimate need. But it is important that no ulterior motive be present.

In some cases the courts have gone further and actually said that there is no liability even if you induce an employee to leave your competitor to join you. For example, in *Sarkes Tarzian, Inc.* v. *Audio Devices, Inc.,* the federal court sitting in California held that there was nothing wrong with trying to induce your competitor's employees to join you—at least that act by itself was not illegal. In that case Audio Devices hired one of Sarkes Tarzian's employees, George J. Eannarino, as its director and manager of a new plant. Eannarino then asked some other employees of Sarkes Tarzian to join him in the new venture. Those employees included a research engineer, a production supervisor, Tarzian's chief of quality control, a technical supervisor, a cost accountant, and a purchasing agent. Sarkes Tarzian claimed that it was being deprived of its key personnel. Chief Judge Leon R. Yankwich, on behalf of the federal district court in California, said that none of those employees had contracts for any specific length of time, so they clearly had the right to leave Tarzian. The court said that since all of the employees had a right to leave at will, and since they could have been terminated at will, the mere fact that they went to work for Audio, a competitor, did not of itself constitute a conspiracy. The facts did not indicate, according to the court, that there was enticement of those employees. They were not lured away. The mere invitation to employees working for your competitor to join you, in and of itself (assuming there are no "term" contracts between those employees and your competitor) does not make you liable to the former employer.

But so far we have been discussing cases where the facts have indicated a relatively innocent hiring of a competitor's employee and a situation where the employee hired did not have a contract for a definite term.

Most employee situations are "at will." That means that the employee, at least in theory, can leave any time he wants. By the same token, the employer enjoys the equal privilege of inviting that employee to leave should the employer decide that the employee's services are no longer necessary or desirable. There is no commitment either way for a definite period of time. A term contract, by contrast, commits both parties for a specified period of time. The distinction is important with respect to liability. In *Carmen* v. *Fox Film Corp.* decided by the federal district court in New York in 1913, Judge Martin T. Manton contrasted the situation where the employee has a contract for a definite term, saying, "To do intentionally that which is calculated in the ordinary course of events to damage and which, in fact, does damage another person in his property or trade is malicious in the law, and is actionable if it is done without just cause or excuse." The distinction was further highlighted in *Terry* v. *Dairymens' League Co-operative Association* wherein the New York State Supreme Court said ". . . the furthering of one's business interests does not ordinarily justify the inducing of the breach of contract for a definite term."

Although the law seeks to encourage employee mobility and seeks to encourage competition, it does not countenance an intentional act that is calculated to cause a breach of contract. Of course the assumption is that the new employer was aware that the employee had a contract with his former employer and that it was for a definite term. That aspect of awareness or "knowledge" brings up one of the more interesting aspects of the law. The law will not allow a person to hide behind a shield of ignorance when there was ample reason to have known a certain fact or at least to have inquired and determined the fact. Most judges realize that in some cases it is extremely difficult to prove actual knowledge. Therefore, if the evidence indicates that one of the parties knew or should have known a certain fact, then a judge will apply the concept of

constructive knowledge. This, in effect, prevents a party from play-
ing the ostrich game to prevent himself from seeing facts that in
fairness he would otherwise have seen or perhaps should have
seen.

For example, in *Carter Products, Inc.* v. *Colgate-Palmolive* Colgate
was charged with stealing Carter's formula for Rise shaving cream.
Colgate had hired Norman Fine, a chemist who had been employed by Foster D. Snell, Inc. Snell was a consultant firm of
research chemists that had worked for Carter and helped it develop the formula for Rise. The facts indicated that Colgate had
been trying to develop a shaving cream for several months and had
been unsuccessful. Fine had been a joint inventor of Rise. Chief
Judge William C. Coleman of the Federal District Court for Maryland noted that Fine was all too willing to be placed by Colgate in
work that was in direct competition with the work that Fine had
done for Carter. On the basis of Fine's contribution, Colgate soon
developed Rapid-Shave and was able to file two applications for
patent on its new shaving cream formula. The evidence indicated
that the work that those patent applications were based on originated and in significant part was performed by Fine while he
worked for Snell on behalf of Carter. "The basis of our decision"
for Carter, said Judge Coleman, "is that Colgate knew, or must
have known by the exercise of fair business principles, that the
precise character of Fine's work with Snell was, in all likelihood,
covered by the agreement which Fine had with Snell not to divulge
trade secrets, and that, therefore, Colgate was obligated to do
more than it did towards ascertaining the extent to which Fine was,
in fact, restricted in what he might disclose to Colgate."

Clearly, Colgate was trying to develop a shaving cream in competition with Carter and it knew that Fine was a joint inventor of
Rise. Therefore, it was wrong for Colgate to permit Fine to work
in direct competition with his prior work for Snell. Colgate, on the
other hand, simply said that it would see to it that Fine lived up
to the limitations imposed on him by his contract. The Maryland
court said that was not enough. The opinion of Chief Judge Coleman indicates that he believed Colgate either knew or should have
known more than it would admit to. Colgate was required to reim-
burse Carter for lost profits and court costs.

Much the same reasoning was applied by Judge A. Sherman

Christenson sitting on the bench of the Federal District Court for Utah in 1958 in *Monsanto Chemical Co.* v. *Miller.* In that case the defendants were Charles M. Miller, who had worked for Monsanto, and the F. C. Torkelson Company. Monsanto claimed that Torkelson was using trade secrets that Miller had acquired while working for Monsanto. Miller, although not employed by Torkelson, worked out of Torkelson's office and worked closely with Torkelson employees on the construction of an electric furnace plant. Judge Christenson said: "the court finds it impossible to believe Torkelson was not, in view of such close consultation and joint work as the evidence indicates, advised of Miller's prior employment, of the policy of Monsanto to regard its operations, design and cost data as confidential, of the impossibility of getting such information directly, and of the inhibitions or restrictions operating upon Miller with respect to disclosure of design data of Monsanto." Torkelson took the position that it did not make any inquiry about Miller's obligation to Monsanto, and that it did not have to make any such inquiry. But the court refused to accept Torkelson's excuse, saying that Torkelson knew or should have known of Miller's obligations to Monsanto and, therefore, of the confidentiality of the information Miller had been revealing.

Thus, "notice" is a key element in determining liability. And notice can be implied from the circumstances. Therefore, when hiring a competitor's employee, it is important that you not overlook obvious facts. While there is no obligation to investigate every prospective employee, by the same token there is no right to ignore facts that in fairness and common sense indicate that the employee being hired may be under some obligation to his former employer. That employee may have signed a contract for a definite term, or may be under a specific fiduciary obligation not to disclose certain confidential information. If the employee being hired has an obligation to the former employer, then it is necessary to determine the extent of that obligation. For example, in the space-suit case involving Donald Wohlgemuth, it was perfectly okay for International Latex to hire Wohlgemuth from B. F. Goodrich provided, however, it did not use Wohlgemuth in its space-suit development program. Remember that Wohlgemuth had been a key employee in Goodrich's development of the space suit and International Latex was now developing its own space suit in competition with

Goodrich. Similarly, there was nothing wrong with American Potash hiring Donald Hirsch from duPont, provided that Hirsch was not going to be working in Potash's program to manufacture titanium dioxide. It is fairly apparent that the concern in these two cases was that the hirings of Wohlgemuth and Hirsch would give rise to the "Rise" type of situation.

As we have seen from *Triangle Film* v. *Artcraft* and *Sarkes Tarzian* v. *Audio Devices,* there is no liability merely because you hire one or more of your competitor's employees—assuming, of course, that there is no term contract between those employees and your competitor and that there is no special obligation of which you have notice or of which you should have notice. In the Sarkes Tarzian case, particularly, all of the employees were employees at will (that is, not under contract for a fixed time period).

But that does not mean that the courts have declared an open field day on competitors' employees. Under some circumstances, the law will protect an employer's relationship with employees at will—even if the employees do not have a special contractual obligation—meaning even if they do not have any trade secrets to impart. For example, where the true objective in hiring employees from a competitor is to monopolize a market or to disrupt and severely cripple the competitor's business, then the courts will not only issue an injunction and allow damages to compensate the former employer for losses, including lost profits, but will permit exemplary (punitive) damages as well.

Take the 1962 New Jersey case of *Wear-Ever Aluminum* v. *Townecraft Industries, Inc.* In that case Townecraft hired Daniel Eisenfeld, a district manager for Wear-Ever. Eisenfeld was in charge of the Philadelphia district. Both companies sold cooking utensils on a door-to-door basis. In that kind of business the personal relationships, including particularly the customer relationships of the individual door-to-door salesman, are unique.

Eisenfeld managed the Philadelphia area with two assistant district managers and four dealers. The dealers were in charge of the door-to-door salesmen for individual territories. According to Wear-Ever, Townecraft instigated a concentrated and systematic plan to raid Wear-Ever employees in the Philadelphia area. It appears that Townecraft first enticed Daniel Eisenfeld to become its zone manager. Eisenfeld, without advising Wear-Ever of his new job, called a meeting at the Cherry Hill Inn in Haddonfield, New Jersey, acting within his capacity as district manager for Wear-Ever. He had his assistant district managers and four dealers present. Eisenfeld was well respected by his assistants and the dealers, and when he advised them that he was leaving to go with Townecraft, he did not have much difficulty in persuading them to join him. The facts indicate that Eisenfeld had contracts with him that evening, and each of his assistants, including the dealers, signed those contracts with Townecraft.

At a later date, the dealers met with their door-to-door salesmen and before long, a total of thirty-five members of Wear-Ever's Philadelphia sales force had been pirated. As a result of that mass exodus, the morale of the rest of the sales force was so depressed that forty-three additional door-to-door salesmen quit Wear-Ever. That accounts for seventy-eight salesmen of a total of eighty. Obviously, Wear-Ever's sales force in that area had been wiped out.

Judge Pashman granted judgment for Wear-Ever, including damages. He characterized the conduct of Townecraft as an act committed with the "malicious intent of inflicting injury." Judge Pashman said that there was nothing wrong with the concept of self-enrichment or with competition, but that when a competitor engages in the systematic enticement of employees with the clear purpose of crippling or destroying an integral part of his competitor's business, then such a commercial piracy is totally unwarranted. Wear-Ever was entitled to be compensated for both its loss of manpower and loss of revenue. In determining its compensation Wear-Ever had a right to take into account such elements as the monetary value of the training of its ex-employees and the cost of recruiting and training new employees to replace them, as well as the profits from the business that it lost. It should be noted that unlike the Sarkes Tarzian case, the loss of the employees was not merely an incident to the hiring of those employees by a competitor; it was "the ultimate consequence envisioned."

Another interesting case is *Eutectic Corporation* v. *Astralloy Vulcan Corporation,* brought in the Federal District Court for Northern Alabama. Both companies sell metallic compositions such as alloys to improve the wear resistance of metal surfaces. Harold Cain had joined Eutectic initially as a salesman, but rose to become vice-president and national sales manager. He had signed an employ-

ment agreement with Eutectic to the effect that he would not
compete with Eutectic for a two-year period following termination
of his employment. He left Eutectic in May 1972 apparently over
some disagreement with management. (Judge Frank H. McFadden's opinion implies that his leaving may not have been entirely
voluntary.)

Cain made the first contact with the president of Astralloy, Harry
Dickenson. Eventually he was hired and placed in charge of sales.
Prior to his being employed, Cain did tell Dickenson of his employment contract and of his obligations to Eutectic. After he joined
Astralloy, seven former Eutectic employees, forming the bulk of
Eutectic's sales force, were hired by Astralloy. Each of those salesmen had signed contracts with Eutectic containing covenants not
to compete for a period of two years, and Eutectic promptly
brought suit claiming "piracy."

Judge McFadden said that because Dickenson knew of the contracts with Eutectic when he hired Cain and Cain's associates from
Eutectic, he had in fact participated in and "induced the fiduciary
breaches." For that reason Astralloy was found liable to Eutectic.
Judge McFadden said that the restrictive covenants were reasonable under the circumstances since they were limited to the same
territories that the men had previously serviced while employed by
Eutectic. He then enjoined Astralloy from competing with Eutectic
through the latter's former employees for a two-year period, and
from hiring any more Eutectic employees during those two years.

Judge McFadden was of the opinion that Astralloy had participated in a raid on Eutectic. And, as in the Wear-Ever situation,
the loss of manpower and loss of revenue to Eutectic was not
merely an incident to the act of hiring its employees but part of the
ultimate consequence envisioned. It appears from the court's
opinion in both cases that Townecraft and Astralloy each knew or
should have known that the direct and necessary ultimate consequence of their action in hiring their competitors' employees
would be to cripple or destroy a significant segment of each competitor's business.

While courts will normally encourage competition and protect
an employee's right of mobility, they will also protect an employer
from unfair competition. And corporate piracy, to the extent that
it is part of a deliberate scheme—part of a malicious act designed

as much or perhaps more to injure the competitor than it is to promote the self-interest of the new employer—is what most courts abhor. Virtually every state in the United States, with the apparent exception of Louisiana, will protect an employer's rights against unlawful interference by competitors with contracts with his employees. Louisiana stands alone in its position that it will not permit a lawsuit for inducing a third person to break his contract.

Recall that we are not concerned here with the innocent independent discovery of a competitor's trade secrets, but with the problems that may arise when hiring an employee, particularly an employee of a competitor, who may be under some obligation to his former employer. That obligation may simply be an unwritten understanding that the employee is not to reveal trade secrets; or, the employee may have been a fiduciary of someone else entrusted with secret information; or he may have actually signed a contract. The contract may be for a definite term or perhaps an "at will" contract (that is, with no specified term) that contained clauses restricting the employee's right to disclose confidential information. The contract might contain a restrictive covenant prohibiting the employee from working for a competitor for a certain period of time. All of those facts are relevant in making a determination on whether there is any liability in hiring the former employee, and in determining what risks you take.

Normally, there is nothing wrong with hiring a competitor's employee. Generally speaking, whether the former employee of your competitor approached you or you approached the former employee, either directly or through a third party such as a recruiter, there is no liability merely because you hired the competitor's employee. Keep in mind the general rule that the law encourages employee mobility and therefore that it must also encourage the hiring of such employees.

But the general rule must be construed in the light of the total situation. The right to hire a competitor's employee does not constitute "open season" for corporate raids. Where one or more employees are hired to fill a legitimate need, there will ordinarily be no problem. But where those employees are hired with the principal thought of gaining access to trade secrets, the law will rear its head to protect the former employer. Remember the Rise situation where the court felt that Colgate should have known better.

When you actually do not know of any obligations that the prospective employee has with your competitor, and the circumstances do not imply facts that warrant further investigation, then you can feel reasonably assured that you are not liable to any ex-employer because you hired that employee. But once you get notice, even after hiring that employee, you do have an obligation to undertake reasonable efforts to discontinue using that employee in a sensitive position, and to avoid making use of any trade secrets disclosed thus far.

If you have already invested considerable sums of money, if you have made a commitment on the basis of information acquired in innocence through that employee, or if you have paid a significant sum of money for information from someone who, it later turns out, was under obligation of confidence to a third party, you are not liable to that third party or former employer. The underlying assumption here is that you acted in innocence when making your investment. That you were a bona fide purchaser and acted in good faith is an essential aspect of your right to continue using the information without liability. "Good faith" requires that you did not know, nor did you have reason to know at the time that you acquired the information, that the person from whom you acquired it was bound not to disclose it.

One of the leading cases that helped resolve this point was *Conmar Products Corporation* v. *Universal Slide Fastener Co., Inc.* Judge Learned Hand ruled in that case that Universal Slide Fastener had no knowledge of any secrecy contract when it hired employees from Conmar Products. Universal had hired former Conmar employees who helped develop new machines for making zippers. Universal invested forty thousand dollars in these machines, which embodied Conmar trade secrets. The evidence suggests that Universal first learned of a contractual obligation of its new employees to Conmar several months after it had made its investment in the new machinery. Furthermore, there was no evidence that Universal knew of Conmar's machinery, or had reason to know that those employees had previously worked on similar machinery for Conmar. Contrast this with the Rise case, where Colgate knew or should have known of

Norman Fine's connection with the discovery of the Rise shaving cream formula.

Judge Hand pointed out that there could be no liability until Universal had received notice of the secrecy obligation of its new employees to a third party. But since Universal had invested substantial sums of money in the machine, relying in good faith on its right to use the information in question, it would be wrong to enjoin Universal from using that information, or to impose an obligation to pay damages, even for the period of time after they acquired the facts.

Thus it appears that when you hire an employee in good faith and you have no reason to suspect any obligation of secrecy to a third party, and if you invest money or get into a new line of business or make other significant capital expenditures in conjunction with making full use of that employee's talents, you are not likely to find yourself compelled to discontinue using that equipment or to put aside that investment at a later date merely because you suddenly learn that the employee was under an obligation of secrecy to a third party. But remember that you cannot act with indifference. You may not simply make the investment while ignoring facts that common sense dictates you should be aware of. In short, you cannot pretend not to know what you should know and would know if you took reasonable precautions. You are not required, however, to conduct elaborate investigations—merely not to overlook the obvious.

It is permissible for you to offer a job to an employee of a competitor, directly or through an agent, such as a recruiter. But if you know, when making the offer, that the employee to whom you are offering a job is under a contract for a definite term to a third party, then you expose yourself to liability to that third party for compensation for whatever damages that third party may suffer, including whatever costs for training and related costs may have been incurred in training the employee you are hiring, and in recruiting and training his replacement. You also expose yourself to liability for punitive or exemplary damages. The fact that you knew the employee was under contract for a definite term and still made the offer exposes you to a charge of malicious interference with the business of that third party. However, where there is no definite term in the employment agreement and the employee you seek to hire is merely an employee "at will," then ordinarily you will not be exposed to liability to the third party employer. Unless, of course, you are purposefully seeking to gain and use trade secrets or you are engaging in a deliberate conspiracy designed to ruin or destroy a significant part of that third party's business. The key here is not whether one or several employees are hired—although the hiring of a group of employees may look more suspicious—but rather whether the circumstances indicate an element of malice—a plan or design to cause injury to the third party as opposed to simply building your own staff. A significant distinction is whether the injury to the third party is merely an incident to the hiring or whether that injury is the ultimate consequence envisioned. Phrased differently, your competitor can hire your "at will" employees provided his real motive is not to get you, injure your business, or get at your trade secrets.

From the viewpoint of the first employer, it now may be understood more clearly why, as part of a security policy, a termination interview should be held with all employees. Certainly whenever an employee leaves and there is even the slightest reason for suspicion that he is joining a competitor, that competitor should be notified of any obligation that the employee has with you. And, of course, on learning of your employee's joining your competitor, you should act quickly not only to put the competitor on notice but to enjoin the disclosure of confidential information, particularly where there is any possibility that the competitor may invest considerable sums of money in reliance on information acquired from your former employee.

9 □ Rights to Employees' Inventions: New Trends

The Laws in Other Countries

In most industrialized countries in the world there are laws governing the rights of employees to compensation for inventions they have made. One need only look to such countries as Italy, Austria, West Germany, the Scandinavian countries, Japan, and recently Great Britain for illustrations of statutory law providing for additional compensation for employee inventions.

In general, these laws provide that employees hired to invent shall not receive additional compensation, although in some of the countries provisions are made for special bonuses or additional rewards should an invention be highly successful. It is in the gray area, the area between the extreme of the employee who was hired to invent and the employee who makes an invention completely on his own, that the legislation applies.

In France and Switzerland, the laws provide for additional compensation to an employee under circumstances where the employee is not hired to invent. In Switzerland there is a commercial law known as the "Law of Obligations." Under that law, inventions made by an employee in the course of his work belong to the employer if the invention was made as part of the duties of the employee, or if the employer expressly retained the right to them. Thus by employment contract, the employer in Switzerland, as in the United States, can require employees to assign all inventions to the employer as a condition of employment. But unlike the United States, the Swiss Law of Obligations requires that the employee be given reasonable special compensation if the invention is of considerable economic value, and that holds true regardless of any pre-existing contract. The point, simply, is that under Swiss law a distinction is made between those special inventions that provide "considerable economic value" and ordinary inventions made in the course of employment. The term "considerable economic value" has been interpreted as something that brings the employer a substantial advantage in the marketplace. By contrast, no such distinction concerning the economic value of an invention exists for employee-inventors in the United States.

The law in Sweden, which is typical of the Scandinavian approach, and which, with some variation, has been adopted in Denmark, Finland, and Norway, distinguishes among four categories of inventions. The first two relate to inventions or discoveries made by an employee as the result of work assigned to him, or where research and activities of an inventive sort are primary tasks. Those two categories are known as "service inventions." A third category covers employee-made inventions that relate to the employer's business activity and are made utilizing the employer's facilities but are not part of the employee's assigned duties. That is the category that often gives rise to the "shop right" in the United States. The fourth category of inventions embraces those made by the employee outside of the course of his employment, not utilizing the employer's facilities but nonetheless relating to the employer's business.

Sweden requires that the employee be provided with reasonable compensation for any invention he makes, and to which the employer takes either full or partial title. That holds true regardless of any contract that may have been entered into as a condition of employment.

The amount of compensation depends on the value of the invention and the category it falls into. With respect to the first two categories—that is, where the idea is directly related to the employee's work or stems from duties specifically assigned—the employee may receive special compensation, but only to the extent that the value of the invention is disproportionate to the employee's compensation. (Note the similarity to the Swiss commercial Law of Obligations.)

The amount of compensation for inventions in the other categories must also be "reasonable." The law provides a special standing board to which both employers and employees may look for guidance, but that board may not issue legally binding opinions unless both parties agree in advance to be bound by the opinion. In the absence of such a mutual agreement, any dispute will have to be resolved by an arbitration board especially created to resolve disputes concerning inventions made in the course of employment and operating under the general Swedish Law on Arbitration.

The law in Denmark is similar, but there is one difference that deserves noting. Denmark recognizes "company inventions." When an invention comes about by cooperation between a number of employees "in an enterprise in such a way that it is not possible to identify certain individuals as the inventors, the enterprise is considered to be the inventor" (Section 4(1) of the Danish Parliament Act of April 29, 1955). By contrast, when several employees in the United States contribute to an invention of which no single inventor can be isolated, all of the individuals are collectively considered "joint inventors." They are then collectively in the same shoes as any individual inventor. Sometimes this has caused a number of problems, particularly where some of the "inventors" are under contract and others are not.

Austria, the Netherlands, Italy, Canada, and Japan somewhat follow a pattern, although with considerable variation. In Austria, agreements between employers and employees providing for an assignment to the employer of title to future inventions made by the employee are valid and enforceable only if they relate to "service inventions." The basic requirement of a "service invention" is that it fall within the scope of the employer's business. (Note that there is no such limitation to employment contracts in the United States.) In addition, under Austrian law, a "service invention" must have been made as part of the employee's job, or it must be shown that the idea for the invention was stimulated by the employee's job, or, at the very least, that his job substantially facilitated the making of the invention.

Where the employee is expressly hired to engage in research or in work where he is expected to invent or to come up with new ideas, then Austria, as most other countries including the United States, recognizes that the employee's compensation is remuneration for that invention. But unlike the United States, Austrian law provides that where the invention has special value to the employer, that is, if it is of exceptional commercial importance, then the employee is entitled to some additional compensation.

Austrian law also contains a provision to the effect that any assignment to a third party by an employer of rights to an invention acquired from an employee is subject to a demand by the employee that the rights be reassigned to him. Thus the employee has the right to reacquire title to his invention in the event that his employer decides at some later stage to part with those rights.

Machinery for resolving disputes is provided by the law in Austria, and jurisdiction in some cases is given to provincial labor courts, in others to ordinary courts.

The law in Canada is limited to certain categories of employees and for the most part does not apply to inventors employed in private industry. But with respect to those employees who are covered—primarily government employees—special provisions are made for transfer of title to the employer, but with special compensation beyond salary to the employee-inventor.

In Japan employers are automatically granted a nonexclusive license with respect to any patent on an invention, made by one of their employees, that falls within the scope of their business. But the employer may not obtain title nor an exclusive license for such inventions by an employment contract entered into *prior to* employment. When the employer takes title or exclusive rights to the invention, the employee has to be compensated in accordance with certain criteria that involve the employer's profits obtained from the use of the invention, as well as the extent of the employer's contribution to the creation of the invention. Once again, we can see that this is not too far afield from the "hired to invent" concept. Thus, in Japan, an employee who comes up with a discovery as part of duties that are assigned to him is not entitled to compensation beyond his salary unless the invention is of exceptional commercial value. Although the law does not expressly read that way, in net effect the standards applied for determining the employee's right to compensation essentially provide for that result. Where the employee was not expected to invent, the employer's contribution is considered to be minimal; hence the employee's right to additional compensation increases.

In the Netherlands the employer has a right to require an assignment of title to inventions made by the employee as part of an employment contract entered into prior to employment. Once again, where the invention is of a special nature, such that its commercial value to the employer is great, the employee is entitled to additional compensation. The key term on which the law revolves is "equitable." The employer is obligated to pay the employee "an equitable sum, having regard to the financial importance of the invention and the circumstances in which it was made." That is an express provision of the law in the Netherlands, and if the employer and the inventor cannot agree on what is equitable, the patent office has jurisdiction to decide that question, and its decision is binding on the parties.

Italy also provides for "reasonable compensation" to the inventor, although the employer may take title to all employees' inventions—provided they are within the employer's "field of activities." Italian law provides for binding arbitration to resolve any dispute over what compensation is reasonable. One unique point of the law in Italy is that inventions, made by employees who are hired or expected to invent, or made as a result of a specific assignment by the employer, belong to the employer not by assignment but rather as an "original" right. The invention is considered made, in effect, by the company. The rationale is simply that the company perceived a problem and specifically hired individuals as its employees or agents to resolve that problem. Any invention arising out of such clearly assigned duties is considered to be the object of the relationship involved and, therefore, under Italian law, considered to be owned by the Italian company as of its own inception. Note the comparison with the "hired to invent" concept in American law. Under the common law, without any contract at all, an American employer is entitled to full ownership of any invention made by an employee under similar circumstances, but title is considered to be *derived* from the employee as a quid pro quo for the compensation paid the employee.

The Federal Republic of Germany (West Germany) has a fairly elaborate system for the payment of compensation to the employee. There are many advocates of similar legislation in the

United States and, indeed, legislation patterned on the West German law has been introduced in Congress by Representative John E. Moss (Dem.–Cal.). Essentially that law allows an employer to take title to inventions of his employees, but subject to "reasonable compensation" to the employee. Here again, various categories of inventions are set forth to distinguish between those made by employees who are expected to invent, as opposed to inventions made by those who come up with an idea outside the ordinary course of their employment. The amount of compensation considered "reasonable" depends both on the category to which the invention belongs and on such factors as the degree of creativeness, the employee's salary level, the functions of the employee in the company, and the commercial or economic value of the invention.

The federal minister of labor in West Germany works with representatives of employer-employee organizations to set forth standardized regulations for computing the value of an invention and the employee's "share factor." There is an involved algebraic formula that is applied to compute the employee's compensation.

Where the employer does not use the invention or does not file application for patent overseas within a certain fixed period of time, rights revert to the employee. An arbitration board in the patent office resolves disputes over compensation.

The law in Great Britain is, of course, the source of American law and therefore quite similar to the law described for the United States. There is, as of 1977, a right to compensation by statute and a provision precluding an employment contract entered into as a condition of employment giving the employer title to all inventions made by the employee. There have been decisions by courts in England to the effect that unreasonable clauses would not be enforced. In one such decision, a contract for the transfer of rights to inventions to the employer that was not limited to the particular service provided by the employee was held to be unreasonable and unenforceable. (*Electrical Transmission Ltd.* v. *Dannenberg.*)

The Soviet Union provides a system for the categorization of ideas and inventions according to different levels. The Soviet system distinguishes between an invention for which a certificate of authorship is granted or a discovery for which a diploma is issued, and a suggestion for "rationalization."

There is an "inventions and discoveries committee" that is authorized to pay a lump sum to inventors of between two hundred and two hundred thousand rubles for inventions and one hundred to one hundred sixty thousand rubles for suggestions for rationalization. (The latter is simply a contribution toward the application of an invention.) Thus the USSR recognizes and rewards the development of know-how.

The different levels of inventions are based on whether the invention makes it possible to start a new branch of production or to produce new and valuable materials, machines, or products. The rules for compensation also take into account the savings generated by useful suggestions.

Since the State, under the Soviet system, owns all inventions, there is no question of a possible dispute or a right to reassignment, or of any contractual issue. All payments are made in lump sums and all decisions made by the Inventions and Discoveries Committee are, as a practical matter, final.

Most East European countries follow the Soviet system. Czechoslovakia, for example, provides special forms of compensation, such as research or travel grants, housing facilities, and other advantages. The key point is that the State always takes title. Even so, some system of evaluating the practical contribution of the discovery or invention is established and a reward or lump-sum payment is made based on that evaluation. Unlike the practice in the West European countries and the United States, such questions as whether the employee was hired to invent, what contribution the employer made, or what use of the employer's facilities was made are irrelevant. The criteria for determining compensation relate solely to the application of the invention and its contribution to the state of technology in that country.

Of all the systems of compensation in the East European countries, that of the German Democratic Republic (East Germany) is the most systematized. There are boards of arbitration set up and a variety of formulas used to assess an inventor's contribution and to provide the inventor with financial compensation. East Germany provides for a basic distinction between exclusive and economic patents. Patents are granted for discoveries that can be put to practice or used in the economy. East Germany relies on an elaborate system of rewards including honors, medals, praise, testimonials, and bonuses. Any additional financial compensation to an inventor is payable as a bonus for work over and above what is ordinarily required of that employee. Payment is also made in the form of a lump sum; there is no royalty to be earned.

Legislative Efforts in the United States

In the United States, for almost two centuries no legislation existed or was proposed governing the right to ownership of inventions or the right to compensation therefor as between employer and employee. Although there were many cases deciding employer-employee disputes, no attempt was made to clarify the judicial precedents, or to embody them in statutory law. The closest we have come to legislation in this area on the federal level, is an Executive Order signed by President Truman on January 23, 1950 establishing a Government Patents Board. That board was designed to establish a government patent policy with respect both to inventions made by government employees and to those made by independent contractors. It did, in fact, establish an administrative system of reward to employees over and above their salaries. Government patent policy today is set by individual agencies such as the Department of Energy, Department of Defense, and Department of Heath, Education, and Welfare. These departments are primarily concerned with establishing policy on title to inventions made by independent contractors, and including those made by employees of contracting companies. And the question for the departments is whether the government or a company under contract to the government will have title to inventions made during the term of contract or as a result thereof. There is still no federal legislation governing the right of non-federal government employees to inventions they create, or to compensation.

In the mid-1960s the California Society of Professional Engineers, in a study of the rights of the employed inventor, concluded that the inventor was being unfairly taken advantage of. The society argued, among other things, that most companies doing business with the government as independent contractors fiercely resist any effort by the government to take title to inventions made in performance of a government contract. Those same companies, however, do not hesitate to require their employees to assign all inventions made in the course of their jobs. According to the society's study, the present system inhibits engineers from coming forward with their best ideas and retards progress in the industrial arts. Indeed, the society contended, employees have been conditioned for so long to accept their salary as full quid pro quo for their inventions that they fail even to recognize their inherent rights. Since the Constitution requires patent applications to be filed in the name of the inventor, the society reasoned, there is an implication that our Founding Fathers intended that inventors be provided with some reward for their creativity. Thus, salary alone is not a sufficient reward.

As a consequence of the society's efforts, California Congressman John E. Moss introduced legislation in the House of Representatives in early 1970 to create a system for determining ownership of inventions and for compensating employees. His bill has been reintroduced repeatedly and is currently pending. Year after year similar legislation is introduced and in time may one day be enacted. As noted earlier, it is patterned after the law in West Germany.

Because it is the first serious effort at introducing legislation on the federal level in the United States in this area the Moss bill is worth looking at more closely. It divides inventions into two categories, (a) the service invention, and (b) the free invention. A service invention is defined as an invention made by an employee during employment, which either grows out of the work he performs or is based on knowledge gained during that employment period. All other inventions are free inventions.

An employee has an obligation to notify his employer of any service invention soon after it is made. That notice must contain a description of the technical problems involved, the solution, and a description of the way in which the invention originated. In addition, the employee must provide sketches or drawings and adequate instructions to permit a full understanding of the invention. If any co-workers participated in or contributed to the invention, the names of all such co-workers must be stated.

Assuming that the notice contains a full description as required by the Moss bill, the employer would then have a limited amount of time, say, two months, after receiving notification to call for

additional information. When all information called for is received, the employer then has a fixed period of time in which to
review and claim title to the employee's service invention. Otherwise it becomes a free invention.

Should the employer choose to claim title to the invention, then
the employee must be compensated according to a formula that
takes into account the market value of the invention, adjusted by
such factors as the conditions and duties of the employee and the
degree to which the operations of the employer contributed to the
making of the invention.

Congressman Moss recommends that guidelines be issued by
the secretary of labor by means of which compensation can be
determined and, in the absence of an agreement, that disputes be
resolved by an arbitration board.

The Moss bill would also establish an office of "adviser on inventions" within the Labor Department, to assist employees in drafting their notices to employers, and to assist both employers and
employees in determining the compensation to be paid for service
inventions.

Many arguments have been made against the Moss Bill, and its
concept is quite obviously difficult to accept in the United States.
One objection often raised is that under the Moss bill if an employer fails to apply for a patent in any country overseas, he forfeits
his rights in that country to the inventor. Furthermore, fear is
expressed that the Moss bill would create two additional bureaucracies in the form of an advisory board in the Labor Department
and an arbitration board in the U.S. Patent Office. One other
objection sometimes made is that the employee, at his discretion,
need not disclose an invention to the employer when he considers
it apparent that it is not within his employer's field.

Although it is not likely that the Moss bill will become law in the
near future, or that the United States will swing wholly over to the
West German system, the bill cannot be taken lightly. As professional organizations become increasingly vocal in their lobbying
efforts, support for some compromise version is likely.

The Moss bill, actually, is not the first attempt at legislation in
the United States, although it is the first to achieve any modicum
of support. In 1963 California Congressman George E. Brown, Jr.
introduced a bill to make it unlawful for an employer to require

employees to pre-assign future inventions as a condition of employment. Congressman Brown was concerned with agreements required of employees as a condition of employment because, in his view, most employees were in no position to bargain as equals and, therefore, in no position to refuse to sign. Congressman Brown would have nullified all the standard employee invention assignment agreements in favor of a return to the common law.

It is interesting to note that a similar conclusion was reached in Great Britain. The Banks Committee, a select group of prominent Britons who agreed to review the British patent laws, found, among other things, that many employers had gone too far in abrogating the common law by insisting on severe employment contracts as a condition of employment. The effect was to encourage a "brain drain" from the United Kingdom and to discourage innovation. That work helped pave the way for The Patents Act of 1977.

Balancing the Equation

If a system of free enterprise is the best system for stimulating business and innovations, and this author believes it is, then there is a need to recognize competing interests. And if competition is a vital and positive element of free enterprise—as it is—then it must be encouraged.

Just as free enterprise depends on the infusion of capital, it depends also on the infusion of ideas. Both elements deserve equal respect and recognition. There is a need to encourage capital investment and to encourage the development of new technology: new ideas, new businesses, new products to invest in. Any system which depresses the growth of one will ultimately depress the growth of the other.

Thus there is a need to provide a mechanism whereby new capital can be introduced with reasonable safeguards, but without discouraging the incentive to discover, to create, to invent. Those safeguards include the right of the investor to assurances of title to the property invested in, including ownership of new developments and spinoffs of ideas related to that business. The right to retain that title through legislation or through contract is not what matters—it is the title itself and the rights that flow from that title that matter. At the same time there is a need to recognize the rights of individuals who are making the contributions, who are actually developing the new products, or inventing new manufacturing methods, or discovering new processes. To the extent that those employees are hired to accomplish that task, it seems reasonable that their salaries, perhaps adjusted to reflect their contribution, be their primary financial reward. Even here many enlightened companies have come to recognize the need for some additional financial incentive, perhaps not as compensation but rather as a tribute or honorarium in recognition of some unique contribution. Many companies have adopted a policy of offering at least some form or token of additional compensation for new inventions. IBM and Exxon, for example, have such systems in effect, and while the sums of money may not be great, the spirit and the circumstances in which they are offered go a long way toward encouraging continued creative efforts by employees.

Exxon, like a fair number of other companies, has adopted a policy of returning patent rights to the employee-inventor if the company does not use the invention within five years of the issuance of a patent. This is a voluntary step similar to the system in West Germany and something like such proposed legislation as the Moss bill seeks to accomplish.

There is still room for further compromise on the part of many companies, with respect to the right of an employee to an invention he was not hired to make. There is a need to acknowledge the lack of bargaining power on the part of the ordinary employee, certainly when negotiating as an individual. There is a need to refrain from insisting on onerous provisions in contracts—provisions that go beyond the scope of the employer's business and beyond the reasonable needs of safeguarding the employer's legitimate business interests.

Many companies, particularly those represented by informed counsel, recognize the advantage to the company of a balanced, reasonable contract designed to protect the company's interests in terms of meeting its more important needs, but without imposing unnecessary hardships on the employee. There is, fortunately, an ever-growing recognition of the rights of employees as individuals, and that recognition is often expressed by the courts in their opinions when they decline to enforce contracts that go beyond protecting the legitimate needs of the employer and make it difficult if not impossible for the employee to continue to work in his field, or to practice a chosen profession.

There also seems to be a growing recognition of the difference in rights that flow from developments made by employees outside the normal course of their employment—particularly outside the reasonable scope of the employer's business—regardless of terms in an employment contract. It is in this gray area that legislation may develop in the foreseeable future. Such legislation may clarify the rights involved and preclude unreasonable agreements by those who would still impose them on their employees.

While the establishment of additional government bureaucracies to determine categories of invention or forms of compensation may be overly cumbersome, some legislation designed to focus on situations where an occasional employer seeks to take advantage of an employee unable to bargain as an equal may be desirable. And legislation may be forthcoming. The objective is not to take rights away from the employer but rather to prevent a few of them—the unenlightened and the misinformed—from hurting themselves as well as others. In short, there is a need for balancing the equation, and some legislation may be helpful toward that end.

Appendix 1 □ Sample Conflict of Interests Statement*

Champion International Corporation

Champion Management,
To. Purchasing and Sales Personnel   *Date.* April 7, 1978
From. Andrew C. Sigler   *Subject.* Conflict of Interests

Each of you is aware that corporate surveys from time to time with respect to the matter of "conflict of interests" have become a standard practice. The Audit Committee of our Board of Directors has expressed the view that such a survey should be conducted annually and a report made on the results thereof to the Board of Directors and the shareholders. The enclosed questionnaire is intended to meet that purpose.

All addressees should realize that the avoidance of any conflict of interests simply means that an employee must not have any relationships or engage in any activities outside of Champion International which might have an adverse influence upon his independent judgment in performing his duties as an employee of Champion International.

For example, if an employee has a financial interest in a contractor or supplier of goods or services who is doing business with Champion International and if that employee is in a position to influence Champion International's business relations with that contractor or supplier, a natural conflict of interest arises which could work against the best interests of Champion International. Also, if an employee of Champion Interna-

*By permission from Champion International Corporation, Stamford, Connecticut.

tional accepts gifts or entertainment of significant value from a contractor or supplier, doing business with Champion International, that employee may either find himself under some sense of obligation or find himself in some manner influencing others to favor such contractor or supplier.

The basic policy is that a Champion International employee must not place himself in a position where he has a personal interest in any outside firm or receives substantial favors or benefits from an outside firm which may influence his decisions or advice about business transactions between Champion International, or any of its subsidiaries, and such outside firm.

We have great confidence in the integrity of each of you. This letter and the required return of the questionnaire have not the slightest implication to the contrary. Each of us has a right to be proud of our record of dedicated service to Champion International and should be ready to open the record for all concerned to approve. Periodic attention on the part of each of us to this matter of conflict of interest also serves a salutary purpose in order to assure that we do not by inadvertence compromise our responsibilities.

In consequence, I am addressing this letter of inquiry to all those whose duties and responsibilities may expose them to a conflict of interest situation. Each addressee is requested to return the completed questionnaire in the enclosed envelope as promptly as possible, and no later than April 24

If you have any questions about the enclosed questionnaire, our Legal Department stands ready to provide further clarification as may be required.

Signed. A. SIGLER

CONFIDENTIAL

Conflict of Interests Questionnaire*

April 7, 1978

1. Do you or, to your knowledge, do any members of your immediate family have any substantial financial interest in any firm or person doing business with Champion International Corporation or any of its subsidiaries?

        Yes   No

        If the answer is yes, please attach a detailed statement covering your relationship with that firm or person and the transactions with Champion International Corporation.

2. Have you received within the past 12 months, or are you now receiving commissions, gifts (other than minor items or casual entertainment), from any firm or person outside of Champion International Corporation that transacts business with Champion International Corporation or any of its subsidiaries?

        Yes   No

        If the answer is yes, please submit a detailed statement of the transactions involved and the amount and form of any commission, gift, reward or compensation you have received.

Print Name   _____

Home Address _____

Title and Location _____

Signature _____

IMPORTANT: Please return the questionnaire in the enclosed envelope via Company mail no later than _____

*Although you may have already disclosed information in answers to a prior questionnaire, please repeat any such information if it is currently applicable.

Appendix 2 □ Idea Submission Policy, Two Approaches

Immediately following is the detailed statement of policy for the Gillette Company on ideas submitted to the company for possible development and/or exploitation. Following that is a letter prepared by Champion International Corporation which must be signed before Champion will consider any suggestion offered from outside the company.

A Word About Ideas*

Each year Gillette receives thousands of letters from all over the world offering suggestions which the writers believe to be new, practical and valuable.

While we do not solicit or encourage the submission of these suggestions, we are always pleased—and grateful—for the interest shown by the public in Gillette and in our products.

Of course, we're interested in new ideas; it's our business to be interested in developments which might expand our product line or make our products more attractive, or which might increase the efficiency of our company's operations.

In the case of ideas offered by the public, however, we're concerned both with protecting the interests of the persons offering the ideas to us and with safeguarding Gillette itself against possible misunderstandings and unjustified claims.

This pamphlet explains something about our own research organization and consultants as well as the problems which face us in handling unsolicited suggestions from the public. It also states our company policy regarding consideration of ideas submitted by the public.

Almost All of Our Ideas Are Home-Grown

Our research scientists and experts are constantly at work in Gillette laboratories creating and developing new ideas . . . ideas that will speed up manufacturing processes . . . ideas that will cut costs . . . ideas that will expand our product line or make our products more attractive. We also retain large numbers of specialists outside the company, including advertising agencies, marketing consultants, and research laboratories.

For a great many years these experts, and their predecessors, have concentrated on the creation and development of ideas relating to new products, new processes, manufacturing, advertising, marketing and other aspects of our business operations.

At considerable expense to us, they have developed thousands of workable ideas now being used by Gillette. They have also created, explored and investigated countless other ideas, many of which may well be used by us in the future. In fact, hundreds of other ideas are even now in the process of being developed for us by our experts and outside consultants.

It's not surprising, therefore, that the vast majority of the suggestions which come to us from the general public duplicate or resemble ideas which we have already developed or know of, or are free to use.

Why An "Idea" Policy?

Because we consider the goodwill of the public one of our greatest assets, we have found it necessary to work out very carefully a clear and consistent policy on consideration of ideas received from the public.

While this policy has the drawback of preventing us from even considering certain types of suggestions, we are convinced it offers the greatest possible protection to persons who have ideas they believe can be profitable both to themselves and to Gillette.

If we were to consider all ideas sent to us, without any restrictions, we would run certain obvious risks.

For instance, if we were to consider patentable ideas before the inventor had complied with the patent laws and Patent Office regulations, misunderstandings and even costly litigation might result **notwithstanding the fact that the ideas were independently developed by us, or were known or freely available to us before they were submitted by persons outside the company.**

Similarly, if we were to consider submitted unpatentable ideas, we would run the risk of incurring ill-feeling or, in some cases, even doubt as to our good faith and integrity if the same ideas had been independently developed by us or were already in the public domain, and were subsequently used by our organization. Also, of course, in the case of unpatentable ideas we would not be able to acquire from the submitter legal rights of any appreciable value, as the ideas themselves may lack novelty and, in any event, would enter the public domain as soon as we used them, and could then be freely copied by others.

For these and other reasons, we have placed definite limitations on the types of suggestions we will consider. These limitations are spelled out in greater detail below.

What Ideas Will Gillette Consider?
We believe the United States patent system furnishes the greatest measure of protection for both the inventor and Gillette in these situations . . . and that the likelihood of misunderstandings arising between us is considerably less when the rights of the inventor are established under and measured by the patent laws.

We therefore will consider suggestions only if they have been fully disclosed in and protected by issued patents or filed patent

applications and are submitted on a completely non-confidential basis.

In other words, such suggestions will be dealt with only on the basis of a possible purchase of the applicable patent rights.

Suggestions Which Gillette Cannot Consider

It follows from what has been said in the preceding section that we cannot accept or consider ideas which either have not been protected by a patent or a patent application or which are inherently incapable of being protected under the patent laws Copyright protection alone is not sufficient to meet the policy requirement of patent protection.

The inherently unpatentable ideas we refer to include suggestions relating, for example, to the advertising or sale of our products, to proposed new uses for present products, to the addition of products to our present lines, or to changes in our methods of doing business.

Such ideas which cannot be legally protected rarely can be of more than nominal value to us—since our only advantage would be in the early use of an idea before our competitors might adopt it. By considering such ideas, Gillette could at best attain only a short-lived competitive advantage at the risk of misunderstanding and even legal claims.

We recognize that this policy does have some disadvantages for Gillette. For one thing, it does not allow us to consider a large number of ideas received from the general public, the people who use our products and on whose good will we depend for our successful operations. We regret this result, but at the same time hope the persons submitting such ideas will understand why we believe the legal risks involved outweigh the benefits which might be obtained from our considering such unprotected suggestions.

How To Submit Ideas And Suggestions

1. If you have an issued patent on an invention, just complete, sign and detach the first copy of the SUBMISSION FORM appearing at the end of this pamphlet and forward it to us with a printed copy of the patent. **If you have a model or specimen of your patented invention, all the significant features of which are disclosed in your patent please feel free to submit it as well.**

2. If you have filed a patent application but the patent has not yet been issued, and only if you are willing to submit the idea in accordance with the policy outlined in this pamphlet, please proceed as follows:

> a. Complete, sign and detach the first copy of the SUBMISSION FORM appearing at the end of this pamphlet and forward it to us with a copy of your filed patent application, but **do not** send us a copy of the "claims" portion of the application;
>
> b. If you desire, you may also submit with your patent application a model or specimen if all of its significant features are disclosed in the patent application. Naturally we cannot accept any responsibility for the safe arrival, handling or return of such models, although we will, of course, take reasonable measures to avoid damage or loss.

Should you be hesitant about disclosing the contents of your patent application under the terms of our policy, we strongly urge that you wait until your patent has been issued and has become a matter of public record before submitting it to us.

3. Submit your idea by letter. Unfortunately, the thousands of suggestions received each year make it impossible to arrange personal interviews to discuss all ideas. All inventions submitted by letter, however, are given the same consideration as if they had been submitted at a personal interview. After an invention has been submitted by letter, a personal interview may be arranged if it appears desirable.

4. In your communications to us limit the disclosures you make to the subject matter shown in your patent or patent application. As a protection to you and to Gillette, material disclosing additional ideas or suggestions will not be cleared for consideration by the company.

Communications With Gillette

All communications relating to the submission of ideas to us should be marked to the attention of **Director, Submitted Ideas Section** at the address shown in the SUBMISSION FORM.

Letters of this nature addressed generally to the company or to any executive or employee, whether by title or by name, are referred immediately to the Submitted Ideas Section and are not shown to or considered by the addressee until the requirements of our company policy have been met.

All letters which do not meet our policy requirements, and which therefore cannot be cleared for consideration on their merits, are retained in the office of the Submitted Ideas Section merely as a record of the correspondence. Related materials accompanying such letters will generally be returned to the submitter. Under no circumstances are any such letters or material revealed to any person connected with any "operating" department of our company such as persons concerned with the research, development, manufacture, sale, marketing or advertising of our products.

One Final Word

We have found that for various reasons, we are not interested in acquiring patent rights in the vast majority of suggestions which we have accepted for consideration. To explain fully the reasons for our lack of interest would, in many cases, require disclosure of our future business plans or of other information which we prefer to keep confidential. For this reason, in instances where we are not interested in obtaining the patent rights offered, we can **only** undertake to notify the submitter that we have considered the suggestion and do not wish to purchase the patent rights he offers us.

The SUBMISSION FORM following provides a means for you to indicate your agreement with and acceptance of our policy relative to submitted ideas. Any inventions or suggestions submitted should be accompanied by the original of this form, completed and signed by the inventor; the copy may be retained for your files.

SUBMISSION FORM

The Gillette Company   . . . ., 19 . . . . .
Prudential Tower Building
Boston, Massachusetts 02199

Attention: Director, Submitted Ideas Section
Gentlemen:
Enclosed is a copy of a patent and/or filed patent application (without the "claims" portion) which, in addition to all models and other related

materials (if any), presented to you now or later, are being submitted to you on a non-confidential basis, and in complete accordance with your policy on submitted ideas as set forth in your pamphlet entitled "A Word About Ideas" (from which this letter was removed), copy of which pamphlet I have received, read and understand.

I represent and warrant that I am the legal owner, or a duly authorized agent of the legal owner, of all rights in and to said patent and/or patent application, or of an undivided interest in said patent and/or patent application and further that all models and other related materials that I submit to you contain only subject matter which is specifically disclosed in my said patent and/or patent application.

In submitting this material to you for review, I agree that you will be under no obligation of any sort, of a trust, equitable or contractual nature, express or implied, or otherwise, my sole purpose being to offer you the opportunity to acquire the aforesaid patent rights. If you choose not to acquire those rights, you will be as free to contest the validity, scope or infringement of the patent or patents concerned as any third party, and just as if this material had never been sent to you.

The following items are submitted herewith:

1. Printed copy of patent No. _____dated . . . . .
2. Copy of patent application Serial No. _____
   filed _____

   (**NOTE:** If you prefer not to disclose the application filing data, merely identify it by its formal title and name (s) of the inventor (s). Please do **not** send us the "claims" portion of your patent application.)
3. Models: (If any are submitted, describe briefly.)

4. Other related material (s) also being submitted on a nonconfidential basis:

Very truly yours,

Sign here: ....
                    (Check the appropriate square, to show your status.)

☐ Patent or Patent Application Owner

☐ Duly Authorized Agent

....

....

(Address)

Suggestion Consideration Request*

Champion International Corporation

Evelyn M. Sommer   Stamford, Connecticut
Patent, Trademark and   06921
Copyright Counsel

Champion International Corporation
Stamford, Connecticut 06921

Gentlemen:

I have been informed by your representatives that you are willing to consider suggestions which may be made to Champion International Corporation by persons outside of Champion International Corporation, but that you require the acceptance by me of certain conditions before considering my suggestion or suggestions. These conditions are:

1. Champion International Corporation is willing to consider any suggestion which may be made, but does so only at the request of the person who has made the suggestion.

2. No obligation of any kind is assumed by, nor may be implied against, Champion International Corporation, unless or until a formal written contract has been entered into, and then the obligation shall be only such as is expressed in the formal written contract.

3. I do not hereby give Champion International Corporation any rights under any patents I now have or may later obtain, covering my suggestion(s) but I do hereby, in consideration of its examining my suggestion(s), release it from any liability in connection with my suggestion(s) or liability because of use of any portion thereof, except such liability as may

*By permission from Champion International Corporation, Stamford, Connecticut.

accrue under valid patents now or hereafter issued, and waive any rights that I may have against Champion International Corporation because of the use by Champion International Corporation of all unpatentable trade secrets and novel subject matter, if any, which are involved in the submitted matter.

I am agreeable to these conditions and ask you to consider my suggestion(s) under them.

_____

_____ , 19____

Appendix 3 □ Sample Consulting Agreements

Following are two sample consulting agreements devised to define and protect the relationship between an employing firm and a consultant hired by that firm for a specific project. Both of these agreements have actually been used by companies referring to consultants for specialized services, the second by a large multinational whose name is virtually a household word. Note the differences between the two with respect to degree of specificity on how confidentiality shall be maintained and protected.

Agreement #1

AGREEMENT made as of this   day of   ,
197_, between Name of Consultant—if individual state home address —if corporation state principal address and state of incorporation
(hereinafter called CONSULTANT), and ABC Corporation, a New Jersey corporation having its principal place of business at Summerview, New Jersey (hereinafter called ABC).

WITNESSETH:

WHEREAS, CONSULTANT has technical knowledge and expertise which will enable him to render professional services to ABC in the solution of problems related to

_____

_____

_____

_____

_____ ; and

WHEREAS, ABC desires to engage CONSULTANT'S services as herein defined; and

WHEREAS, CONSULTANT represents that he is under no obligation to any third party that would interfere with or conflict with his rendering professional services to ABC as hereinafter defined; and

WHEREAS, CONSULTANT desires to render professional services to ABC in the solution of specific problems in CONSULTANT's field of expertise;

NOW, THEREFORE, in consideration of the premises and of the mutual promises and covenants herein contained, the parties hereto agree as follows:

ARTICLE I

1. As part of his professional services hereunder, CONSULTANT shall, during the consulting period, advise and assist ABC in developing

_____

_____

_____

_____

2. CONSULTANT'S professional services shall include, but not be limited to, advising ABC on technical matters and suggesting solutions to technical problems in connection with ABC's programs as they involve or relate to the field of endeavor and/or products or processes described in Paragraph 1 above.

3. CONSULTANT shall in no sense be considered an employee of ABC nor shall he be entitled to or eligible to participate in benefits or privileges given or extended by ABC to its employees.

4. The consulting period shall extend from _____ to _____unless sooner terminated as provided herein.

5. CONSULTANT and ABC contemplate that CONSULTANT shall devote _____(   ) number of hours per week during the consulting period to the professional services required of him hereunder. In consideration thereof ABC will pay CONSULTANT a consulting fee at the rate of *(Amount written out)*
($ same amount in figures) payable *(monthly—semi-monthly, etc.)*

ARTICLE II

1. Any CONFIDENTIAL INFORMATION acquired by CONSULTANT with respect to any of ABC's existing or contemplated products processes, techniques, or know-how, or any information or data developed pursuant to the performance of the consulting services contemplated hereunder shall not be disclosed by CONSULTANT to others or used for CONSULTANT'S own benefit without the written consent of ABC. The obligations of CONSULTANT under this paragraph shall survive termination of this Agreement, provided, however, that CONSULTANT'S obligation to keep confidential shall not apply to information which
   a) was known to CONSULTANT, as evidenced by his written records, prior to the receipt of the disclosure; or
   b) was generally known to the public at the time of disclosure; or
   c) hereafter becomes generally known to the public through no fault of CONSULTANT.

2. CONSULTANT will not render services, directly or indirectly, to any person or organization which is engaged in or about to become engaged in research on or development of, or the production, marketing or selling of a product, process, or service which competes with a product, process or service of ABC during the term of this Agreement and for a period of

one (1) year after termination of this Agreement, without the written consent of ABC

3. Any inventions, improvements, or ideas made or conceived by CONSULTANT in connection with and during the performance of services hereunder and related to the business of ABC and for six (6) months thereafter, shall be the sole property of ABC and shall be reported to ABC promptly.

4. CONSULTANT, without charge to ABC shall execute, acknowledge and deliver to ABC all such papers and documents including applications for patent, as may be necessary to enable ABC to publish or protect said inventions, improvements, or ideas, by patent or otherwise in any and all countries and to vest title to said patents, inventions, improvements, and ideas in ABC, its successors or assigns. CONSULTANT shall render all such assistance as ABC may require in any Patent and Trademark Office proceeding or litigation in Federal or State Courts involving said inventions, improvements, or ideas, and shall be reimbursed for reasonable expenses incurred in connection therewith.

5. CONSULTANT, as part of the services to be performed hereunder, shall keep written notebook records of his work, properly witnessed for use as invention records, and shall submit such records to ABC when requested or at the termination of CONSULTANT'S services hereunder. CONSULTANT shall not, except at the direction of ABC reproduce, in whole or in part, any of said written notebook records.

ARTICLE III

1. ABC shall have the right to terminate this Agreement upon thirty (30) days written notice in the event of a breach or default of any of the terms of this Agreement by CONSULTANT or in the event that as a matter of policy, ABC decides to withdraw from further work or further investment in the field of endeavor described in Article I, Paragraph 1 of this Agreement for which the services of CONSULTANT were engaged.

2. It is expressly understood and agreed that in the event this Agreement is terminated, for any reason whatever, CONSULTANT's obligations herein with respect to confidential information, conflict of interest, and inventions, improvements, or ideas as set forth in Article II of this Agreement shall survive termination.

3. If any provision hereof is held invalid or unenforceable by a court of competent jurisdiction, it shall be considered severed from

this Agreement and shall not serve to invalidate the remaining provisions thereof.

_____   By   _____
(Consultant)   (Title) ABC Corporation

If consultant is a company, use
line for company name and have
title of officer who executes
agreement typed under his
signature.

Agreement #2

AGREEMENT made as of this   day of
         19   , between   residing at
                         (hereinafter called
CONSULTANT), and ABC Company, Inc.
a New Jersey corporation having offices at Summerview, New Jersey,
(hereinafter called ABC).

WITNESSETH

WHEREAS, CONSULTANT has technical knowledge and expertise which will enable him to render professional services to ABC in the solution of problems related to research and development in the field of

WHEREAS, ABC desires to engage CONSULTANT's professional services as herein defined; and

WHEREAS, CONSULTANT represents that he is under no obligation to any third party that would interfere with his rendering to ABC professional services as hereinafter defined; and

WHEREAS, CONSULTANT desires to render professional services to ABC in the solution of specific problems in CONSULTANT'S field of expertise;

NOW, THEREFORE, in consideration of the premises and of the mutual promises and convenants herein contained, the parties hereto agree as follows:

ARTICLE I

Where used in this Agreement, the following terms shall have the meaning attributed to them herein:

CONFLICTING PRODUCT means any   , product, process, machine or service or any person or organization other than ABC in existence or under development which competes with a product, process, machine or service upon or with which CONSULTANT has worked during the term of this Agreement with ABC and whose use or marketability could be enhanced by application to it of CONFIDENTIAL INFORMATION to which CONSULTANT shall have had access during the consulting period.

CONFLICTING ORGANIZATION means any person or organization which is engaged in or about to become engaged in research on or development, production, marketing, or selling of a CONFLICTING PRODUCT.

CONFIDENTIAL INFORMATION shall mean information disclosed to CONSULTANT or learned by CONSULTANT as a result of his rendering professional services hereunder not generally known in the trade or industry in which ABC is engaged, about products, processes, machines and services, including research, development, manufacturing, purchasing, finances, data processing, engineering, marketing, merchandising, and selling; and corresponding information about the products, processes, machines, and services of ABC affiliates, acquired by CONSULTANT during the consulting period.

ARTICLE II

1. As part of his professional services hereunder, CONSULTANT shall, during the consulting period, advise and assist ABC in developing products involving the use of   technology in the   field, including without limitation, the development of   and other   devices such as   . CONSULTANT'S professional services shall include, but not be limited to, advising ABC on technical matters and suggesting solutions to technical problems in connection with ABC's programs as they involve   technology. In particular, CONSULTANT will devote his consulting efforts hereunder to developing   for use with the   and/or being developed by ABC.

2. CONSULTANT shall in no sense be considered an employee of the Company nor shall he be entitled to or eligible to participate in any benefits or privileges given or extended by the Company to its employees. Nothing herein, however, shall prevent ABC and CONSULTANT, at any time, from mutually agreeing in writing to change CONSULTANT'S status to that of a regular employee of ABC.

ARTICLE III

1. The consulting period shall extend from   to   unless sooner terminated as provided herein.

2. CONSULTANT shall be obligated, during the term of the consulting period to provide ABC with professional services as herein defined.

3. ABC shall have the option, in its sole discretion, to terminate the consulting period on   , 19   , provided, however, that ABC shall advise CONSULTANT in writing of its decision to so terminate the consulting period not later than   , 19

4. CONSULTANT and ABC contemplate that CONSULTANT will devote thirty-two (32) hours per week during the consulting period to the professional services required of him hereunder. Upon agreement from time to time between ABC and CONSULTANT, CONSULTANT'S hours may be varied to suit the mutual convenience of CONSULTANT and ABC.

5. For that portion of the consulting period from   to   ABC will pay CONSULTANT a consulting fee at the annual rate of   Dollars. CONSULTANT shall be paid One-Twelfth ($^{1}/_{12}$) of said annual rate on the last day of each month beginning with   ,   19   and ending in   , 19

6. If, prior to   , 19   , ABC has developed a   on which CONSULTANT has been working and decides to subject same to   testing, or if ABC does not exercise its option under paragraph 3 of this ARTICLE III to terminate the consulting period, ABC shall pay CONSULTANT, on or about   , 19   , a bonus of   Dollars. ABC shall have the sole right to decide whether said   shall be subjected to   testing.

7. The bonus referred to in paragraph 6 of this Article shall be separate from, and in addition to, the consulting fee payable under paragraph 5 of this Article.

8. If ABC does not exercise its option under paragraph 3 of this Article,

then for that portion of the consulting period extending from
                , 19   to   , 19   ABC shall pay
CONSULTANT   a   consulting   fee   at   the   annual   rate   of
                        Dollars. CONSULTANT shall be paid One-Twelfth
($^{1}/_{12}$) of said annual rate on the last day of each month beginning with
                        , 19   and ending in   , 19

9. If ABC does not exercise its option under paragraph 3 of this Article, and if CONSULTANT performs his obligations hereunder, ABC shall pay to CONSULTANT, on or about   , 19   , a bonus of   Thousand Dollars. The bonus referred to in this paragraph shall be separate from, and in addition to, the bonus referred to in paragraph 6 of this Article and from the consulting fee payable under paragraph 8 of this Article III.

10. If ABC in exercise of its option under paragraph 3 of Article III, terminates the consulting period effective   , 19   ·,· and if ABC has not decided prior to   , 19   , that it will test a   on which CONSULTANT has been working, then ABC shall pay CONSULTANT, on or about   , 19EM   , the sum of   Dollars in addition to the consulting fee payable under paragraph 5 of this Article.

ARTICLE IV

1. Any CONFIDENTIAL INFORMATION acquired by CONSUL-TANT with respect to any of ABC's existing or contemplated machines, products, processes, techniques, or Know-how, or any information or data developed pursuant to the performance of the consulting services contemplated hereunder shall not be disclosed by CONSULTANT to others or used for CONSULTANT'S own benefit without written consent of ABC. The obligations of CONSULTANT under this paragraph shall survive termination of this Agreement, provided, however, that CONSULTANT's obligation to keep confidential shall not apply to information which

   a)   was known to CONSULTANT, as evidenced by his written
        records, prior to the receipt of the disclosure; or
   b)   was generally known to the public at the time of disclosure; or
   c)   hereafter becomes generally known to the public through no
        fault of CONSULTANT.

2. CONSULTANT will not render services, directly or indirectly, to any CONFLICTING ORGANIZATION in the United States, Canada, or any of the countries in the European Economic Community (Common Market) for a period of two (2) years after termination of

this Agreement with ABC except that CONSULTANT may render services to a CONFLICTING ORGANIZATION whose business is diversified and which is, as to that part of its business in which CONSULTANT agrees to render services, not a CONFLICTING ORGANIZATION provided ABC prior to CONSULTANT'S rendering such services shall receive written assurances from such CONFLICTING ORGANIZATION and from CONSULTANT, that CONSULTANT will not render services, directly or indirectly, in connection with any CONFLICTING PRODUCT.

3. Nothing herein shall require CONSULTANT to divulge to ABC information received in confidence from a third party.

ARTICLE V

1. Any inventions, improvements, or ideas made or conceived by CONSULTANT in connection with and during the performance of services hereunder and related to the business of ABC and for six (6) months thereafter, shall be the sole property of ABC, and shall be reported to ABC promptly.

2. CONSULTANT, without charge to ABC other than reasonable payment for time involved in the event the services contemplated hereunder shall have terminated, but at ABC's expense, shall execute, acknowledge, and deliver to ABC: all such further papers, including applications for patents, as may be necessary to enable ABC to publish or protect said inventions, improvements, and ideas by patent or otherwise in any and all countries and to vest title to said patents, inventions, improvements, and ideas in ABC, or its nominees, their successors or assigns, and shall render all such assistance as ABC may require in any Patent Office proceeding or litigation involving said inventions, improvements, or ideas.

3. CONSULTANT, as part of the services to be performed hereunder, shall keep written notebook records of his work, properly witnessed for use as invention records, and shall submit such records to ABC when requested or at the termination of CONSULTANT'S services hereunder. CONSULTANT shall not, except at the direction of ABC, reproduce, in whole or in part, any of said written notebook records.

ARTICLE VI

1. This Agreement shall be construed, and the legal relations between the parties determined, in accordance with the laws of the State of New Jersey.

2. CONSULTANT shall not originate any publicity, news release, or other public announcement, written or oral, whether to the public press

other public announcement, written or oral, whether to the public press or otherwise, relating to this Agreement, to any amendment hereto or to performance hereunder, without the prior written approval of ABC.

3. If either party of this Agreement defaults or materially breaches the terms of this Agreement other than by reason of force majeure, the other party shall have the right to cancel this Agreement by giving written notice by Registered Mail to that effect to the defaulting party thirty (30) days in advance of the date of cancellation specified in the notice. However, if the default or breach is corrected or made good by the party receiving notice within thirty (30) days after the notice of termination has been received, this Agreement shall not be cancelled but shall remain in full force and effect.

4. If any provision hereof is held invalid or unenforceable by a court of competent jurisdiction, it shall be considered severed from this Agreement and shall not serve to invalidate the remaining provisions thereof.

ABC COMPANY

_____   By _____
CONSULTANT   (Title)

Appendix 4 □ Sample Employment Agreements

The first two agreements following are in use by a large American chemical corporation. Note the difference between that required for nontechnical employees and that required for technical employees.

The third employment agreement is one made with a key employee of a company being sold. In this instance there is an explicit acknowledgment that the employee is considered one of the company's major assets, and the purpose of the agreement is clearly to assure the employee's remaining with the company through the period of sale.

The fourth agreement here is an example of a deferred compensation agreement containing a restrictive covenant designed to discourage the employee from later entering into competition with his present employer.

ABC Company, Inc. and Subsidiaries

Employment Agreement (Nontechnical Employees)

This Agreement is signed by me as a condition and in consideration of my employment by ABC Company, Inc. ("ABC") or, if employed by a Subsidiary, of my employment thereby. For the purposes of this agreement, "Subsidiary" means any corporation fifty percent or more of the voting capital stock of which is owned directly or indirectly by ABC, and "the Company" means ABC or the Subsidiary by which I am employed at the time.

1. With respect to all information, whatever its nature and form and whether obtained orally, by observation, from written materials or otherwise, except such as is generally available to the public through publication, obtained by me during or as the result of my employment by ABC or a Subsidiary and relating to any products, apparatus or processes, to any uses thereof or therefor, to raw material or product prices or costs (including manufacturing costs) or to any research, technical, manufacturing or commercial activities or plans of ABC or any Subsidiary, I agree:

   a. To hold all such information, in strict confidence, and not publish or otherwise disclose any thereof except to or with the prior consent of an authorized representative of the Company.
   b. To use all reasonable precautions to assure that all such information is properly protected and kept from unauthorized persons.
   c. To make no use of any such information except such use as is required in the performance of my duties for the Company.
   d. Upon termination of my employment by the Company, or upon request of the Company, to deliver to the Company all written materials and all substances, models, mechanisms and the like containing or relating to such information, all of which written materials and other things shall be and remain the sole property of the Company. For this purpose, "written materials" shall be deemed to mean and include letters, memoranda, reports, notes, notebooks, books of account, data, drawings, prints, plans, specifications, formulae and all other documents or writings, and all copies thereof.

2. My obligations under Paragraph 1 above shall remain in effect both during my employment by ABC or any Subsidiary and thereafter, whatever the reason for termination of such employment, and shall survive any termination of this agreement.

3. I shall not be requested or required to violate, and I agree to respect, any valid obligations I now have to prior employers or others relating to proprietary or confidential information.

4. I agree to perform and carry out diligently, faithfully and to the best of my ability all duties assigned and instructions given to me by authorized personnel of the Company, to comply with the rules, regulations, policies and procedures of the Company, and to act and comport myself at all times in the best interests of the Company.

5. This agreement supersedes any prior agreements executed by me with or in favor of ABC or any Subsidiary, any such prior agreements being deemed to have remained in effect up to the date hereof.

IN WITNESS WHEREOF, I, _____, have signed this agreement in duplicate, retaining one signed and dated copy, this . . . . .day of _____, 19 . . . . .

_____L.S.

WITNESS: _____

ABC Company, Inc.
and Subsidiaries

Employee Agreement
(Technical Employees)

This Agreement is signed by me as a condition and in consideration of my employment by ABC Company, Inc. ("ABC") or, if employed by a Subsidiary, of my employment thereby. For the purposes of this agreement, "Subsidiary" means any corporation fifty percent or more of the voting capital stock of which is owned directly or indirectly by ABC, and "the Company" means ABC or the Subsidiary by which I am employed at the time.

1. With respect to information, inventions and discoveries, including improvements, developed, made or conceived by me, either alone or with others, at any time, within or without normal working hours, during my employment by ABC or a Subsidiary, arising out of such employment or pertinent to any field of business or research in which, during such employment, ABC or any Subsidiary is engaged or (if such is known to or ascertainable by me) is considering engaging, I agree:

   a. That all such information, inventions and discoveries, whether or not patented or patentable, shall be and remain the sole property of the Company.

   b. To disclose promptly to an authorized representative of the Company all such information, inventions and discoveries, and all information in my possession as to possible applications thereof to industry and other uses thereof or therefor.

c.   Not to file any patent applications relating to any such invention or discovery except with the prior consent of an authorized representative of the Company.

d.   At the request of the Company, and without expense to me, to execute such documents and perform such other acts as the Company deems necessary to obtain patents on such inventions and discoveries in any jurisdiction or jurisdictions and to assign to the Company or its designees such inventions and discoveries and any patent applications, whether or not active, and patents relating thereto.

2. With respect both to information, inventions and discoveries referred to in Paragraph 1 and to all other information, whatever its nature and form and whether obtained orally, by observation, from written materials or otherwise, except such as is generally available to the public through publication, obtained by me during or as the result of my employment by ABC or a Subsidiary and relating to any products, apparatus or processes, to any uses thereof or therefor, to raw material or product prices or costs (including manufacturing costs) or to any research, technical, manufacturing or commercial activities or plans of ABC or any Subsidiary, I agree:

a.   To hold all such information, inventions and discoveries in strict confidence, and not publish or otherwise disclose any thereof except to or with the prior consent of an authorized representative of the Company.

b.   To use all reasonable precautions to assure that all such information, inventions and discoveries are properly protected and kept from unauthorized persons.

c.   To make no use of any such information, invention or discovery except such use as is required in the performance of my duties for the Company.

d.   Upon termination of my employment by the Company, or upon request of the Company, to deliver to the Company, all written materials and all substances, models, mechanisms and the like containing or relating to such information, inventions or discoveries, all of which written materials and other things shall be and remain the sole property of the Company. For this purpose, "written materials" shall be deemed to mean and include letters, memoranda, reports, notes, notebooks, books of account, data, drawings, prints, plans, specifications, formulae and all other documents or writings, and all copies thereof.

3. My obligations under Paragraphs 1 and 2 above shall remain in effect both during my employment by ABC or any Subsidiary and thereafter, whatever the reason for termination of such employment, and shall survive any termination of this agreement.

4. All inventions and discoveries developed, made or conceived prior to my employment by ABC or a Subsidiary which as of the date of commencement of such employment I owned or in or to which I had an interest or right, other than those patented prior to such employment, are identified on the back hereof. Any such inventions or discoveries not so patented or listed shall be deemed made or conceived during such employment. Subject to the foregoing, I shall not be requested or required to assign or disclose any inventions or discoveries developed, made or conceived prior to such employment, or information relating thereto.

5. I shall not be requested or required to violate, and I agree to respect, any valid obligations I now have to prior employers or others relating to proprietary or confidential information and to my inventions and discoveries. I have supplied or promptly shall supply to the Company copies of written agreements containing any such obligations.

6. I agree to perform and carry out diligently, faithfully and to the best of my ability all duties assigned and instructions given to me by authorized personnel of the Company, to comply with the rules, regulations, policies and procedures of the Company, and to act and comport myself at all times in the best interests of the Company.

7. This agreement shall bind my heirs, executors, administrators, legal representatives and assigns, and supersedes any prior agreements executed by me with or in favor of ABC or any Subsidiary, any such prior agreements being deemed to have remained in effect up to the date hereof.

8. No waiver or amendment of any provision of this agreement shall be valid or effective unless in writing signed by the party against whom enforcement thereof is sought.

IN WITNESS WHEREOF, I, _____, have signed this agreement, retaining one signed and dated copy, this . . . . .day of ___ _____, 19 . . . . .

_____L.S.

WITNESS: _____

Agreement with Key Employee of a Company Being Sold

THIS AGREEMENT made and entered into this
day of   , 19   , between American, Inc., a
Delaware Corporation, having its principal office at

(hereinafter called the "Company") and John Q. Smith, whose
address is
                        (hereinafter called the "Employee").

W I T N E S S E T H :

WHEREAS, Employee is presently employed by the Company in its
Famous Product Subsidiary (hereinafter called FPS) located in Alaska,
and it is represented and acknowledged between the Company and Employee that Employee is a "key" employee of FPS who works for the
Company in a position of mutual trust and confidence, and in such capacity said Employee is privy to confidential information of the Company
relating to said FPS, including, but not limited to, information relating
to research, development, purchasing, accounting, engineering, marketing, merchandising and selling; and

WHEREAS, the Company is negotiating for the sale of FPS to National
CORPORATION, a New York corporation, having its principal office at
260 Madison Ave., New York, New York 10016 (hereinafter called National) and

WHEREAS, the Company desires to retain the services of said Employee for FPS and further desires the right to transfer said services to
National as part of the sale of FPS to National and

WHEREAS, Employee desires to remain with FPS in the event of its
sale to National.

NOW, THEREFORE, in consideration of the mutual premises hereinafter set forth, the parties agree as follows:

I. *Definitions*

As used in this Employment Agreement, the terms defined below shall
have the following meanings:

(a) The "Company" means American, Inc. or any affiliated or related
company including its successors and assigns.

(b) FPS means the Famous Product Subsidiary, a component of National Corporation, including the successors and assigns to said FPS
component.

(c) "Confidential Information" means information not generally known, about FPS's processes and products including information relating to research, development, manufacture, purchasing, accounting, engineering, marketing, merchandising and selling.

(d) "Inventions" means discoveries, improvements and ideas (whether patentable or not) related to any activities of FPS.

(e) "Conflicting Product" means any product or process of any person or organization other than FPS, in existence or under development, which resembles or competes with a product or process upon which Employee worked during the last two years of his employment by the Company or about which he acquired Confidential Information through his work with the Company.

(f) "Conflicting Organization" means any person or organization engaged in, or about to become engaged in, research on or development, production, marketing, or selling of a "Conflicting Product."

II. In consideration of the representations made by the Employee and the obligations he assumes in this Agreement, the Company agrees:

A. To retain the services of the Employee for a period of two (2) years from the date of this agreement unless terminated in the manner provided herein or at the death of the Employee, whichever occurs first.

B. That the Employee shall receive an annual salary of $, to be paid in twelve (12) monthly installments.

C. That he shall promptly be given the title of   and that his responsibility, duty and authority shall be reasonably consistent with that title.

D. That he shall not be transferred geographically to a location outside of Alaska without his written consent thereto.

III. The Employee hereby makes the following representations and commitments:

A. I, the undersigned Employee, represent and acknowledge that I am a key employee of FPS, that I play an instrumental role in the business of FPS and in that capacity I am familiar with and in possession of "Confidential Information."

B. I am aware of the pending sale of assets of FPS to National and I recognize that this Employment Agreement is in contemplation of such sale and shall have no force and effect in the event said sale is not consummated prior to January 1, 198   or such later date as American and National may agree upon in writing.

C. I agree that for the remunerations and other considerations set forth in this Agreement, and in recognition of the fact that as a key employee of FPS, my continued loyalty to FPS is an essential element of its sale to National, I accept and will abide by the following terms and conditions:

(1.) From and after the date of this Agreement, I will not engage in any business or other activity except as required in the normal course of my work as an employee for FPS and furthermore, I agree not to engage in any business or other activity, or render services, directly or indirectly, to or for any Conflicting Organization in connection with research, development, manufacturing, purchasing, accounting, engineering, marketing, merchandising, and selling of Conflicting Products for a period of at least one (1) year subsequent to termination of my employment with FPS. Furthermore, I agree not to accept any employment during said one (1) year period without giving the Company at least thirty (30) days written notice prior to engaging in such employment and that the notice shall specify the name and address of my new employer.

(2.) If I am unable to obtain employment consistent with my training and education, solely because of the conditions of Paragraph IIIC(1.), such provisions shall bind me only as long as the Company shall make payments to me equal to my monthly rate of pay at termination (exclusive of extra compensation or employee benefits) for each of said month of unemployment, provided I comply with all of the other provisions of this Agreement. I will, during each month of such unemployment for which I claim payment, give the Company a detailed written account of my efforts to obtain employment, and such account will include a statement by me that although I conscientiously sought employment, I was unable to obtain it solely because of the provisions of this Paragraph.

I understand that the obligation of the Company to make payment as provided herein shall be incurred only after it receives a claim for payment in writing. I understand further that the Company shall be relieved of making a monthly payment to me for any month during which I have failed to account to the Company and make a claim for payment as provided above.

The Company is obligated to make such payments to me upon my fulfillment of the conditions set forth above for twelve (12) consecutive months unless the Company gives me written permission to accept available employment, or gives me a written release from my obligations as stated in Paragraph IIIC(1.).

The Company's obligation to make such monthly payments shall, in any event, either expire one (1) year from the termination of my employment with the Company or upon my obtaining employment during said year which does not conflict with my obligations under this Agreement.

The Company shall not be liable, under this Agreement, or any action relating thereto, for any amount greater than the equivalent of twelve (12) monthly payments.

D. With respect to "Inventions" made or conceived by me, either solely or jointly with others, I agree that during (i) my employment, or (ii) within one year after termination of my employment:

(1.) I will promptly and fully inform the Company in writing of such "Inventions."

(2.) I shall assign (and I do hereby assign) to the Company any and all rights to said "Inventions," and to applications for Letters Patent and to Letters Patent granted upon said "Inventions."

(3.) I acknowledge and shall deliver promptly to the Company (without charge to the Company, but at the expense of the Company) such written instruments and shall do such other acts as may be necessary in the opinion of the Company to obtain and maintain Letters Patent and invest the entire right and title thereto in the Company.

E. EXCEPT as required in my duties to the Company, I will never use or disclose any "Confidential Information."

F. Upon termination of my employment with the Company, all records of "Confidential Information" including copies thereof in my possession, whether prepared by me or others, will be left with the Company.

G. Except as expressly set forth on a schedule attached to this Agreement, or as set forth in the records of FPS, I make no claims to any prior Inventions and I shall not assert any rights under any Inventions as having been made or acquired by me prior to my being employed by the Company.

IV. This Agreement may be terminated:

(i) By the Employee or the Company, following the two-year period provided for in Paragraph II above, effective at such time as shall be specified by notice in writing to the other party, which time shall not be less than (30) days from the date of giving such notice; or

(ii) By the Employee at such time following two (2) years from the date hereof as he shall elect to retire in the event that he is eligible for retirement under any applicable provisions of the Company's pension and retirement plans.

(iii) By the Company effective at such time as shall be specified by notice to Employee in the event of his disability or incapacity, which time shall not, however, be less than (30) days from the date of giving such notice, provided, however, that such notice shall be of no effect and this Agreement shall continue in full force and effect if prior to the date of termination specified in such notice such condition has ceased to exist.

For the purposes hereof "disability" or "incapacity" shall mean Employee's inability to perform the duties assigned to him hereunder by reason of physical or mental impairment which can be expected to result in death or to be of long-continued and indefinite duration' and such condition shall be deemed to exist (or, if having been found to exist, shall be deemed no longer to exist) when so certified in writing by a disinterested licensed physician or psychiatrist selected by the Company or, if Employee so elects by notice to the Company, by two out of three such physicians or psychiatrists selected by the Company, or when determined to exist (or no longer to exist) by a court of competent jurisdiction. Such disability or incapacity shall be deemed to have commenced (or no longer to exist) upon the date determined by and specified in a certificate of such physician(s) or psychiatrist(s) or upon the date determined by a court as aforesaid. Employee agrees to submit to examination and diagnosis by such physician(s) or psychiatrist(s) selected by the Company or by such court. In the event of termination for disability under this paragraph, Employee will receive those disability benefits normally provided by the Company to its employees.

(iv) In any event it is understood and agreed that this Agreement may be terminated for cause by the Company at any time solely on the discretionary determination by the Company that the Employee is not performing his duties in a satisfactory manner. However, the Company shall not exercise such discretion in an unreasonable manner.

(v) The provisions of Paragraph III shall survive termination.

V. This Agreement shall be binding upon and shall inure to the benefit of the heirs, executors, administrators, legal representatives, successors and assigns, as the case may be, of each party hereto, and this Agreement, its rights and obligations shall be assignable by the Company, but not by Employee without the written consent of the Company.

It is expressly understood and agreed that this Agreement is entered into in contemplation of assignment to National as part of a transaction whereby National acquires the assets of FPS. Such assignment is to take place on the closing of the transaction pursuant to which American will assign the assets of FPS, which closing shall take place on or before   , or on such later date as American and National may agree upon in writing, and National agrees that it will at said closing accept such assignment and agree to be bound by the terms and provisions of this Agreement from and after the date of closing. In the event that the Agreement between American and National described herein shall not be closed as provided above, this Agreement shall be null and void.

In the event this Agreement is assigned to National as provided above, Employee shall be eligible for and receive all of the employee benefits including but not limited to compensation plans, insurance, disability, hospitalization and retirement benefits on the same terms and conditions that National normally provides to its employees.

It is further understood that in the event of the assignment of this

Agreement to National, Employee shall execute whatever forms are customarily required of National employees and shall not, during the term of his employment by National, receive or accept remuneration for services rendered to anyone, for any endeavor, other than from National, except and unless authorized to do so in writing by an official of National. This provision shall not bar receipt of income from investments or from sources not requiring the rendering of any personal services to a conflicting organization.

VI. Any notice permitted or required to be given by this Agreement shall be in writing and shall be deemed given if sent by Registered Mail to the address first above written.

VII. No waiver by either party of any breach of the provisions of this Agreement shall operate or be construed as a waiver of any other or subsequent breach thereof.

VIII. This Agreement contains the entire understanding of the parties hereto and none of its provisions may be waived, amended or modified or supplemented, nor any discharge with respect thereto effected orally, but only by an instrument in writing signed by the Company and myself.

IX. This Agreement shall be construed and governed by the laws of the State of Delaware.

IN WITNESS WHEREOF, the Company has caused these presents to be signed by its duly authorized officer and its corporate seal to be hereunto affixed and attested, and I, the Employee, hereunto set my hand and seal, all as of the day and year first above written.

AMERICAN INC.
By _____

_____
John Q. Smith (Employee)

National hereby accepts the obligations made by it pursuant to the provisions of Paragraph V of this Agreement and with respect thereto has caused these presents to be signed by its duly authorized officer and its corporate seal to be hereunto affixed and attested as of the day and year first above written.

NATIONAL CORP.

By _____

Deferred Compensation Agreement (With Restrictive Covenant)

THIS AGREEMENT, made and entered into this
day of   , 19   , by and between THE AMERICAN
CORPORATION, a Delaware corporation (Company), and John Q.
Smith (Officer).

WITNESSETH:

Company is engaged in the purchase, transportation, marketing and
sale, of health care products.

Officer, for the compensation fixed from time to time by the Board of
Directors of Company, is employed in an executive capacity.

To provide an incentive and reward to Officer to contribute his ability,
industry and loyalty to advance the success of Company, to induce Officer
to continue in the service of Company and to discourage competition by
Officer should his employment by Company be terminated, Company
and Officer hereby covenant and agree as follows:

I.

Amount:

When Officer's employment is terminated by Officer or by Company,
whether because of death, retirement, disability, resignation or any other
reason, Company, subject to the other terms, provisions and conditions
set out below, agrees to pay, in the manner and at the times set out below,
to Officer, or to his surviving widow, or to his minor children, the amount
of deferred compensation ("DCA") specified and/or calculated as below,
to-wit:

A. If, at the time of termination of his employment by Company,
Officer has been in the employ of Company for at least 120
months (10 years) from January 1, 19   , the DCA shall be
$

B. If, at the time of termination of his employment by Company,
Officer has been employed for less than 120 months (10 years)
from January 1, 19   , the amount shall be a sum calculated

by multiplying .8 1/3% of the amount specified in I A above by the number of months, and   fractions thereof, during which Officer was employed by Company; provided, however, if Officer's employment by Company is terminated by reason of disability, which, in the opinion of a physician designated by Company, is total, or by reason of his death, then the DCA shall be the amount specified in A above, regardless of the duration of his employment by Company.

II.

Method of Payment:

A. The DCA herein provided shall be paid in 120 equal monthly installments, save and except that Officer may elect, as evidenced by written instructions to Company, to have the DCA paid, in equal monthly installments during any number of months in excess of 120 but not more than 240.

B. The first of the monthly payments herein provided and contemplated shall be payable not later than the fifth day of the month next succeeding the month during which Officer dies, retires, or is totally disabled, or during which his employment by Company is terminated for some other reason, and the succeeding installments shall be paid on or before the fifth day of each month thereafter.

III.

Payee:

A. If the termination of Officer's employment by Company is for some reason other than his death, the DCA shall be paid to Officer.

B. If the termination of Officer's employment by Company is caused by his death, or if he should die prior to payment by Company of the entirety of the DCA, the DCA, or the balance thereof remaining unpaid at the time of his death, as the case may be, shall be paid to his wife, if he be survived by a wife, or, in the absence of a surviving widow, to the children of Officer who are then living and who are under 20 years of age.

C. If, in accordance with the provisions of immediately preceding subparagraph B, all or a portion of the DCA is payable to the surviving widow of Officer, and if such surviving widow should die prior to the payment by Company of the entirety of the DCA, the balance of the DCA remaining unpaid at the time of the death of the surviving widow shall be paid, in equal shares, to the children

of Officer who are then living and who are under the age of 21
years at the time of the death of the surviving widow, provided,
however, that no payment shall be made to any such child after
such child shall have attained the age of 21 years. The amount
being paid to any such child, upon his or her death prior to reaching 21 years or upon his or her attaining age 21, shall be paid,
proportionately to such other child or children of Officer who are
under age 21.

D. Payments to any child under the age of 21 years shall be made
to such child or to the trustee of a trust for the benefit of such child
in the manner designated by Officer before his death, or, in the
absence of such designation by Officer, by Officer's surviving
widow.

E. Such payments may be made with the check of Company and,
in the event any change in beneficiary, Company shall be entitled
to suspend and defer further payments until Company shall have
been furnished with written proof, satisfactory in form and content
to Company, evidencing such change of beneficiary.

F. Notwithstanding any provision herein contained to the contrary, the obligation of Company to pay the DCA and/or the unpaid balance thereof, shall terminate upon (1) the date of death of
Officer, (2) the date of death of his surviving widow, if any, or (3)
the date the youngest of his surviving children who is then living
attains the age of 21 years, whichever is the latter date.

IV.

Termination [*Restrictive Covenant*]:

Officer covenants and agrees that after his employment by Company has terminated he will not, directly or indirectly, in any capacity whatsoever, own, become associated with, or engage in or
render service, aid, or comfort of any kind to any business engaged
in the purchase, transportation, marketing and sale, of health care
products.

If Officer should violate this covenant, Company's obligation to
pay the DCA and/or the balance of the DCA remaining unpaid at

the time of such violation, shall immediately terminate and be of no further force or effect.

V.

Service of Employee:

A. Prior to termination of his employment by Company, Officer covenants and agrees to perform, to the best of his ability, his duties in the capacity in which he is employed in accordance with the directions of Company and to devote to the performance of such duties his full time and attention, and will not become associated with or engage or render service to any business other than that of Company.

B. Subsequent to termination of Officer's employment by Company, Officer agrees to render to Company such services of an advisory or consultative nature as Company may reasonably request so that Company may continue to have the benefit of his experience and knowledge of the affairs of Company and of his reputation and contacts in the industry.

VI.

Assignment:

Subject only to the privilege granted in Paragraph III D above, neither Officer nor any of the beneficiaries specified in Paragraph III above may assign, mortgage or otherwise hypothecate, without the written consent of Company, any of the rights herein granted by Company.

VII.

Successors:

The provisions hereof shall inure to the benefit of and be binding upon Company, its subsidiaries and its successors, if any, irrespective of the mode or manner of succession, be it by statutory merger, consolidation, the result of sale of all or substantially all of the assets of Company or its successors, or otherwise.

VIII.

This DCA is in lieu of all other retirement benefits in American
Corporation. The employee receiving a DCA
will not participate in any other American Corporation retirement
benefits unless mutually agreed on by and between the Company
and employee.

WITNESS THE EXECUTION HEREOF this   day of
, 19

_____

Officer

THE AMERICAN CORPORATION

_____

By: President

Reference List of Cases Cited

Aetna Bldg. Maintenance Co., Inc. v. *West et al.* 39 Cal. 2d 158, 246 P. 2d 11 (1952)

Alex Foods, Inc. v. *Metcalfe & Torgerson* 137 Cal. App. 2d 415, 290 P. 2d 646 (1955)

Anchor Alloys, Inc. v. *Non-Ferrous Processing Corp.* 39 A.D. 2d 504, 336 N.Y.S. 2d 944, 176 USPQ 125 (1972)

Aronson v. *Quick Point Pencil Co.*, 440 U.S. 257, 59 L.Ed. 296, 99 S. Ct. 1096 (1979)

Banner Metals, Inc. v. *Lockwood et al.*, 178 CA 2d 661 125 USPQ 29 (1960)

Blacksmiths of South-Mims, 2 Leo. 210, 74 Eng. Rep. 485 [C.P. 1587]

Block, H & R Inc. v. *McCaslin*, 541 F. 2d 1098 Cert. denied 430 US 946 (CA 5, 1976)

Carmen v. *Fox Film Corp.*, 258 F. 703 reversed for other reasons 269 F 928 (1913)

Carter Products, Inc. v. *Colgate-Palmolive Co.*, 130 F.Supp. 557, 104 USPQ 314 (1955) affm'd. 230 F. 2d 855, 108 USPQ 383

Casey v. *Educational Technology Inc.*, NYLJ, 9-1-72 p.16 (S. Ct., N.Y., 1972)

City Ice & Fuel Co. v. *McKee*, 57 S.W. (2d) 443 (1933)

Conmar Products Corporation v. *Universal Slide Fastener Co., Inc.*, 172 F. 2d 150, 80 USPQ 108 (1949)

Crouch, A. C. et al. v. *Swing Machinery Company, Inc.* 468 S.W. 2d 604 (1971)

Davies v. *Carnation Company*, 352 F 2d 393 147 USPQ 350 (1965)

Doughtry v. *Capital Gas Co., Inc.*, 229 So. 2d 480 (1969)

Dunlop Holdings Ltd. v. *Ram Golf Corp.*, 524 F. 2d 33, 188 USPQ 481 (1975) Cert. denied, 424 U.S. 958, 96 S.Ct. 1435 189 USPQ 256 (1976)

Dunn v. *Frank Miller Associates, Inc.*, 237 Ga. 266, 227 S.E. 2d 243 (1976)

duPont, E. I. de Nemours & Co. v. *American Potash & Chemical Corp.*, 200 A. 2d 428, 141 USPQ 447 (1964) *duPont, E. I. de Nemours & Co.* v. *Christopher,* 431 F. 2d 1012, 166 USPQ 421 (1970) cert. denied 400 U.S. 1024 168 USPQ 385 (1971)

Dyer's Case, Y.B. Mich. 2 Hen. 5, f.5, pl. 26 (C.P.1414)

Educational Sales Programs, Inc. v. *The Dreyfus Corporation* 169 USPQ 117 (1970)

Electrical Transmission Ltd. v. *Dannenberg,* 66 R.P.C. 183 (U.K., 1949)

Engineering Associates, Inc. v. *Pankow,* 268 N.C. 137, 150 S.E. 2d 56 (1966)

Escott v. *Bar Chris Construction Corp.,* 283 F. Supp 643 (S.D. NY 1968)

Eutectic Corporation v. *Astralloy-Vulcan Corporation,* 510 F. 2d 1111, 182 USPQ 321 (1974)

Gaines v. *Jones,* 486 F. 2d 39 (1973) Cert. denied 415 U.S. 919

Gilder v. *Housebow Hotels,* 419 S.W. 2d 70, Supreme Court of Missouri

Goodrich, B. F. Co. v. *Wohlgemuth,* 117 Ohio App. 493, 192 N.E. 2d 99, 137 USPQ 804 (1963)

Graham v. *John Deere Co.,* 383 U.S. 1, 86 S.Ct. 684, 15 L. Ed. 2d 545 (1966)

Guth v. *Minnesota Mining & Mfg. Co.,* 72 F. 2d 385 22 USPQ 89 (1934) Cert. denied 294 U.S. 711

Head Ski Company v. *Kam Ski Company,* 158 F.Supp 919, 116 USPQ 242 (1958)

Hecht Foods, Inc. v. *Sherman,* 43 A.D. 2d 850 351 N.Y.S. 2d 711 (1974)

Hillman v. *Hodag Chemical Corporation,* 96 Ill. App. 2d 204, 238 N.E. 2d 145 (1968)

Houghton v. *United States,* 23 F. 2d 386 (1928) Cert. denied 277 U.S. 592

Ingle Bros. Pacific, Inc. v. *Scott,* 478 S.W. 2d 210 (1972)

Jackson v. *Walton,* 2 La. App. 53 (1935)

Jamesbury Corp. v. *Worcester Valve Co.,* Inc. 443 F 2d 205 170 USPQ 177 (1971)

Kadis v. *Britt,* 224 N.C. 154, 29 S.E. 2d 543, 152 ALR 405 (1944)

Kenco Chemical and Manufacturing Co., Inc. v. *G. Brett Railey, Jr.,* CCH 1973-2 Trade Cases 74, 834

Lektro-Vend Corp. v. *Vendo Company,* 403 F.Supp. 527 reversed for other reasons 433 US 623 (1975)

Lochner v. *New York* 198 US 45 (1905)

Loescher v. *Policky,* 173 N.W. 2d 50 (1969)

Markson Bros. v. *Redick,* 164 Pa. Superior Court 499 (1949)

McCombs v. *McClelland,* 354 P. 2d 311 (1960)

Mitchell v. *Reynolds,* 1 P.Wms. 181, 24 Eng.Rep. 347 (Q.B. 1711)

Monsanto Chemical Co. v. *Miller,* 118 USPQ 74 (1958)

Motorola, Inc. v. *Fairchild Camera & Instrument Corp.,* 366 F.Supp. 1173, 177 USPQ 614 (1973)

New Jersey Zinc Co. v. *Singmaster,* 71 F. 2d 277, 22 USPQ 105, Cert. denied, 293 U.S. 591 (1934)

Operations Research, Inc. v. *Davidson & Talbert, Inc.* 241 Md. 550, 217 A. 2d

375 (1966)

Osborn v. *Boeing Airplane Co.*, 309 F. 2d. 99 (1962)

Peabody v. *Norfolk*, 98 Mass. 452, 96 Am.Dec. 664 (1868)

Post v. *Merrill Lynch, Pierce, Fenner & Smith, Inc.*, 421 N.Y.S. 2d 847, 48 N.Y. 2d 84 (1979)

Printing & Numerical Registering Co. v. *Sampson*, L.R. 19 Eq. 462 (1875)

Public Relations Aids, Inc. v. *Wagner*, 37 A.D. 2d 293, 324 N.Y.S. 2d 920 (1971)

Ralph v. *Karr Mfg. Co.*, 314 N.E. 2d 219

Rensselaer v. *General Motors Corp.*, 223 F.Supp 323 (1962) Affm'd 324 F. 2d 354

Roessler v. *Burwell*, 119 Conn. 289, 176 A. 126 (1934)

Rousillon v. *Rousillon*, 14 Ch.D. 351 (1880)

Rudman v. *Cowles Communications, Inc.*, 330 N.Y.S. 2d 33, 30 N.Y. 2d 1 (1972)

Sarkes Tarzian, Inc. v. *Audio Devices, Inc.*, 166 F.Supp 250, 119 USPQ 20 (S.D. Cal. 1958) Affm'd 283 F. 2d 695 (1960) Cert. denied, 365 U.S. 869, 81 S.Ct. 903 (1961)

Schneller v. *Hayes*, 176 Wash. 115, 28 P. 2d 273 (1934)

Schwayder Chemical Metallurgy Corporation v. *Baum et al.* 45 Mich. App. 220, 206 N.W. 2d 484, 177 USPQ 600 (1973)

Sloan v. *Mud Products, Inc.*, 114 F.Supp. 916, 98 USPQ 443 (1953)

Solari Industries, Inc. v. *Malady*, 55 N.J. 571, 264 A. 2d 53 (1970)

Standard Brands, Inc. v. *Zumpe*, 264 F.Supp 254, 152 USPQ 731 (1967)

Standard Parts Company v. *Peck*, 264 U.S. 52, 44 S.Ct. 239, 68 L.Ed. 560 (1924)

Telex Corp. v. *International Business Machinery Corp.* 510 F. 2d 894, 184 USPQ 521 (1975)

Terry v. *Dairymen's League Co-operative Association*, 157 N.Y.S. 2d 71 (1956)

Triangle Film v. *Artcraft*, 250 F. 981, 7 ALR 303 (1918)

United States v. *Battone*, 365 F. 2d 389 Cert. denied 385 US 974 (1966)

United States v. *Dubilier Condenser Corp.*, 289 U.S. 178, 53 S. Ct. 554, 77 L. Ed. 1114 (1933)

United States v. *Mayfield, E. D.* N.Y. Criminal Action No. 65 CR 143 (1965)

Universal Winding Company v. *Clarke*, 108 F.Supp. 329, 94 USPQ 295 (1952)

Ward v. *Consolidated Foods Corp.* 480 S.W. 2d 483 (1972)

Warner-Lambert Pharmaceutical Co. v. *John J. Reynolds, Inc.* 178 F.Supp. 655, 123 USPQ 431 (1959) Affm'd 280 F. 2d 197, 126 USPQ 3

Wear-Ever Aluminum, Inc. v. *Townecraft, etc., Inc.*, 75 N.J. Super. 135, 182 A. 2d 387 (1962)

Wesley-Jessen Inc. v. *Reynolds*, 182 USPQ 135 (1974)

Wexler v. *Greenberg*, 399 Pa. 569, 160 A. 2d 430 (1960)

Selected Bibliography

"A Geneva court has convicted Robert Aries in absentia." *Chemical Week,* October 1966, p. 19.

Allen, Kenneth R. "Invention pacts: between the lines." *IEEE Spectrum,* March 1978, p. 54.

Arnold, Tom. "Internal Security Measures for Protection of Confidential Information." *Problems of Business and Industrial Security,* New York: Practising Law Institute, 1971, p. 27.

Arnold, Tom and Graham, John G. "Trade Secrets and the Peripatetic Employee." *Trade Secret Course Handbook,* Practising Law Institute, 1973.

Arnold, Tom and McGuire, David. "The Law and Practice of Corporate Information Security." *Journal of the Patent Office Society* (in 2 parts, March and April 1975).

Aronstein, Claude Serge. *International Handbook on Contracts of Employment.* Kluwer (Deventer, The Netherlands, 1976).

Banton, William B. "A Study in the Law of Trade Secrets." *University of Cincinnati Law Review* 13 November 1939, p. 507.

Baram, Michael S. "Trade Secrets: What Price Loyalty?" *Harvard Business Review,* November–December 1968, p. 66.

Barlay, Stephen. *The Secrets Business.* New York: T. Y. Crowell Company, 1973.

Bender, David. *Computer Law: Evidence and Procedure.* New York: Matthew Bender, 1978.

———. "Trade Secret Protection of Software." *George Washington University Law Review* 38 (1970), p. 909.

Bergier, Jacques. *Secret Armies.* New York: The Bobbs-Merrill Company, 1975.

Berryhill, Jack W. "Trade Secret Litigation: Injunctions and Other Equitable Remedies." *University of Colorado Law Review,* winter 1977, pp. 189–214.

Blake, Harlan M. "Employee Covenants Not to Compete." *Harvard Law Review* 73 (1960), p. 625.

Banks, M.A.L. *Report of the Committee to Examine the Patent System and Patent Law.* London: Her Majesty's Stationery Office, 1970.

Browne, Allan. "Guarding Against Unfair Competition and Business Piracy Through Preventive Law." *Los Angeles Bar Journal,* October 1975, p. 153.

Bryenton, Gary L. "Validity and Enforceability of Restrictive Covenants Not to Compete." *Western Reserve Law Review* 16 (1964), p. 161.

"Business Sharpens its Spying Techniques." *Business Week,* 4 August, 1975, p. 60.

"Bypassed Bosses: The Man Who Misses Big Promotion Poses Hard Problem for Firms." *The Wall Street Journal* 8 May, 1968, p. 1.

Carpenter, Charles E. "Validity of Contracts Not To Compete." *University of Pennsylvania Law Review,* January 1928, p. 244.

Clinic Report on Trade Secrets. The PTC Research Institute of The George Washington University, 1970.

Coleman, Lawrence A. and Cole, Charles B. "The Effect of Shifting Employment on Trade Secrets." *The Business Lawyer,* January 1959, p. 319.

"Companies Use Codes to Ward Off Thieves and Safeguard Secrets." *The Wall Street Journal,* 16 June, 1978, p. 1.

"Computer Expert Accused of Theft of $10.2 Million to Buy Diamonds." *The New York Times,* 7 November, 1978, p.1.

"Corporate Security." *The Lawyer's Brief.* Cleveland, Ohio: Business Laws, Inc. 5 (20 October, 1975), No. 21.

Costa, J. S. *Law of Inventing in Employment* (New York: N. Y. Central Book Co., 1953).

Doerfer, Gordon L. "The Limits on Trade Secret Law Imposed by Federal Patent and Antitrust Supremacy." *Harvard Law Review* 80 (May 1967), p. 1432.

"DuPont Buys Nuttin' Hot." *Oil, Paint & Drug Reporter,* 21 March, 1966.

Ellis, Ridsdale. *Trade Secrets.* New York: Baker, Voorhis & Co., Inc., 1953.

Ewing, David W. "Civil Liberties in the Corporation." *New York State Bar Journal,* April 1978, p. 188.

———. *Freedom Inside the Organization.* New York: E. P. Dutton, 1977.

————. "Wanted: A 9–to–5 Bill of Rights." *The New York Times,* section on business and finance, 2 October, 1977, p. 16.

"Executive, 'Lured' by Control Data, Wins $4.2 Million." *National Law Journal,* 6 November, 1978, p. 3.

"Executives and Others, High on the Economy, Are Job-Hopping Again." *The Wall Street Journal,* 15 March, 1973, p. 1.

Fetterly, Daniel D. "Historical Perspectives on Criminal Laws Relating to the Theft of Trade Secrets." *The Business Lawyer* 25 (1970), p. 1535.

Gordon, John A. "Misuse of Confidential Information and the Employer-Employee Relationship." *15th Annual Institute on Mineral Law,* Louisiana State University Press, 1969, p. 133.

Greene, Richard M., Jr. *Business Intelligence and Espionage.* Homewood, Illinois: Dow Jones-Irwin, Inc., 1966.

Harding, Victor M. "Trade Secrets And the Mobile Employee." *The Business Lawyer,* January 1967, p. 395.

"How a Job Shook Prices in 2 Stocks." *The New York Times,* section on business and finance, 18 August, 1968, p. 2.

"Ideas for Sale: More Firms Buy, Sell the Fruits of Research to and from Outsiders." *The Wall Street Journal,* 18 February, 1976, p. 1.

"If You Quit, I'll Sue." *Forbes,* 15 December, 1968, p. 40.

"Industrial Espionage." *Harvard Business Review,* November-December 1959, p. 6.

"Industrial Espionage—big and growing." *Chemical & Engineering News,* 20 January, 1969, p. 20.

"In Search of a Secret Formula." *The New York Times,* section on business and finance, 9 April, 1978, p. 4.

"In the Driver's Seat: Lee Iacocca." *The Wall Street Journal,* 2 November, 1978, pp. 1 and 41.

Janssen, Henry H. "Antitrust Considerations in Proceedings Against Former Employees Who Compete Against Their Former Employer." *The Business Lawyer* 31 (July 1976), p. 2063.

Jehoram, Herman Cohen. *The Protection of Know-How In 13 Countries.* Kluwer (Deventer, The Netherlands, 1972).

Jorda, Karl F. "The Propriety of Holding Patentable Matter As a Trade Secret." *Trade Secret Course Handbook,* Practising Law Institute, 1977, p. 233.

Kaufman, Sanford D. *Industrial Espionage, Trade Secrets and Property Protection.* New York: J. J. Berliner, 1969.

Kreider, Gary P. "Trends In The Enforcement of Restrictive Employment Contracts." *University of Cincinnati Law Review* 35 (1966), p. 16.

Laude, K. E. "The Compensation for Employee Inventions in Germany." *Journal of the Patent Office Society,* vol. 44, p. 772.

Leonard, J. W. "The Protected Rights of the Employee Inventor in his Invention." *Journal of the Patent Office Society* 49 (1967), p. 357.

Lieberstein, Stanley H. "How to Keep Laboratory Records and Notebooks." *Seminar Course book,* Fairleigh Dickinson University, October 1974.

————. "How to Profit From Licensing Know-How." *Trade Secret Course Handbook,* Practising Law Institute, 1971.

————. "Keeping a Trade Secret Secret." *The Wharton Magazine,* fall 1978, p. 44.

————. "Lawsuits Against Former Employees." *Journal of the Patent Office Society,* November 1977.

————. "The Computer and The Law." *Dun's Review,* March 1970, p. 58.

————. "The Legal Traps of Executives." *Dun's Review,* May 1969, p. 60.

————. "Patents and Other Valuable Intangible Rights." *Encyclopedia of Professional Management.* New York: McGraw-Hill, 1979, p. 868.

————. "The Rights of the Employed Inventor." *Trade Secret Course Handbook.* Practising Law Institute, 1971.

————. "The Theft of Trade Secrets," *Problems of Business And Industrial Security,* Practising Law Institute, 1971, p. 49.

————. "Trade Secrets and the Mobile Executive." *Dun's Review,* October 1968, p. 60.

Liebhafsky, Douglas S. "Industrial Secrets and the Skilled Employee." *New York University Law Review* 38 (April 1963), p. 324.

Lewis, R. David. "Contracts in Restraint of Trade: Employee Covenants Not To Compete." *Arkansas Law Review,* summer 1967, vol. 21, p. 214.

Martin, Alfred B. "Enticement of Employees." *The Business Lawyer,* July 1973, p. 1341.

"Mayfield Pleads Guilty in Theft of Crest Plans." *Advertising Age,* 9 August, 1965, p. 2.

Menk, Carl W. "What Are the Chances of Being Fired?" *The New York Times,* section on business and finance, 18 June, 1978, p. 1.

Meyer, Herbert E. "The Headhunters Come Upon Golden Days." *Fortune,* 9 October, 1978, p. 100.

Meyer, Pearl. "When To Use Employment Contracts." *Harvard Business Review,* November-December 1971, pp. 70–73.

Milgrim, Roger M. "Get the Most Out of Your Trade Secrets." *Harvard Business Review,* November-December 1974, p. 105.

———. *Trade Secrets.* New York: Matthew Bender, 1967. This excellent two-volume legal treatise is updated to present biannual cumulative supplements.

"Mobil Corp. Accuses Superior Oil in U.S., Canadian Suits of Luring Key Personnel." *The Wall Street Journal,* 6 February, 1978, p. 4.

Murray, Thomas J. "The Case of the Disloyal Executive." *Dun's Review,* December 1967, p. 35.

Needham, Roger A. *Problems of Business and Industrial Security,* Practising Law Institute Course Handbook, No. 29, 1971.

Neumeyer, Frederick. "Employees' Rights in Their Inventions: A Comparison of National Laws." *Journal of the Patent Office Society* 44 (October 1962), p. 674.

Neumeyer, Frederick and Stedman, John. *The Employed Inventor in the United States.* The Massachusetts Institute of Technology, 1971.

Nolte, A. C. Jr. "Shop Rights." *The Encyclopedia of Patent Practice and Invention Management.* New York: Van Nostrand-Reinhold, 1964.

O'Meara, Roger J. *Employee Patent and Secrecy Agreements.* New York: National Industrial Conference Board Study, No. 199, 1965).

———. *How Smaller Companies Protect Their Trade Secrets.* New York: The Conference Board, Inc., 1971.

Orenbuch, Louis. "Trade Secrets and the Patent Laws." *Journal of the Patent Office Society* 52 (October 1970), p. 638.

Orkin, Neal. "The Legal Rights of the Employed Inventor." *Journal of the Patent Office Society* (in 2 parts), October–November 1974.

Parsons, Gerald P. "U.S. Lags in Patent Law Reform." *IEEE Spectrum,* March 1978, p. 60.

Perham, John. "How to Protect Corporate Secrets." *Dun's Review,* August 1977, p. 48.

———. "The Great Game of Corporate Espionage." *Dun's Review,* October 1970, p. 30.

Popper, Herbert. "Trade Secrets, Industrial Espionage, And the Clam-Up Concept." *Chemical Engineering,* 15 July, 1968, p. 134.

Posedly, Gloria. "Shootout Over Patent Protection." *The New Englander,* April 1978, p. 20.

"Protection and Use of Trade Secrets." Law Note, *Harvard Law Review* 64 (1951), p. 976.

"Recruiting in Silicon Valley: Persuasion and Prizes in the Quest for Scientific Skills." *Time,* 7 August, 1978, p. 67.

Rezac, William T. "Assignments of Inventions to Employers Here and in Europe." *N.Y.U. Intra Law Review* 15 (1960), p. 219.

Rich, Giles S. "Laying The Ghost of the "Invention" Requirement" (text of a speech delivered before a combined meeting of the New Jersey and Philadelphia Patent Law Associations 12 October, 1972), *APLA Quarterly Journal* (December 1972), p. 26.

———. *The Vague Concept of "Invention" As Replaced by Sec. 103 of The 1952 Patent Act.* IDEA, P.T. & C. *Journal of Research and Education,* George Washington University Conference, No. 46 JPOS 855.

Rines, Robert H. "A plea for a proper balance of proprietary rights." *IEEE Spectrum,* April 1970, p. 41.

"Rough Going: More Office Workers Battle Being Fired By Suing Their Bosses." *The Wall Street Journal,* 18 June, 1975, p. 1.

Schiller, A. Arthur. "Trade Secrets and the Roman Law." *Columbia Law Review* 30 June 1930, p. 837.

Schmidt, Cecil C. "Inventions and Proprietary Information: A Tug of War Between Employees and Employers." *Law Notes,* 7 January 1971, p. 39.

"Secrets for Sale—Industrial Spying: $6 Billion Drain on U. S. Business." *Los Angeles Times,* 19 August, 1974, p. 1.

Seidel, Arthur H. and Panitch, Ronald L. "The Opening Stages of Trade-Secret Litigation." *The Practical Lawyer,* April 1973, p. 17.

Skornia, Thomas A. "Employment Contracts." *Chemtech,* January 1977, p. 7.

Smith, Lee. "People Raiding on Wall Street: The Mauling Merrill Lynch Never Expected." *Fortune,* 23 October, 1978, p. 78.

Sommers, Howard N. "Trade Secrecy—A Magna Charta." *Law Notes,* summer 1975, p. 39.

Stedman, John C. "Trade Secrets." *Ohio State Law Journal* 23 (1962), p. 4.

Stessin, Lawrence. "Don't Count on Employment Contracts." *The New York Times,* section on business and finance, 23 July, 1978, p. 14.

———. "How To Guard Trade Secrets." *The New York Times,* section on business and finance, 30 September, 1973, p. 1.

Stessin, Lawrence, Wit, Ira S., and Ellentuck, Elmer I. *How to Protect Your Business.* New York: Man & Manager, Inc., 1968.

Stessin, Lawrence and Wit, Ira S. *The Disloyal Employee.* New York: Man & Manager, Inc., 1967.

"Superior Seduction: Mobil sues to protect secrets." *Time,* 20 February, 1978, p. 76.

Sutton, John P. "Trade Secrets Legislation." *IDEA,* P.T.&C. *Journal of Research and Education,* George Washington University 9 (1965), p. 587.

Symposium on "The Employee Inventor." April 8, 1965. *Journal of the Patent Office Society,* 47 July 1965, pp. 469–513.

"The Gatorade Dispute." *Chemical & Engineering News,* March 1970, p. 14.

"The Great Computer Heist." *Newsweek,* 20 November, 1978, p. 99.

"The Obligation of a High-Level Employee to his Former Employer: The Standard Brands Case." Comment, *The University of Chicago Law Review* 29 (1962), p. 339.

Trade Secrets: A Management Overview, Management Bulletin 64, New York: American Management Associations, 1965.

"Trade Secrets: The Technical Man in Legal Land." *Chemical & Engineering News,* 18 January, 1965.

Turner, Amédée E. *The Law of Trade Secrets.* London, Sweet and Maxwell Ltd., 1962.

Vandevoort, John R. "Trade Secrets: Protecting a Very Special Property." *The Business Lawyer* 26 (1971), p. 681.

"Vigilant Firms Strive to keep their Secrets by Plugging Up Leaks." *The Wall Street Journal,* 28 July, 1972) p. 1.

Wade, W. "Industrial Espionage and Mis-Use of Trade Secrets." Ardmore, Pa.: Advance House, 1965.

Wetzel, Carroll R. "Employment Contracts and Non-Competition Agreements." *The University of Illinois Law Forum,* 1969, p. 61.

"When workers become directors—The German Experiment, A mixed blessing." *Business Week,* 15 September, 1973, p. 188.

Whiteside, Thomas. *Computer Capers: Tales of Electronic Thievery, Embezzlement, and Fraud.* New York: T.Y. Crowell, 1978.

"Why Executives Say 'I Quit.' " *Management Review,* October 1971, p. 2.

Index